HAROLD HOLDWAY
20th CENTURY CERAMIC DESIGNER

Harold Holdway and Ruth Holdway

Opposite page: Harold in his studio with design work behind him. Photograph: Kinocraf Films Ltd.

HAROLD HOLDWAY
20th CENTURY CERAMIC DESIGNER

Harold Holdway and Ruth Holdway

Landmark Publishing

Published by

Ashbourne Hall, Cokayne Ave
Ashbourne, Derbyshire DE6 1EJ England
Tel: (01335) 347349 Fax: (01335) 347303
e-mail: landmark@clara.net
web site: www.landmarkpublishing.co.uk

ISBN 13: 978-1-84306-192-2

ISBN 10: 1-84306-192-9

British Library Cataloguing in Publication Data:
a catalogue record for this book is available
from the British Library.

Print: Biddles Ltd, King's Lynn, Norfolk

CONTENTS

PREFACE

Having a natural flare for art, especially ceramics, and to be able to use these skills professionally over fifty years alongside so many talented fellow craftsmen and women, and to be reasonably successful in satisfying customers, enables me to reflect and look back with pride at being given this opportunity. Therefore I would like to share a few details of the many great characters I knew and worked with who really do deserve due credit.

So many fine potters and artists have served a lifetime at numerous factories, but relatively few are remembered. I hope that I can redress the balance in some small way.

Harold Holdway. 1993

Unfortunately, Harold's eyesight failed before he completed his memoirs. After graduation I had agreed to act as my Grandfather's eyes and to help him finish off the story before a valuable social history was lost. Unfortunately, Harold died in 2002 before we started, thereby ending his memoirs in the 1950s. Therefore for the final chapters I have pieced together fragments from his colleagues, friends and his extensive archive in an attempt to 'complete' the story. I hope that I have not done anyone an injustice.

Ruth Holdway. 2006

A colour trial painted by Harold. I have included it simply because Harold has made a routine exercise so decorative and precise.

ACKNOWLEDGEMENTS

Although writing a few words of thanks is a pleasurable experience, I am dreading omitting someone's vital contribution, especially since I am completely ignorant of who my Grandfather consulted in writing his memoirs. I only hope I am doing no one an injustice, especially when attributing a design to someone, as often the person that took the credit for it was reliant on the hard work of someone else, if they were credited at all.

First I must thank my family and close friends for putting up with me when at times this book took over every waking (and some non-waking) hours. Taking practically all the photographs in three weeks, or rather bullying my Father into taking all the photos, was an incredibly intense period and I am very thankful that my Father did not go on strike.

Thank you to Pam Wooliscroft, Curator of Spode Museum, Robert Copeland and Bill Coles for filling in all the photographic gaps of our family collection. I am also extremely grateful to Graham Barlow for patiently scanning in my Grandfather's slides. After I learnt the hard way about corrupting disks and had destroyed all evidence of his hard work, without bating an eyelid, he did them all over again.

Although our family seems to keep everything, thereby creating our own Spode archive, there are invariably gaps in our collective knowledge. I am very grateful to the following people for sparing the time to speak to me: Robert Copeland – a veritable mine of information, anecdotes and humorous insights; Paul Wood, Managing Director of Spode; Gordon Hewitt; Janet O'Malley; Mike Kitt; Michael Sinclair; Jean Bettany; Gill West; Lynne Joyce and Douglas Hawley (now deceased).

I am also very grateful for Pam Wooliscroft's time finding elusive patterns and people and, along with Robert Copeland, for guiding me in the pattern safe.

Once written comes the laborious task of checking and proofreading and I am thankful of the time my Aunt, Eileen Clarke, Robert Copeland and my immediate family have spent reading the text.

Finally this book would not have been possible without a grant from Ceramica-Stiftung Basel. It is a shame that many great stories and much research are not published due to commercial restraints. The financial help enabled me to reduce the cover price by fifty per cent, making a valuable social history more affordable and accessible.

As my Mother says, fault-finding and criticism is inevitable once a book or article is published, but unless the author is brave and makes a statement, the work would never be finished and as a resource would be wasted and practically useless. If I have made a mistake, I am sorry, but please be kind to me, it's my first time.

INTRODUCTION
A TALENTED DESIGNER:
MY GRANDFATHER

To be a talented artist is one thing, but to be a successful designer is another. Being an art director needs the skill of an artist, the foresight of a sales manager and the discretion of a manager. Many talented artists do not have the skill to survive commercially. Harold, however, had the skill to design for an ever-changing market, which ensured his longevity at Spode. As Harold commented on two very talented artists working at Worcester, they produced works of art but the buying public do not necessarily want to buy them. "Some artists, by virtue of their reputation, feel that their work is beyond criticism and that we, the buyers have to take whatever is offered. As a practising artist I personally have always welcomed intelligent criticism from informed people. All agree that artists should enjoy freedom of expression for part of their working time to create ideas which express their own individuality but this should be carefully controlled and only practised when we have sufficient completed models which satisfy both company and market requirements." Harold was a commercially aware artist with the company's interests at heart.

Harold's life was summed up in his retirement press release, "Harold has been described as a 100% Spode man." He was dedicated to the company and was steeped in its proud tradition. In a letter to Lyn T. Davies, Managing Director, 22.12.77, Harold expressed his devotion to the job:

"In the eyes of many people long service with one company is a sign of stagnation and lack of ambition – but this is not the case with my own career at Spode. There has always been a challenge and it is my good fortune that I have been given the gift of creativity, the outcome of which has been fruitful from time to time. I feel the future of Royal Worcester Spode is assured and I am glad I have had the opportunity of helping to cement a fine partnership."

Harold carried out a diplomatic role, interpreting the Copeland directors' traditional ideas into new products for the changing lifestyles of younger customers that would help prolong the survival of the poorly funded company. Harold's era at Spode was the end of a high period of potting. It was a time

of technical change with the last of the bottle ovens being fired as new firing, making and decorating techniques were being developed in order to be competitive with other factories. It was as if Harold spanned several centuries of potting tradition. The black and white photographs of the smoky scenes of the pot banks of the 1930s when Harold started could have dated back to Josiah Spode II. The techniques and atmosphere had hardly changed for centuries. Harold adapted to a factory much more in line with the twentieth century by the time he retired in the late 1970s. The techniques had been modernised and the tastes of the customers had changed considerably. The technology of the 1970s would have been unimaginable when Harold left Art School. As Mike Kitt, one of Harold's designers, says:

"During Harold's art Directorship the company emerged from wartime conditions to meet again the demand for fine decorative china and earthenware. The quality of making and decorating was immense and Harold demanded excellence using the traditional skills and interpreting the needs of the carriage trade both in Britain, Europe and North America."

Even during the low points in the company's history such as the late 1960s, Harold continued to produce quality designs. Douglas Hawley, export sales manager, said in his memoirs, "Harold Holdway, one of the best designers the factory ever produced, as art director, was among the men who continued to maintain the prestige of Spode."

The management and the sales staff appreciated Harold's skill as a designer as his designs sold well. Gresham Copeland wrote a sincere letter of appreciation on his retirement in October 1958. "It is with the very deepest regret indeed that I have to leave you. No senior executive, much less a director, could have ever expected or had such a loyal and devoted member of a team. Mere words obviously cannot express my real feelings of gratitude for the support you have given me." At a much later date Harold was chosen as one of the company's most valued workers to appear in their 1972 Annual Report and was invited to a black tie dinner in America. The caption accompanying the photograph said, "A Spode designer for thirty-eight years and art director since 1957, Harold Holdway is today the acknowledged dean of British pottery art directors, his creativity matched only by his leadership, guidance and training."

Harold was a staunch believer in good quality design and would accept nothing that was second best. In an article for *Homes and Gardens*, January/February 1971, he gave his views on the importance of producing quality work. "It is essential for someone who wants to design for a large pottery to be able to draw really well. An academic training, with drawing from life, architecture and classical casts is necessary schooling for the type of artist we need." The journalist Corinna Wildman commented, "It is refreshing in an age where freedom of expression is often considered the only quality necessary to make an art form acceptable, to meet someone who believes that there are no short cuts and that disciplined training is as important to the artist now as it ever was." Harold was an approachable teacher and he passed on his skills to his department. "Although he somewhat regrets the lack of time at his disposal for designing, it is obvious that his thorough understanding of the needs of a large pottery suit him well for his present role, where he can pass on his knowledge through his assistants."

Harold had a firm view that tableware designs should be high quality and functional. He was keen to draw on the tradition and craftsmanship of the mature company yet he wanted his designs to be pure, refined and elegant. He described the perfect plate as a good frame around food. "The ideal plate is plain white or is one of the pale body colours inherent in the various materials from which different types of chinaware are made. If the shape is not good, no amount of painted decoration can save it. A good shape is one which has strength, character, simplicity and is the right weight and size for the job." However, he was well aware that a pottery would have difficulty in remaining solvent if only plain or slightly decorated ware was produced. He was equally apt at designing the decorative plate as well as the functional dinner service and produced many stunning commemoratives in his latter years at Spode.

A designer is lucky in that his life and achievements live on forever in his designs. As Corinna Wildman said, "It is probable that in years to come his designs will be as much an inspiration to a new generation of potters as the old Spode patterns are to him now." Harold mused in a letter, "Who knows? Maybe some day you might find an example of my work at Sotheby's!!" (18.09.90). Even if in the future the prices of his pottery never equal those of some of his contemporaries, his designs have already given many people across the world hours of pleasure.

Harold posing with a Renaissance pattern bowl that he designed based on the antique Camilla pattern.

PROLOGUE

War clouds were beginning to form over Europe in the summer of 1913, when another member of the Holdway family was born. On 10th June I was born in a small two-up, two-down terraced house in Shelton, near Stoke-on-Trent railway station where my father was a goods guard. At a very early age, my parents recognized that I was able to draw with a skill beyond my years (or so I was told). I vaguely remember drawing locomotives and track layouts, which childish efforts my father often showed to his fellow workers with great pride.

Another early memory was of my carving of a World War One tank using a worn-out mould made of Plaster of Paris, which had been thrown away from a nearby factory. I only have faint memories of the war. My father, being in a reserved occupation, did not join the forces, but in 1918, as the war was drawing to a close, he contracted the dreaded Spanish Flu and died after a short illness.

While the peace celebrations went on around us, my mother, left alone with four children, was determined to keep the family intact. We were a close-knit unit consisting of my mother, two older brothers, myself and one brother two years younger than me. So, she decided to try and get a job, though these were difficult times, with men returning from the forces anxious to savour the better world they had been promised. Fortunately because of my father's past employment with the railway company, Mother was offered, and accepted, a job of ticket collector at one of the local stations. My eldest brother, William, aged thirteen had just started work with Boots the Chemists. My brother Hugh was seven years older than me. I joined the Infants' class in the primary school while a friendly neighbour looked after my younger brother, Arthur.

My progress though elementary school was not a pleasant experience apart from art lessons, where I showed promise; so much so, that I was chosen to take the test for the two-year Art School scholarship.

Now the story of my life as an artist and designer can begin………………

Art School design for coffee cup and saucer. Print and enamel. October 1933.

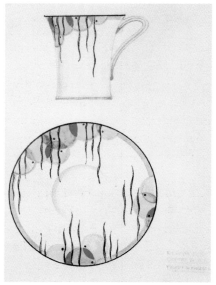

Art School design for teaware in print and enamel. Circa early 1930s.

Art School design for a "modernistic" tea cup and saucer.

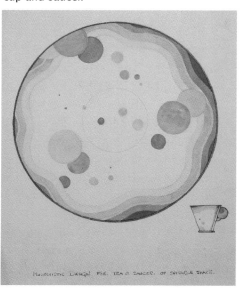

THE BEGINNING 1926–1934

Early in 1926, aged twelve and a half years and attending Cauldon Elementary School in Shelton, I was selected, together with another lad named Douglas Haig, to sit for a two-year Art School scholarship at Burslem. There were forty places for the whole of the Potteries and over 200 selected applicants sat the examination.

Although natural ability in art skills was essential, an above average standard in general education had to be demonstrated as well, so the test included English, mathematics, history and geography. I was the lucky one from our school. In my opinion, poor Douglas was more competent in art subjects than I was, so I can only assume that his general education was not of a high enough standard to meet the requirements of the examiner. I have often thought since that many natural artists must have been deprived of an artistic education because of their failure to master academic subjects.

As there were no grants for the scholarship I had to make the journey to Burslem by train. This was made possible because my mother was able to get a concessionary fare ticket for me as a result of her employment with the railway company. As money was scarce, I suggested that she should allow me to have a bicycle, which could be paid for by weekly payments, the cost of which equalled the rail fares. After a lot of thought, she agreed and so I became the proud possessor of a new machine. Of course, I had to use the cycle in all weathers, hail, rain, ice and snow, winter and summer, but I now had a means of transport, which I could use for pleasure. It also enabled me to practise my skills of painting and drawing of outdoor subjects.

In September 1926, I started my artistic education at the Burslem School of Art in the junior art department. The headmaster, Mr H. Landon, and his assistant, Miss E. Reeves, both taught art and general education subjects. Mr W. Mills taught modelling, historical ornament and 'light and shade' in drawing. Plant form and animals from life were taught by Mrs Millie Brough, who was a part-time teacher. At this time, the resident Head of School and Superintendent of Art Instruction for the Potteries was Mr Gordon Forsyth.

Our entry consisted of twenty-two boys and eighteen girls of varying ages up to fifteen years. I was the youngest member of the class being thirteen

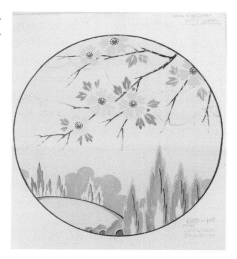

Design for lacquer plaque. October 1932.

Floral vase design entered in a Royal Society of Arts Industrial Design competition.

Millie Brough

A teacher at Burslem School of Art, Millie was also a renowned local artist. She was born in Bentilee, Stoke-on-Trent in 1889 named Hannah Amelia Bartlam. She studied at Longton Technical College before going to the Goldsmiths College, London. In the 1930s she became renowned for painting pot banks and barges in the Potteries and the Manifold Valley.

She taught at Burslem School of Art from the mid 1920s to the mid 1950s. During this period she developed techniques in other media such as etching, lithograph and linocut. Millie died in 1972.

years and three months old. For the first time in my short life, school had become a pleasure and I worked very hard and found the competitive spirit exhilarating.

I soon realised that I was leading the field in nearly all the art subjects, such as history of ornament, ceramics and anatomy. All of the subjects were fascinating to me and gave me great pleasure. An important feature of the course was the great amount of homework that was set, including many design projects. Regular examinations in all subjects soon showed who were the leaders and I fared very well indeed.

Art School Report 1927: "A very promising student. Excellent work in art subjects." E. Reeves.

As time slipped by we all began to wonder what the future held for us. A month or two before the end of our second year's tuition, various manufacturers were contacted with a view to our future employment with their companies. Occasionally, a student was allowed to gain factory experience by working half time, either morning or afternoon, and I was one of the lucky few that had this special dispensation. Two months before I was due to finish school; I was fixed up as a designer, working half time with George Jones & Sons, Crescent Potteries, Stoke-on-Trent. In

the midst of so much unemployment, I felt extremely lucky to have made the grade and to have been awarded the job of my choice.

My first employers occupied a large factory in South Wolfe Street, Stoke, adjacent to Minton's and separated from them by the canal, which formed the boundary. They were manufacturers of china and earthenware, employing several hundred work-people. George Jones & Sons produced all types of tableware, also toilet ware and fancies, made to a high standard and they were able to command reasonably high prices for their wares. Much of the china was richly decorated with enamels and often finely gilt by gold printing and by handwork. In the past they had been responsible for much fine hand-painting by men, but this type of work was losing its popularity, largely because of its high price. The large quantity of earthenware that was produced included very fine self-prints and many on-glaze enamel decorations. There were also a great number of lithographed patterns, 'lithos', sometimes with enamels added by hand. As the firm had its own facility for litho sheet printing, it was able to be highly competitive in price.

The standard of goods produced by George Jones was always considered to be of higher quality than the Longton producers, who were mainly producing inexpensive china tea ware, but they were never able to compare and compete with the "fine china" firms such as Wedgwood, Spode, Minton, Royal Worcester, Royal Doulton and Crown Derby. Those firms aimed at the highest standards both of design and quality, which commanded much higher prices.

I began full-time work at George Jones in August 1928. I had assumed that as I had been paid 15s. per week for half-time work prior to leaving school, I would be paid 30s. per week when I put in a full week. Alas, it was not to be! The job was a staff appointment, which meant holidays with full pay, also full wages if I was away from work through illness. The working week was five and a half days, resulting in 44 hours: Monday to Friday 8.30am to 5.30pm, with one hour for lunch, and on Saturdays 8.30am to 12.30pm. As I lived in Shelton, I was able to go home for dinner – which in the Potteries meant lunch – and be back at work within the hour.

Our art director was Mr Charles Birbeck. To me, as a youth, he appeared quite elderly; he was a smallish, portly man, balding with a trim of white hair and he possessed a fairly quick temper when roused. He had been a ceramic painter in the past and he later applied his skills to other branches of pottery decorating. Mastering lithography for ceramics was one of his greatest achievements and he was responsible for the firm acquiring a litho-printing department with a small team of operators, located on its own site. During his time at the factory he produced many fine floral litho decorations. In addition to creating the original artwork he was also able to produce all the colour separation plates needed for the printing of transfers.

By the time I arrived at the factory he had ceased doing any of this type of work because his eyesight was not good enough for the fine draughtsmanship required. Nevertheless, he was a good teacher by past example and in showing me the standards he had once achieved, he hoped I would strive to equal them. Needless to say, I never did equal the high quality that he had attained but the knowledge I gained was to stand me in good stead in later years.

My early days were spent working in a small office-cum-studio with the resident designer, Mr Cyril Shingler, a man in his thirties, with a very gentle, refined manner. He possessed great creative talent and was responsible for many fine decorations. It must have been an awful blow for him to have to suffer the mindless chatter and the endless barrage of questions and queries that were constantly fired at him by an eager-to-learn junior. I admired his skill enormously; for he was the only man I ever met who simply took a sheet of paper and created good designs and decorations without resorting to books of reference and inspiration from the work of others. There were some days when ideas just did not materialise and all round the edges of his paper a mass of thumbnail doodles would appear, delicately drawn, which would be rubbed clean when an idea was eventually registered in line and colour in the centre of the drawing paper.

He taught me a great deal, advising me on which works to study and how to master the many techniques needed to achieve maximum effect in ceramic design. It was a sad day for me when he announced that he was leaving the employ of George Jones and I never did know why he "called it a day." He had set a wonderful example to an impressionable youth and I was to miss his guidance in the future.

Years later, in 1962, I was to meet him again. I accompanied Mr Spencer Copeland, with Mr Leonard Whiter, sales manager and historian, as representatives of Spode on a visit by the Fine China Manufacturers Federation to Cong in Ireland. There we met Mr Arthur Dutton, one of the Royal Worcester

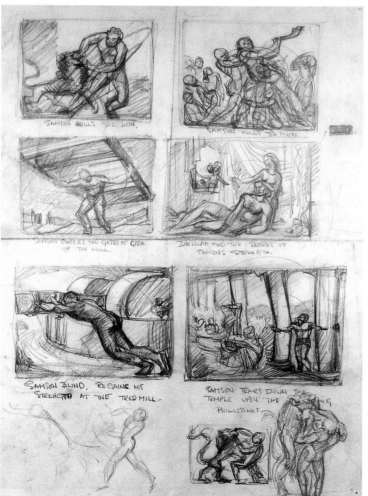

Right: Art School two-colour linocut and below, sketch of the canal, possibly Sideway, Stoke, 1935.

Below and left: Samson and Delilah pen and ink and preliminary sketches.

Above and left: Green Art School nude model, front and back.

Right: Alternative cat model designs.

Below: Blue/grey Art School nude model.

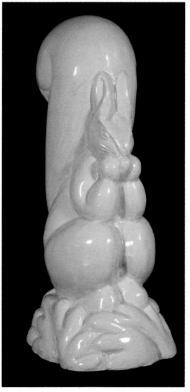

Left: Squirrel model and above, alternative design.

14

Left: Forsyth vase designed and painted for Royal Lancastrian. The motto around the base reads: "Tandem Fit Surculus Arbor" meaning, at length the sprig becomes a tree.

Below left: Backstamp featuring Forsyth's four scythes rebus.

Above: Gordon Forsyth: Thaxted Church, Cambridgeshire.

Left: Vase designed and painted by Harry Tittensor, titled Friday, featuring a monk and fish for Royal Doulton.

Below: Dartmouth streetscene by Albert Wagg.

Below: Reginald Haggar: Skyscape (possibly the Sutherland monument, Tittensor, Stoke-on-Trent) dated 5th September 195?

contingent and a member of their board. He invited Leonard Whiter and myself to visit their factory as his guests, and we accepted with pleasure. After a most interesting tour, he invited us for lunch to a country hotel, and surprise, surprise, he had brought along none other than Cyril Shingler, curator of the Dyson Perrins Museum at the Royal Worcester Factory. Meeting him again after thirty years was a delightful experience for me. Although I had no idea that he was engaged in such a pleasant occupation, he was well aware of his junior's career progress following the departure from George Jones and Sons. He was still the same kindly man (although a little older, like me) for whom I held the greatest respect.

Shortly after Cyril Shingler left George Jones, another senior designer was appointed to take over the duties of Charles Birbeck who, following a serious illness, had to spend the rest of his life in a residential home. The man appointed was Mr Leon Grice ARCA, who was installed in the office of Mr Birbeck and was, of course, in charge of myself and responsible for my training. Once again I was lucky in my choice of boss, for he was a man of great ability and, unlike Mr Birbeck, he could 'show me how' by sitting down beside me and demonstrating his skill.

These were happy days for me for there was so much to learn and many opportunities for one to work hard, as I was. As well as working full time at George Jones, I continued to attend art classes at the Burslem School of Art as a senior student. Instead of paying a fee, I sat for a bursary award examination to cover the three-year period to study advanced subjects. I was successful in being awarded the bursary, which included a fifteen-pound per year cash grant. The award was conditional upon my making a minimum of six attendances during the weekly morning, afternoon and evening sessions. Because of my full-time commitments, I opted to attend five evening and one of the afternoon classes. Fortunately the firm gave me permission to take the one afternoon a week off, thinking no doubt that they would reap the benefit in the long term.

I studied several advanced subjects, including design, historic ornament, history of potting, life drawing, anatomy and plant drawing. One of my joys was having tuition from two great masters of art subjects, Mr Gordon Forsyth and Mr Harry Tittensor – each with equal art qualifications – ARCA and RI. They were great friends and yet at the same time keen rivals. They often spent their vacations together at home and on the continent, painting delightful watercolours, particularly interiors of cathedrals and churches. I think Gordon Forsyth just about held the lead in ability because of his tremendous versatility. He was a master of stained glass making, painting huge murals and even wrought iron design. At exhibitions of painting one could hardly recognize the difference in style of the two men and observers would often have to check the signatures to make sure which was which.

Having scored a hit with Mr Forsyth in my Junior Art School days it was a great pleasure to continue the association. Mr Tittensor was my tutor in advanced design and life drawing and throughout my life, I never met a more talented man in these subjects. By virtue of his being a freelance pottery designer of great repute he was a brilliant teacher who could sit down beside you and 'show you how'! Mr Bernard Wood and Mr Billy Mills also gave supporting tuition in several subjects. The years spent as a senior student were very rewarding and I had no difficulty in achieving first-class results in every subject.

Towards the end of my student days at the Burslem School, I met a charming and lovely girl, whom I was to court and eventually marry. Because of my Art School commitments this meant a certain amount of restricted courting because the evening art classes did not finish until 9.15pm which meant a 'hell-bent' dash on my bicycle to meet the girl of my dreams on Tuesday and Thursday evenings of each week. I think the record time for the journey from Burslem to Oakhill – a distance of about six miles – was twenty minutes.

A few years later, a Mr Light, who was head of the Stoke School of Art, decided to retire and Mr Forsyth offered the job to Mr Tittensor. As there was no daytime class commitment he accepted the appointment. He, in turn, invited me to accompany

Two Art School bookend nude models. Harold also produced a version in white.

him as a teacher of general art subjects. This was an honour, which I readily accepted, and I started this spare time activity with great pleasure, but at the same time experiencing a slight feeling of sadness in severing my connection with the 'mother school'. This new experience was most enjoyable and rewarding, for I recruited quite a number of girls and boys who were apprentices at the Copeland factory, who in turn were most keen to have their 'boss' teach them to try and become real artists. I am not sure how long this fruitful period lasted – it was all too short – for it came to an abrupt end when I learned that Mr Tittensor had suddenly died and a new headmaster had been appointed.

I was certain that it would be virtually impossible to find a replacement for such a man, who, blessed with such charm, kind disposition, and an over-abundance of skill and ability, was always ready to share this with others. The new man was none other than Mr Reginald Haggar ARCA who had spent a few years as art director at Minton's prior to teaching at Burslem School of Art. He was an expert watercolourist and favoured the delicate portrayal of his subjects and was a particularly fine draughtsman. He had built up quite a reputation for fine work and he was fully versed in what the pottery industry needed.

I cannot say that I took an immediate liking to him, and I am sure that his feelings for me were similar. However, with some reservations, I agreed to stay on as a teacher for one or two nights a week and in addition, conduct my own personal experimental design work without interference from anyone. I suppose I was just a little arrogant in my attitude and Mr Haggar and I did not always see eye to eye over certain decisions that he made.

One of my pleasures was to sit in at the life class sessions and one day the new life class master appointed by Mr Haggar – (the former head had always taken the life class himself) – made some over-critical comments about my work. My style had strength, boldness and good proportion, developed over a number of years and approved by the master men, Messrs Forsyth and Tittensor, and the new man tried to get me to change my style to a weak and insipid method which he personally favoured, having been taught this at the Royal College of Art in London. This I refused to do and reminded him that men of greater experience than his had approved of my workmanship. Mr Haggar was a trifle upset at my attitude towards his new master and the outcome was that I never attended the life class again to save any further embarrassment.

Another occasion was the annual show of student's

A 'rolly-polly' Art School model with alternative sketches. Also in his class was Ann Potts who became noted for similar models.

work, which always took place at the end of term and was held at the Burslem School of Art. I had produced practically the whole of the Stoke Art School's display of glazed pots and vases, which I had thrown and turned in a variety of incised designs. I informed Mr Haggar that the previous year most of my exhibits, which should have been returned to the Stoke School, were missing, and in consequence, I did not receive a single piece for myself. I intended to make sure that this would not happen again. Reg was again upset at my attitude and stated that I had no right to any of the items as they were the property of the Stoke School and he would make sure that this stipulation was carried out to the letter. As this was the end of term I decided to write to the boss – Mr Forsyth – and explain my problem. He sent a letter in reply giving me permission to have whatever I needed in view of the poor return from the previous year.

In the olden days, there was such a thing as an orange box, which measured 4ft x 18in x 18in. This useful object my young brother and I carted onto a train to Burslem. At the Art School, closed for the summer recess, I showed the letter to the caretaker. The exhibition had closed but had not yet been dismantled, and the caretaker was delighted to help when he heard my story. The three of us packed every piece I had exhibited. With my orange box now full

Left: Birbeck Rose plate and backstamp named after William Birbeck, the George Jones painter and brother of Charles Birbeck who mentored Harold's early days. The artist has signed his name by the stem.

Right: Harold enjoyed learning the process of transforming a design into a lithograph at George Jones & Sons Ltd.

Left: "Holdway Centres" the first lithograph produced for George Jones & Sons. Original artwork and magazine cutting. 1930.

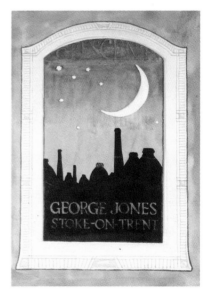

Right: Hand painted sketch of a George Jones display logo by Cyril Shingler. Pre-1932.

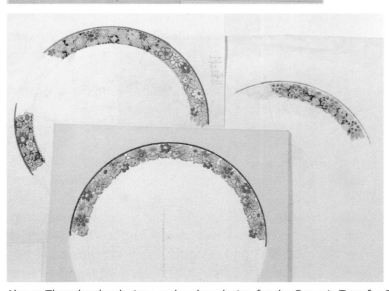

Above: Three border designs and a plate design for the Ceramic Transfer Co. Ltd. 1933. Note the logo in the top right corner.

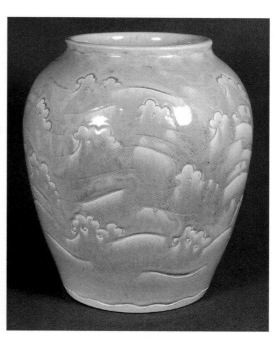

Art School glazed
pottery vases
1933–1935.
Handthrown and
incised.

to the bursting, my brother and I staggered to the station and arrived in Stoke safe and sound with nary a broken piece. End of the story – almost! September had dawned and the Stoke School opened as usual for the autumn term. Mr Haggar made a beeline for me as soon as I entered, shook me by the hand and said: "Harold, I shall never cross swords with you again!" He never did and they remained firm friends from then on.

Fate stepped in to halt my activities at the Stoke School. Complete harmony reigned over Mr Haggar and myself and he was overjoyed at the amount of practical work that was being produced. In a ground floor room at the back of the school we had a gas-fired kiln, which was regularly used for firing student's work. It was capable of firing both biscuit and glazed ware, and also enamel decorated pieces.

As the kiln flues were badly in need of cleaning, Mr Eric Owen, the modelling master, took on the task and did a fine job. I had produced enough items to fill the kiln for the first firing after the cleaning of the flues, so after placing my pieces into the kiln, I set the time switches to cover the firing cycle, which would end at 9pm. On a number of occasions during the cycle I checked to see if the firing was being done efficiently. Everything worked perfectly, the firing temperature had reached the pre-determined peak temperature required, so I duly turned off the gas supply to the burners and made sure all was safe. It was always noticeable that the walls of one side of the life classroom were very hot when the kiln was fired; this was because the flue fed into a chimney breast, which was built onto the outside wall.

I lived in Shelton, which was less than a mile from the school, and I was awakened in the early morning by the sound of a fire engine bell passing the end of the street. I jumped out of bed and started to dress and my mother woke up and wondered if I was sleepwalking. When I told her that I thought the Art School was on fire she insisted I must have been dreaming, telling me to forget it, go back to bed and go to sleep. Next morning, I awoke surprisingly early, rushed my breakfast, grabbed my bicycle and before 8am I was standing outside the front of the Art School building. It looked just as usual with its blackened brickwork from the many years of exposure to he smoke-laden atmosphere of Stoke. I thought Ma must have been right - it was a dream after all!

On second thoughts, I walked round to the back of the school where I was startled by a solitary fireman who was still damping down the embers of a fire. So after all, it was a reality. To make matters worse the firemen had opened the heavy doors of the kiln,

directed their hoses on the contents and smashed every piece. The whole of the kiln room and the life room, including part of the roof and the contents were in ashes. It was a sorry sight to behold and I had personally lost several folios of life class studies made at the Burslem and Stoke Schools.

The insurance assessors stated that the fire was caused from the kiln igniting a floor joist protruding into the chimney breast, causing it to smoulder and burst into flames some hours later. Mr Haggar had been informed and when I met him on his arrival we wondered if the school would ever be used again. It was many months before it was repaired to its former state – this time without a kiln.

In the meantime, I attended art classes at Hanley School of Art, where I had an enjoyable time and became very friendly with the masters and senior students. The headmaster of Hanley Art School was Mr Percy Lloyd, a very fine artist and designer employed locally. The school was only open for evening classes and I studied design with Mr Lloyd and life drawing with Mr Albert Wagg. Albert Wagg was an obvious admirer of the work of Mr Forsyth and Mr Tittensor for his watercolour drawings were superb and in this field he ran them a very close second. He was also a very talented lithograph artist and designer and highly respected 'by those with eyes to see.' In my opinion he was never accorded the acclaim he deserved in his lifetime.

This last episode more or less completed my senior school training, but I must mention here a few words of praise about the variety of the course, covering precision and figure modelling, throwing, turning and mould making, which the Stoke School was well known for. The excellence in these skills was fully appreciated by the many students who attended the classes, particularly those of Mr Eric Owen, the head modeller from Minton's. Under his guidance I executed a number of original models. As well as giving advice with the modelling, he helped with the moulding and casting of the subjects and, although I never reached a very high standard with this form of artistic expression in clay, I enjoyed the time spent on it enormously. The throwing and turning instruction also proved to be of inestimable value, which I made full use of in later years at the Spode factory.

However, much of this lay in the future and we must return to my days with George Jones, where I stayed for five years. As I have said, they were happy years, made so by the joy of learning my craft and liking for the people I worked for. But my career with George Jones & Sons was to come to an end quite suddenly, for the factory was to be taken over by new owners. Once amalgamated with other firms, new heads were to guide our destiny. First Leon Grice left the employ of the company, followed shortly afterwards by myself. This was a sad episode for me because the old factory had so much to offer in furthering the career of an aspiring designer. I could, however, look back on a rewarding time in which I had gained much valuable experience.

During my stay at George Jones, part of my training had been to study in depth the strengths and weaknesses of all the decorating processes so that full consideration could be given to them when creating new designs. For the best part of twelve months I studied the difficult craft of hand-painting under the guidance of Mr William Birbeck, the brother of Charles. He was the last survivor of a number of artists employed at the factory. 'Billy', unlike his brother, was a tall man, with a slightly shuffling gait. He had a shock of greying hair and a heavy moustache, nicotine-stained from the large pipe he smoked.

As the demand for hand-painting dwindled over the years, William Birbeck had had to apply himself to try and cope with a variety of subjects and such were his skills that he managed to portray all the popular subjects – flowers, fruit, landscape, fish and birds – which were likely to be asked for on dinner, tea and dessert services. The technique required for ceramic painting is very difficult to master and it was only after weeks of practice that I managed to produce an example which was only promising at best. At the end of my stint of instruction, dear Billy was pleased with the progress I had made and hoped that I might be persuaded to take up ceramic painting as a full-time occupation and eventually succeed him.

During the course of my search for knowledge, one of the greatest thrills I experienced was in trying to master the art and skill of lithography. First, one had to learn to appreciate the limitations of the process. Once a design had been created, careful analysis was made of the number of colour separations needed. The artwork involved was substantial and tedious but after this was completed, producing the first printing of the design was most exciting. Various colour combinations could be tried and sufficient prints of each scheme could be produced on a small sample-printing machine to provide a number of fired examples for approval.

I was particularly interested in this process and had several designs accepted for production in bulk, which was quite an achievement for a teenager. One design that gave me great satisfaction was a series of floral centres and sprays, using many different colours, which was entitled 'Holdway Centres'. There were also several ornamental border decorations with interspersed flower motifs and centre arrangements. Throughout my career I have often wondered why more factories did not avail themselves of the lithograph printing facility, especially in later years, when new materials made lithos easier to produce and apply to wares.

When I left the employ of George Jones during 1933 it seemed a tragic event to me, almost the end of my world. Following my departure, I spent a short time with one of the lithograph manufacturers[1] as a member of the design staff, churning out many scores of inexpensive decorations which were peddled around the Potteries by travellers in the hope of making a sale to various pottery producers. If a sale was made of the design, then usually a trial sample was made and with luck a large order given for transfer sheets. The standard of design was lamentable and the taste of the average manufacturer left a lot to be desired. The best I can say was that it was a job, but one with little or no pleasure for myself.

Fortunately I did not have to suffer the indignity of doing this kind of work for long, because early in 1934 I noticed an advertisement in the *Staffordshire Evening Sentinel*; the great firm of W.T. Copeland

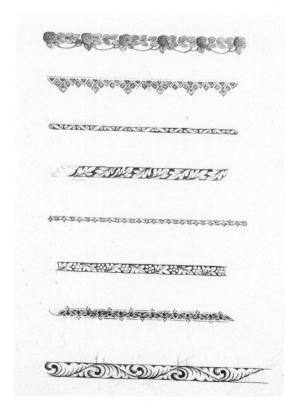

Border designs sketched on the back of a scrap of paper for the Ceramic Transfer Co. Ltd.

[1] Ceramic Transfer Co. Ltd, Jenkins Street, Bursiem.

& Sons required a junior designer to act as assistant to their art director. Hurriedly, I rushed off an application by post to the general manager, Mr William Longsdale, giving him a résumé of my past experience and qualifications. Well over a hundred applications were received and I was one of a shortlist chosen for interview. This was to be conducted by Mr Ronald Copeland, Chairman of the company, at a date to be arranged.

The day came and, armed with a bulging folio of my work, I arrived at the Spode factory, where I was ushered into Mr Ronald Copeland's splendid office. It was of a most dignified appearance, the walls covered with diplomas and Royal Warrant Holder's Certificates, together with finely painted framed slabs and plaques by the great Copeland floral artist, Charles Ferdinand Hurten. Another wall was occupied by a large display cabinet housing many examples of fine china. To me it was breathtaking.

Mr Copeland, a tall, grey-haired gentleman, dignified and autocratic, was sitting at a large antique desk when I entered. He rose, extending his hand to greet me, and, dismissing the general manager with an imperious gesture, he asked me to take a seat. After a long conversation, which lasted over an hour, he indicated that he thought that I would be most suitable for the job vacancy. I tried in vain to show him my designs and artwork, which I had brought along for the interview, but he waved my efforts aside and said it was not necessary.

Ronald Copeland. Drawing by Harold.

He then sent for Mr Longsdale and, in my presence, instructed him to arrange for a suitable work studio to be made available as soon as possible and fix a date when I should report for duty. Whilst all this was happening, one thought was constantly recurring in my mind. Why had I not met the most important character in my future career, the art director whose assistant I was to be? Little did I realise that everything would be revealed in the near future, in no uncertain manner!

Within a fortnight, at the given time and date, I reported for duty and was welcomed by the general manager. He introduced me to my future lord and master, Mr Thomas Hassall, Art Director of W.T. Copeland & Sons Ltd. He was then aged 56 years, short, fat, balding, bespectacled with a most fearsome countenance. To me he presented a frightening image. After the formal introduction, Mr Longsdale left me, as he put it, in Mr Hassall's good care. I then underwent a lecture, which must have lasted about two hours, during which Mr Hassall gave me a complete outline of the history of the company, emphasising the insignificance of any contribution I might make towards its future fortunes. The fact that I had had a successful Art School training seemed to be quite insignificant in his eyes.

Gradually the truth dawned on me that this good man did not wish me to play any useful part in the general scheme of things and was most hostile in his attitude. Fortunately I was the protégé of Mr Ronald Copeland, and, providing I proved my worth, there was nothing the art director could do about me. He had been instructed to introduce me to all the heads of the factory departments, which he did and then escorted me to my workroom and left me to my own devices. This was not an auspicious start to my new job – 20th February, 1934 was indeed a day to remember!

My workroom was situated on the first floor of one of the factory's multi-storey buildings. On the second floor, directly above my room, was the office of Mr Hassall. Each day he had to pass my door many times, but never once did he come in. At the start of each working day, Mr Hassall arrived at the factory at 9am and climbed the thirty-six steps, passing my glass-panelled door without so much as a glance, nod or any other sign or greeting, preceded by Mrs Hilda Beech, an ex-burnisher, who tidied his office in addition to looking after the works' museum and small showroom. Under his arm he carried his daily newspaper, which he read avidly, making comments on the news of the day to anyone within earshot.

This routine lasted for about an hour, until at 10am

Mother T's underglaze painting workshop.

precisely he would make his first regular duty call, which was a visit to a small brick-built workshop situated on the far side of the factory, which housed about a dozen underglaze paintresses and which was the domain of Mrs Turner – Mother T – who was in charge of the small group. On opening the door of the workroom, he would be greeted by the lovely aroma of cooking, for on the stove-pot would be a perfectly cooked breakfast dish, ready for serving to the visitor.

A three-legged stool was in position and the newspaper-covered bench space stood ready to receive the tasty dish. Mr Hassall would then proceed to tuck into this repast with gusto – he really did enjoy this first task of the day. After he had finished he would sit back and relax for a while, with a freshly filled pipe aglow, often remarking that the world was not such a bad place after all. Nothing was ever said about this practice – one should always remember that there was no internal telephone system of communication in these early days, and on a factory site covering nine acres it was not too difficult to hide away and not be found.

However, at the beginning of my life at Spode, I knew nothing of Mr Hassall's habits. I had assumed that I would be given some specific task to perform but nothing was forthcoming. I was not the type to sit in my room and read my paper, so I paid a visit to the glost warehouse and had a fair quantity of ware delivered to my room. I then proceeded to produce a quantity of designs carefully painted in watercolour on these pieces. I continued like this, producing many ideas without any sign of a visit from Mr Hassall, which was very mystifying to me.

However, this situation was to change in a dramatic way. One day, I was working as usual on a design, when I heard the voice of Mr Ronald Copeland on the stairs, asking Mr Hassall to accompany him to see what progress I was making. I was very nervous for I

had no idea if I was doing what was expected of me, but so was Mr Hassall! For all he knew I had been sitting doing nothing all this time. But Mr Copeland, on seeing my array of designs, became very excited about my work and was loud in his commendation. As it was nearly lunchtime, they both soon departed, leaving behind a very happy young man. I went home to lunch and told my mother of Mr Ronald's praise, not anticipating what awaited me on my return.

This time Mr Hassall did not pass my door. He simply burst into the room, ranting and raving at me, with threats of what he would do if I ever repeated the exercise. He insisted that in future he would tell me what I should do and when. I bowed my head under the onslaught, but this was the last time he ever ignored my presence. It was the start of a turbulent partnership of great variety and interest. The following day, he visited me in my room and gave me an instruction to familiarise myself with the product range. I was to spend my day watching the decorated ware being delivered into the enamel receive area, ready to be fired. I was to inspect the pieces and report any faults in decorating to the foreman or forewoman of the department from which it came. To make life more interesting, I used to visit all the decorating departments and after a short while I was considered to be a good judge of quality.

It was a few weeks before I saw a watercolour brush and colours again, and when I did it was to help with the recording of new shapes and patterns in the record books, in accordance with an instruction I had received. The head of the pattern book department was Sam Williams, an ex-gilder, who did quite a reasonable job of illustrating the entries in the books. He was a veteran of the First World War and he kept me enthralled with his vivid and colourful account of his exciting army days. He enjoyed his pints of ale in the evenings and was a regular drinking companion of Mr Hassall.

I was gradually being accepted by Mr Hassall as a useful member of staff as slowly but surely I absorbed a wealth of general knowledge about the way things were run at the factory. The whole of the design facility was shrouded in mystery. New decorations were being produced, some of which were very fine indeed, and I discovered that the main source of inspiration came from the hands of an ex-ceramic painter named Harry Hammersley and his workmate, Charles J. Deaville, an ex-gilder, who also possessed great skills. These craftsmen worked in a dingy room and were given projects by Mr Hassall, who approved or rejected their work when it was submitted to him. I was quite envious of their ability and felt very sorry that they did not receive just recognition for their fine work.

In the mid-nineteen-thirties, with three million unemployed, everyone with a job worked hard to keep it. Lots of short-time working was the norm and most of the potteries were struggling to keep their heads above water. The time when new products are needed is when orders are short and because of the urgent need, Mr Hassall allowed me to submit ideas for consideration. By now, he had accepted my position as his assistant and life became a lot more enjoyable for me. Patience had had its reward.

Although we were never allowed any real credit for our work as artists, it was still very satisfying to have one's own decorations produced and offered for sale to the public. Each design was always submitted to prospective customers by the art director and all comments were passed on by him to each of the designers – a pat on the head if the design was liked and a real blast if it was rejected. The earnings of senior designers were based on a day wage system and were never high. In consequence, they had a poor standard of living, but all workers at the factory were badly paid, so we hoped that our designs would be successful and bring massive orders and increased prosperity for the firm and for us.

Young self-portrait aged 23, 1936, drawn with the minimum of lines in pen and ink.

THE FACTORY'S MANAGEMENT

W.T. Copeland & Sons was our firm's correct title but it was always simply referred to as Copeland's. The factory itself was often known by its original name – the Spode factory. It was very much of a family firm and it was noted for the characteristics this implies. Like many others in the district, the relationship between worker and owner was a distinctly 'touch your forelock' one. The hierarchy of those who controlled our destinies must receive early attention here.

The board of directors was headed by the chairman, Richard Ronald John Copeland, known to all as Mr Ronald. Alfred Gresham Copeland, known as Mr Gresham, and Arthur Edward Hewitt, Mr Ted, were joint managing directors. The chief executives were Frank L. Thorley, the sales manager, and Thomas Hassall, the art director.

Richard Ronald John Copeland ruled with a rod of iron and humble workpeople trembled at the sound of his voice. So did everyone else, up to and including the senior management. Fortunately for the peace of mind of all concerned, Mr Ronald spent more of his time away from the factory than within it. His demeanour on one of his infrequent visits depended on whom he first met on his arrival and what tales were poured into his ear; it could range from the kindly to downright satanic. He was a man of commanding appearance whether he was wearing his exquisitely tailored business suits or his sporting tweeds. He was often to be seen minus his jacket and waistcoat, shirtsleeves rolled up and conspicuous braces supporting his high-waisted trousers. In this garb he looked a true master potter.

In addition to his responsibilities to the company he had many other interests to which he gave unstinting time and effort. His philanthropic interests included the founding of the Children's Orthopaedic Hospital at Biddulph, Staffordshire, a truly magnanimous act, and a lifetime of support for the Scouting Movement in North Staffordshire. As President of the Scouting Association, he provided a permanent campsite of many acres on his estate at Kibblestone. He was also a Freemason of the City of London and, in 1946, Prime Warden of the Worshipful Company of Goldsmiths.

Mr Ronald Copeland was married to Ida, daughter of Camillo Fenzi of Florence and of Mrs Leonard Cuncliffe of Trelissick, Cornwall. Ronald and Ida had two sons, Richard Spencer Charles, later to head the firm, and Ronald Geoffrey Galton, who became a captain in the 11th Hussars and, after serving in World War Two, was killed on active service in 1952. Mrs Ida Copeland was a Fellow of the Royal Society of Arts, and led a very active public life. She was a Member of Parliament for Stoke-on-Trent from 1931 to 1935. Mr Ronald Copeland was appointed Justice of the Peace in 1932, High Sheriff in 1939, Deputy Lord Lieutenant in 1946 and was created Commander of the British Empire in 1948. In later years, Mrs Ida Copeland inherited the stately house at Trelissick in Cornwall and she and her husband took up residence there.

Before Mr Ronald moved to Trelissick, he lived in a fine house at Colwich, near Stafford, where he housed many of the loveliest pieces in his collection. There was also a large representation at the factory, which he had had displayed in a special gallery, built in 1939. His taste was impeccable, probably too refined for the average customer and he often said that most buyers had little true artistic appreciation. One of his greatest joys was to bring beautiful blooms from his garden to the factory where the artists could make studies of them and, it was hoped, receive inspiration for new patterns. Mr Ronald unfortunately suffered from extreme short-sightedness and needed very strong spectacles to correct his vision. Because of his affliction he did miss a lot of detail but he had a wonderful knowledge of fine china and he was an avid collector of early Spode.

Gresham Copeland drawn by Harold in 1963.

25

Alfred Gresham Copeland was younger than his brother Ronald and differed from him in almost every way. In my early days I had little to do with him because, as Mr Gresham's main responsibility was for maintaining high production standards at the factory, his chief contacts were with the departmental managers and foremen. The area of the firm's activity that he covered ranged from raw materials to packing the finished goods and it really was a full-time job. Mr Gresham conscientiously fulfilled every aspect of his onerous duties, reporting for work every weekday and being kept constantly busy. He was responsible for the ordering of all commodities into the factory and he made sure that standards were rigidly adhered to, paying particular attention to the purity of ceramic materials and making sure that adequate supplies were always available. A particularly important commodity in his care was the nugget gold. He personally ground this on the factory's mill and mixed it himself following secret recipes, which he guarded carefully.

Mr Gresham was a truly Christian gentleman and he was always ready to lend a helping hand to anyone in need. He held strong religious views and was very happily married with two sons, John and Thomas Robert. The family home was a large house a few miles south of Stoke, known as Tittensor Chase, set in lovely woodlands covering many acres. Because of Mr Gresham's intense industry he was highly respected by the workforce. The firm and its interests were his main concern and he collected early Spode blue and white printed wares, having one of the finest collections in existence. Specialists from all over the world sought his expert opinion and he collaborated with several authors who wrote on the subject.

Arthur Edward Hewitt was the agent for Mrs

A circular Gibbons' Rotalec enamel kiln installed by A.E. Hewitt.

Ida Copeland, the wife of Ronald Copeland, and managed the successful campaign that resulted in her election in 1931 as Conservative Member of Parliament for Stoke-on-Trent. The association and friendship were nurtured and in 1932, he joined the Board of W.T. Copeland & Sons Ltd. He was a knowledgeable pottery owner, being head of Jackson and Gosling, a good quality Longton china company that he ran very successfully. Copeland's were very much in need of a top-level executive at this time, with the energy and drive necessary to inject some enthusiasm and to introduce new ideas and methods.

This appointment took place two years before I joined the company and Mr Hewitt was well established when I arrived. He was causing quite a stir at the old factory. He was a natural leader and as a captain during the First World War he won the Military Cross. His war experience stood him in good stead in the battles that lay ahead at the Spode factory.

One of his major moves early in 1934 was his negotiation of a large contract to supply earthenware for a gift scheme.[2] It took over twelve months to complete and he built a gas-fired glost oven for earthenware with the profits from the order. This was a notable example of his foresight but there were many other lesser ones and he continued in this progressive way throughout his association with the company. His achievements are too numerous to mention in this brief personal account, but they were very great and his arrival was the start of a prosperous period for the firm.

In addition to his many responsibilities within the factory he undertook many outside it. He was a very

Arthur Edward Hewitt: Joined the Copeland board in 1932.

[2] One of the first giftware schemes was a Sunlight Soap promotion offering a Blue Italian fruit or salad bowl to celebrate their 50th anniversary.

King George VI and Queen Elizabeth's visit to the factory in 1941. Photo courtesy of Spode Museum Trust.

active member of the local council, chairing a number of important committees and playing a large part in bringing Stoke up to date. He made valiant efforts to promote clean air and rid the city of its smoke-laden atmosphere. With this in mind, he advocated the firing of ovens and kilns by gas and electricity instead of coal and, as an example, he followed up his successful gas-fired tunnel oven at the factory with two circular Gibbons' Rotalec, continuously-operated enamel kilns which were heated by electricity. They proved a great success.

During the early years of the Second World War he became Lord Mayor of the City and during his term of office he was host to Their Majesties King George VI and Queen Elizabeth when they paid a visit to the factory in 1941. During the visit, I had the honour of being presented to Their Majesties and I escorted them around the enamel banding and finishing department, explaining the various processes to them. They were fascinated with the skill displayed and were particularly interested to see colour bands being applied to ten-inch dinner plates being decorated with Christmas Tree pattern.

The King wanted to examine a piece more closely and picked up one of the plates by the edge. It had a band of colour already applied and he left a perfect thumbprint on it. He most courteously expressed his regret for spoiling a finished piece. I told him it was only the job of a minute to clean off the colour and re-apply the band, but after they left the department I retrieved the plate and scratched a descriptive explanation through the unfired colour on each side of the thumbprint. I then personally placed the piece in the hands of the head enamel fireman, Frank Simpson, and told him how special it was. I watched him place it in the kiln so that it would be fired and ready for collection the following morning. Bright and early, I arrived at the factory and asked for the

plate, but, with red faces, the firemen said it had not been seen and that it could not be found. It had simply vanished into thin air! It was a sad end to the story but I have no doubt that this unique plate will turn up one day. Hopefully, it will be returned to the factory, where it belongs amongst its treasures and mementoes.

A big move in Mr Hewitt's plan for the firm and one which he made early in 1934 was to engage the services of an ace sales manager, Mr Frank Thorley of Wedgwood. He had spent all his working life with Wedgwood, rising through the ranks to become their sales manager. He was middle aged, of serious demeanour and a lover of outdoor pursuits, particularly with horses and dogs. He was well known as a very forceful salesman with a powerful personality and boundless energy. He gave great support to Mr Hewitt and his ideas, and gained a lot of respect from everyone when orders began to flow into the company, largely because of his enthusiasm and drive. During this period we had a fine showroom in London, with a manager and assistants, and our London stockists made full use of their expertise and help. We also had a representative for the North, Charles Audley, and one who covered the South, Edwin Leadbeater. The latter was one of the few commercial travellers who did not possess a motor car for transport. He did all his travelling by rail with large trunks to hold his samples.

In the early Thirties few private motor vehicles were to be seen on the streets and roads of Stoke-on-Trent and very few pottery workers ever aspired to owning such a luxurious form of transport. Even motorcycles were rarely owned by working men and seldom if ever used for journeying to and from their place of employment. The suspicion in the mind of the worker was that if the bosses saw workers with such luxuries, it would be assumed that their wages were too high and that they were aping their betters. My own form of transport, like so many others, was a pedal cycle, which was also used for leisure. For a number of years I had been an active member of one of the local cycling clubs and enjoyed riding many thousands of miles exploring the countryside and beauty spots which abound the outskirts of Stoke-on-Trent, including the picturesque counties of Cheshire, Derbyshire and Shropshire. Armed with a pencil, sketchbook and watercolours, I enjoyed recording many scenes.

The rough-surfaced streets and cobbled main roads were seldom, if ever, crowded with vehicles. The electric tramcars, with their overhead conductors running on polished tracks, emitted strange tunes as their bogie wheels squeaked and squealed in motion. Horses and carts were still in abundance and eager young boys armed with buckets and shovels followed them hoping to collect the horse droppings to help fertilise the smoke-blackened patches of soil in the backyard gardens of their humble abodes. Perhaps Mr Leadbeater was wise, as motoring in those conditions can hardly have been a pleasure.

Mr Thorley had to work with Mr Hassall, the art director, particularly when he was in need of new shapes and patterns to stimulate trade. They clashed on many occasions and throughout their working relationship Frank Thorley was never considered to

be a 'true Copeland man' in the eyes of Tom Hassall. I was often a victim of their disagreements, having to be loyal to Mr Hassall, even when I knew he was at fault. Mr Thorley used to take advantage of any absence of Mr Hassall from the factory, usually caused by some trip or other. He would then seek me out and insist on accompanying me round all the decorating departments to see the state of the orders being processed and what new ideas were forthcoming. I was always sworn to secrecy by Mr Thorley about these and this made life very difficult for me.

Mr Thorley was responsible for a number of the overseas markets as well as home sales but a major exception was North America. This was handled by a company known as Copeland and Thompson, which held the sole rights to sell Copeland products throughout the USA and Canada. The German and Italian markets were also excluded, being in the capable hands of Herr August Warnecke of Hamburg. Mr Thorley's area of responsibility was still wide and of vital importance to the factory's future. He came to Copeland's in the dark days of the 1930s Depression. He had faults but he was a success and he played a big part in the steady build-up of the firm's business before the Second World War.

Thomas Hassall, who features prominently in this account, was born in 1878 and died on 7th April

Thomas Hassall: Art Director. Drawing by Harold. April 1940.

Thomas Hassall inspecting Coronation mugs and beakers, 1937.

1940. He was happily married with five children, three boys and two girls, and the family lived at The Croft in Penkhull. It was his habit to walk to and from the works twice every day for he always had lunch at home and considered these walks good exercise.

During my early years with the company my future success depended on my ability to unravel the mystery and aura that surrounded him. He worked at Copeland's all his life. Following his father's example, he became a qualified ceramic painter after serving his apprenticeship at the factory. He then became one of the numerous artists employed during this period. Most of these were specialists in specific subjects and, as far as I was ever able to ascertain, Mr Hassall was mainly known for his floral painting. Very few examples are to be found to help make a true assessment of his skills. His work as an artist attracted the attention of Ronald Copeland. According to his obituary, he held the position of art director for thirty years, so he must have been promoted after a relatively short time. He had detailed knowledge of all the various processes and this enabled him to fulfil the function of decorating manager in addition to his duties as the art director.

When I was appointed as his assistant he had been in his position for twenty-four years and was a law unto himself. As art director, his main task was to direct the efforts of a talented staff of artists and designers. He had considerable success in this and he also saw to it that the characteristics of the early Spode designs were maintained in the designs currently being produced. He constantly made use of the finely recorded entries in the early pattern books as a guide and inspiration.

One of his skills was his ability to mix the various colours for the decoration processes. He did this without using any recipe and he never kept a record for future reference. This became a worry to the directors and I was instructed to learn this skill as quickly as possible in case an emergency arose. It was a cat and mouse situation, because I am sure he was conscious of my being a little over-zealous and too attentive so he would often take a break during the colour-mixing sessions on some pretext or other and would then return later to complete the job without me in attendance. I overcame this difficulty, however, by instructing the lady in charge of the colour shop to make a note of which colours he used and with this information, it was only a matter of trial and error before I was able to mix any colour to make a good batch.

I spent only six years of my career working with Thomas Hassall but during this time we built up a very close love–hate relationship. In spite of his many shortcomings I had a deep respect for his ability to cope with any situation and I gladly pay tribute to the major part he played in the revival of the fortunes of W.T. Copeland & Sons Ltd in the 1930s.

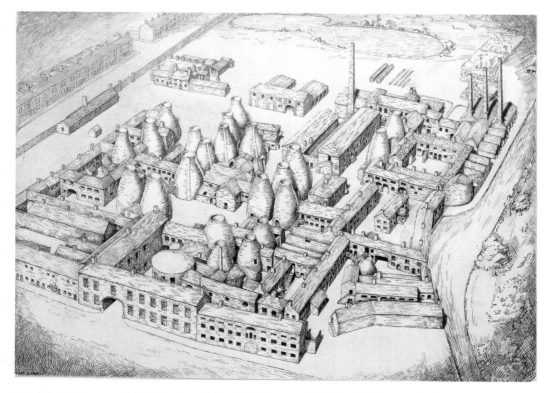

Harold's 1951 pen and ink drawing of the 1833 clay model of Spode's factory has been used many times in publicity material.

Left: Bill wheeling best coal into the china bottle oven with Jim Evans, china biscuit fireman until the change over to tunnel firing in 1960.

Right: Snow on a cold bottle oven, 9th February 1940.

Right: Award-winning photo of Spode's bottle-ovens taken by Harold Holdway.

Below: Copeland's chimney for drying slip.

Below right: A publicity stunt with a lorry balanced on four teacups, following a similar achievement by Wedgwood using coffee cans. Apparently Harold eventually captured this photo during his lunch break after many failures. Each wheel was jacked up in turn, but as they moved to the next one the cups kept slipping out, making a noise like a gunshot.

DESIGN DEPARTMENT SPECIALISTS

Design departments tend to be collections of specialists and that of Copeland's in the 1930s possessed three of outstanding ability: Harry Hammersley, Charles J. Deaville and Eric Olsen. The work of the last of these was to one side of the mainstream of the factory's tradition but that of the other two was central to it.

A few months were to elapse after I joined the company before I had chance to meet Harry Hammersley. My curiosity had been aroused because I used to occasionally catch a glimpse of a piece of his artwork or a floral arrangement, usually in the hands of Mr Hassall, which I admired enormously. Eventually I tracked him down in his place of work. It was only a few yards from my own workroom, but such was the secrecy that existed at this time in Copeland's art department!

It was a dark and dingy room with four tall windows, two on each side. On opening the door, one could see two elderly figures at work, seated at benches. Lots of paraphernalia cluttered their workspace and the whitewashed walls were sadly in need of repainting. Dusty floorboards creaked with every step one made. Such was the domain of Mr Harry Hammersley and Mr Charles J. Deaville. Never in my life had I seen such a pathetic sight as these two brilliant craftsmen working in such depressing surroundings. They had heard of my existence via the factory grapevine and I was welcomed in a most genuine manner, being offered any help or advice that it was in their power to give.

When I studied the work of Mr Hammersley and watched his skilful fingers deftly composing groups of flowers and other subjects with such ease, I asked myself how I could ever hope to compete with such ability and acquire such knowledge. He had learned his skills in the hard school of experience, for, like his father before him, he was a Copeland-trained artist. He was a contemporary of Arthur Perry, John Arrowsmith and many other first-class painters – a band that was gradually dwindling away in the Twenties.

Following his own appointment, Mr Hassall made good use of the talents of Mr Perry and Mr Hammersley to enhance his own reputation, particularly when designs or special painted services were required. Arthur Perry decided that living in the shadow of Mr Hassall did not suit his future plans and in 1926 he left the employ of W.T. Copeland & Sons and joined Royal Doulton. There he spent the remainder of his working years, painting many fine services, finally retiring at the age of seventy-six years. Arthur Perry's departure meant that more creative work was required from Harry Hammersley and Charles Deaville. Both of them had great creative ability as well as the additional skills of being able to make highly finished drawings and produce artwork in watercolour for presentation purposes. China painters they were, and of the first order, but their talents were of a rarer and, to a factory, more precious kind.

The Alcock Vase, gilded by Charles Deaville and painted by Samuel Alcock. Photo: Bill Coles, courtesy of Spode Museum Trust.

Arthur Perry with Harold, 1965. Photograph: H.K. Bowden.

Gainsborough designed by H. Hammersley. Photograph: Jones.

One of the finest designs ever created by Harry Hammersley was one on which he was working when I joined the firm. Gainsborough was an under-glaze, transfer-printed floral decoration on a shape with slightly embossed rims that was painted by girls. Floral design was Harry's speciality and this one was a freely arranged group of flowers and leaves which covered most of the plate's surface and had a delightful and unusual quality. Each piece had a different arrangement of flowers and when the service was viewed as a whole, it was difficult to believe that anyone could have come up with such a variety of arrangements. What amazed me was the ease with which Harry Hammersley composed his flower groups and the speed with which the pencil in his fingers moved over the paper.

Gainsborough was aimed mainly at the American market and when it was launched there, it was a runaway success. Our agent's method of marketing was to allow only one dealer per town or city to stock any particular pattern. In general this worked very well, but as everybody wanted Gainsborough, an additional alternative pattern with similar characteristics and the same appeal was urgently needed to take advantage of such a wonderful selling opportunity. This would have been impossible without Harry Hammersley's great skill. He was able to produce, not one, but two alternative decorations in a similar vein. They were named Romney and Lawrence, and the ploy satisfied the demands of the American market for a number of years. Gradually, however, the alternative designs began to lose popularity and fade away, but Gainsborough went on from strength to strength, becoming one of the factory's all-time best sellers.

The creator of this phenomenon was a slight, rather short man with greying hair; a fine conversationalist, extremely generous and mild in manner. He was happily married and lived in Penkhull. I was always fascinated by the way he rolled his own cigarettes – very little tobacco and lots of paper. After lighting one of these so-called cigarettes he would take just one or two puffs and lay it down on the edge of his bench, where it almost immediately went out. No ashtrays were used when dusty floorboards were so convenient! At the end of the day there would be a small area around his feet strewn with nicotine-stained butts. The habit seemed hardly inappropriate to the sordid surroundings in which he was obliged to work. Before Harry Hammersley reached retirement age he was taken ill and he died shortly before the war began. His death came as a great shock to me but it was even more of a shock to Thomas Hassall for he knew he had lost one of his most faithful servants and he knew he would never replace him.

Despite Harry Hammersley's great value to the firm, in all the time I knew him he never held a staff appointment, being kept on the establishment as a day wage worker even when doing creative work. When he was painting special services he was paid at a piecework rate, just like any factory operative. A year or so after his death his widow, who was in straitened circumstances, brought to the factory a bundle of sketches that Harry and his father had produced during their lifetimes. She asked if they would be of any use to the company. The sketches were accepted and a trivial sum of money changed hands. Strange and ungrateful world, where a just reward for honest endeavour seemed so hard to come by!

There must be many treasured, richly painted services in the world featuring Harry Hammersley's work and signed with the initials HH. I think particular praise should be given to him for the crossed fruit and flower dessert services, which he painted so skilfully. The examples of them in the Copeland section of the Spode Museum are an honour to his memory.

Harry Hammersley's work companion, Charles J. Deaville, was the elder statesman of the craftsman gilders. He was responsible for some of the finest examples of gilding ever to have graced stately homes, royal palaces and international exhibitions. His work is exemplified in the gilding of the large vase painted with classical figures by Samuel Alcock, which is on display in the Spode Factory Museum. This vase has a very unusual feature for it bears the initials CJD discreetly hidden in the gold embellishment in the foot. It is indeed a rare occurrence for a gilder to be allowed to sign his work and Deaville is the only one I know in the history of the firm to have enjoyed the privilege. Sometimes he signed his name in full.

I first met Mr Deaville when I was a small schoolboy and he was in charge of the Stoke branch of the Boys' Brigade. As a very junior member of this body I was in awe of the Captain who looked impressive and dignified in his uniform. It was many years later at the Spode factory that I renewed the acquaintance and he was by that time an elderly man, although he still had the bearing of a well-drilled soldier. He was very helpful to me and gave me lots of good advice on ornamental design and arrangements suitable for various types of decoration.

I only wish I could remember some of the stories he used to recount of the old days. One particular story that I do remember concerned a vacancy that was on offer for the post of head gilder at the factory of Josiah Wedgwood & Sons at Etruria. Mr Deaville and his fellow gilder Mr Ted Goodwin were rivals and companions at Copeland's, each vying with the other in craftsmanship. If one of them could take the Wedgwood position each would become cock of the walk in his own sphere and they decided to toss a coin as to who should apply for the vacancy at Wedgwood. Mr Deaville won the toss and chose to stay at Copeland's. Mr Goodwin applied to Wedgwood and was successful. Years later he was appointed Wedgwood's Art Director, a most elevated position which he held until his retirement in the late Thirties. I am sure Charles Deaville often wondered if he had been wise in his choice when the coin came down in his favour.

Charles Deaville was a very happily married man, deeply religious and abstemious. He had a son, Leslie, who served as a highly skilled engraver at the factory for many years.[3] Charles retired before the beginning of World War Two and died on 4th January 1939. In all, his service to Copeland's had totalled more than sixty years. Towards the end of his career his creative designs proved very successful, which gave him and Thomas Hassall great satisfaction.

In almost every way Eric Olsen was a complete contrast to Charles Deaville and Harry Hammersley. Of Norwegian birth and with no Copeland background or training, he was bought into the firm by Mr Ted Hewitt shortly before I joined in 1934. He was an artist sculptor and his style of work was 'Modern', extremely so in the context of the Copeland factory. He was allowed a free run in his choice of subject and

he had his own studio. This was in splendid isolation, well away from the normal modelling facilities run by Mr Hassall. He was allowed to use all the processes available on the factory to produce his pieces and this included ordering supplies of special glazes and clays. He was more or less his own master and his output of work was prodigious.

He produced a series of sculptured animals, which included a polar bear, bison, tiger, elephant and various dogs. All were in a very simplified form. He favoured a semi-matt glaze for the finish, either in an ivory colour or in a pale green called Royal Jade. This project, which gave him his first commercial success, produced good sales for a number of years. Using the same glazes, he also produced a large number of low-relief modelled vases, bowls, trays and other items, which had a lot of charm and sold well.

In his time at the factory he held a private exhibition of his individual creations in a London gallery. The wares were full of character and they mainly consisted of vases and bowls decorated with subtle textures and glazes. These he sold as original specimens of his craft, as opposed to his commercial work. The *Studio Art Magazine* was most impressed and reproduced in colour many of his creations to illustrate an approving article on his work.

Early in the Second World War, he modelled two toby jugs, one of Churchill and the other of Roosevelt, and such was their popularity, particularly the Churchill one, that a small department was set up to satisfy the demand. They were modelled in typical toby jug style, but his next venture, following their success, was naturalistic. He produced a small bone china figure of Mr Churchill in his familiar pin-striped suit, Homburg hat and cigar, carefully painted in proper colours. This was quite an expensive item but it was still a great success.

Rabbit designed by Eric Olsen in onyx ware.

[3] Leslie is rumored to have been a little eccentric. Whilst on lookout duty during the war he used to ride around the factory on his bike naked!

His ability as a draughtsman and a designer for applied decorations could have been only rarely put to the test and I remember only two instances: a very pretty modern design for china tea ware featuring seagulls and a bold botanical-style apple design for earthenware. The first proved popular but the second, although nicely executed, had no real success.

Shortly after producing the Churchill figure model he volunteered for service in the Norwegian Army, where he had a distinguished military career as a camouflage expert. After the war he went to America and became a successful art director for a famous ceramic factory, Haegar Potteries, New Jersey. On rare occasions we saw him again when he paid visits to the Spode factory to see old friends.

Shortly after I joined the firm in 1934, the crest painter, Mr Frank Slater – who was not in good health – died and was succeeded by Mr Joe Austin, who had been on short-time working at Minton's. Joe was to play a very important role in the future design sphere. I was from time to time allowed to show my personal creative skills and enjoyed some success. Mr Geoffrey Cholerton, then a junior painter, was also invited to do a small amount of artwork during this period.

The deaths of Mr Hammersley and Mr Deaville were a great loss to the firm and left Mr Hassall desperately trying to fill his vacancies. After a lengthy time a Mr Jack Price, a Doulton painter, signed on. Although his ceramic painting had a certain skill, I never saw any evidence of any creative design work. After painting some services, mainly of game subjects, he bade Copeland's farewell, leaving Mr Hassall with the realisation of the unlikelihood of his ever replacing the skills of Mr Hammersley. This meant more design work being done by the remaining few, of which I was one.

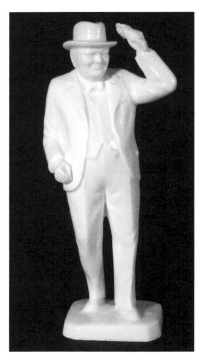

Left: Unpainted Winston Churchill statuette designed by Eric Olsen. The painted version has striped trousers. Courtesy of Bill Coles and Spode Museum Trust.

Right: Winston Churchill toby jug designed by Eric Olsen. Photo: David Walsh.

Figure-maker finishing the statuette of Winston Churchill in the clay stage before firing in the bisque oven.

Placers carrying clay Winston Churchill toby jugs to the bisque oven, the quality being checked on the way by the foreman. Both photos courtesy of Spode Museum Trust.

PAINTERS AND GILDERS

At Copeland's I had the opportunity to study in depth a large variety of products and it was quite a revelation to me. The small select group of fine china companies, of which Copeland's was one, produced goods to a very high standard. One of the craft departments that the firm was still able to maintain and which interested me greatly was that of the men painters. Whereas George Jones had but a solitary painter, Copeland's employed several. As with other factories, the demand for fine hand-painting had diminished, but in the mid-1930s there were still enough orders from high quality shops to justify the employment of four men who were well qualified and a few who were less so.

One of my main duties as assistant to Mr Hassall was to pay a daily visit to the men painters' department to check their work, count the number of pieces painted and arrange for the finished work to be taken to the enamel kilns for firing. At this time, the staff consisted of eight painters. They were all paid on a piecework basis, set so that none of them was able to earn high wages.

The two senior painters of the greatest ability were Fred Micklewright and Joe Fenn. The former was a very quiet, dignified man, well past middle age. He was the nearest to a specialist among the four, mainly painting landscapes featuring stately homes, castles and ruins, etc, all done in a very individual style. Joe Fenn was in his early sixties and, like me, had

previously worked at George Jones, but he had spent most of his working life there. He was a man with much ability and he was able to paint most of the subjects that were asked for, landscapes, flowers, fish, game and fruit.

Jesse Savage was an elderly painter who possessed average ability but he was a very conscientious worker and could handle a variety of subjects. So also could Harry Wakefield, the final member of the quartet and the youngest by far, being in his mid-thirties.

The four junior painters, often called the "boy painters", had completed a form of apprenticeship but they had a very limited knowledge of fine painting and little prospect of enlarging it, for their day-to-day occupation was to fill in outline prints with enamel colours to produce the famous Herring Hunting pattern. This was a menial task for the boy painters as it required only limited skill. The price paid was thus known as "Tuppenny Hunting." It sold in vast quantities and so effectively sabotaged any chance that these young men might be given any serious challenge for their skills.

The only change of work they had was when they were called upon to paint Billingsley Rose. This was another bulk earthenware pattern with outline prints, consisting of a single rose bloom in the centre of the plate, which was painted in pink, with surrounding buds, green leaves and forget-me-nots. Painting Billingsley Rose was no better paid than Herring

Herring Hunting painted by Kathleen Holdway.

Gold burnishing Maritime Rose, a variation of Billingsley Rose.

Hunting and they needed to work hard. All orders were scrupulously divided into lots and the price for the work ensured that total effort had to be put into each day's work. Any slacking or time-wasting meant a smaller wage packet and slipshod work was not tolerated under any circumstances; the only reward for this was dismissal.

What the future held for the boy painters was obviously a matter for speculation. Although they were described as journeymen, they had had so little training and practice in the finer skills of the craft they could not be termed qualified painters. They showed hardly any interest in attending art classes to improve their knowledge and little encouragement was given to them by their supervisors or the senior artists in the department. They were in a vulnerable position and, in later years, the work that mainly occupied them was, indeed, done by women and girls and the quality of workmanship (or workwomanship) was equal to anything the men ever produced.

A sign of the times was the occasional practice of getting both Micklewright and Fenn to make drawings of some of their artistic compositions. These were then engraved on copper plates and inexpensive transfer prints were made to reproduce their work, together with their signatures, which were also engraved. After the subjects were printed on the ware, women enamellers filled them in and the total cost was a fraction of the original freehand painted work of the men. The male artists were naturally very disturbed by this practice because it was just one more step in cutting out the need for the craftsman painter. The finished ware was still described as hand-painted, a discreditable misstatement, but the low price should have made it apparent to those who had not the eyes to see the difference.

The first of the young painters to bring his artistic career to a premature end was the oldest, Bill Eccles. Shortly after my start with the company, a vacancy occurred for an earthenware enamel warehouseman which he applied for and he was taken on in this capacity. He opted for a regular weekly wage instead of the piecework job of a painter; like so many others he had decided that there was very little future in ceramic painting. Throughout his working life as a warehouseman he was a very happy man and was head of his department for many years. Quite often finished ware was rejected for some slight defect in the decoration and Billy was often to be seen with his brush, repairing faults which were then re-fired to make best ware. The skills of his early training came in useful from time to time!

But, to me, this had appeared as a lamentable waste of this man's early working experience. He had been fortunate enough to have received his initial tuition from a man who was a living legend, Arthur Perry, one of the greatest china painters of the turn of the century. It has always been a great sadness to me that I never had the experience of seeing this superb artist practise his skills, for he left the employ of Copeland's in 1926, years before my arrival. To Billy, however, as he had recently married a most attractive paintress, a secure job was of more importance than the glamour of being called an artist.

In his youth, Bill Eccles was a notable sportsman and played football for Stoke City and cricket for one of the leading local teams as a first-class batsman and wicketkeeper. In middle age, he kept his links with the sporting fraternity by officiating as a football referee. When he reached the factory retirement age of 65 he carried on working for an extra two or three years. The reason for this decision was, as he told me, quite simply that he felt that he could not afford to retire. Pottery workers make no fortunes!

As a young painter, Bill Eccles had three colleagues; Eric Bate, a tall, slim young man with a notable sense of humour, Arthur Gaskell and Geoffrey Cholerton. Arthur Gaskell was a rather short man, of stocky build but athletic bent. He had natural artistic aptitude and it was a pity that so few opportunities were given to him to progress as an artist. Occasionally, when new design samples were required to be painted by hand and the older men were fully occupied, Mr Hassall would call upon the young painters to try out their skills. Quite often their efforts were acceptable to him but these opportunities were rare occurrences and the chance of real appreciation and progress was very slight.

Geoffrey Cholerton was twenty-three years of age when I first met him, in 1934. He was tall and not at all athletic, a slow mover but with a keen brain. He was a very poor timekeeper and had to put in many hours of overtime to make up a full week's work. Despite repeated warnings, this habit was a weakness with him throughout his career. He spent a short period at Hanley Art School, attending evening classes, and he had a natural flair for art subjects, but after one or two sessions, he tired of the type of tuition he was receiving. He decided that evening classes at art school had little to offer him and ceased attending.

Although, like his colleagues, he had to endure the slavery and monotony of piecework filling in of prints, when the opportunity presented itself he showed that he could easily surpass the efforts of the others and he was the first to be called upon by Mr Hassall for an artistic effort. Any such activity was covered by the cloak of secrecy since no artist was encouraged to wander around the factory with anything of his own creation. Artwork could be seen by Mr Hassall's eyes alone. Even so, by stealth and ingenuity, Geoffrey's presence and work were noticed by the right people and this was to prove a valuable asset to him in later years.

The other craft department that Copeland's were able to maintain, which was of great interest to me, was that of the gilders. Mr Tom Brough, an old-time gilder himself, was the foreman in charge of it and allocated the orders, checked the items of gilt ware and was responsible for the general standard of workmanship. He was also the foreman in charge of the china-printing department and that he was able to combine the two posts was a tribute to the calibre of the gilders, who were so experienced that they really needed no supervision.

In the year 1934, I doubt if any other china manufacturers had such a large number of highly skilled gilders as Copeland's. They had acquired their skills in the palmy days of the late Victorian and Edwardian eras, when highly ornate and elaborate ornamental pieces were in demand from rich and often aristocratic customers. Such times had long passed but there was still sufficient call for expensive services to justify the employment of Fred Hulme, Harry Boothby, Percy Mallaburn, Jack Stone, Albert Thompson, Arthur Heapy, William Ball and Alec Kelsall. They were all the finest craftsmen, regularly employed without any short-term working and they were capable of producing the most intricate designs

Geoffrey Cholerton: Ceramic artist.

to act as a finish or framework for colour decorations. Their type of work was known as freehand pattern gilding. Like painters, they were all paid on a piecework basis.

I christened this elite band 'Snow White and the Seven Dwarfs', Snow White being Fred Hulme, their father figure, who had a shock of white hair and a white moustache to go with it. He was the doyen of the old-timers who had spent most of their working lives in the employ of Copeland's.

Fred Hulme, who was over seventy years of age in 1934, was famous in his day for the many beautiful pieces and services he gilded and even in his advanced years his workmanship could not be faulted. He was a colourful character and a good-looking man. When one viewed him from the rear he resembled a slim youth and he had a jaunty and sprightly walk. His handsome face had the unusual colour and quality of parchment, with a finely wrinkled skin, his hair and moustache were very white. His dress was immaculate and I have no doubt that he must have been a real dandy in his youth.

The whole department worked on piecework and no one got rich, but 'Old Fred', as he was affectionately known, must have invested his money wisely in earlier days, for he owned a fine tobacconist's shop in Shelton which was run by his wife and daughter. He enjoyed a very busy social life, seeking whatever pleasures were on offer every night of the week. He once gave me what he considered to be good advice: "Harold, get up early in the morning and go to bed late at night and remember you're a long time dead!"

A spare-time activity that was enjoyed by engravers and gilders was watch and clock repairing, for which their steady hands and eyes and their long training in precision suited them well. In this field too, Fred Hulme had done well, being a partner in a repair business, which had a shop on Liverpool Road, Stoke. This was the source of a well-loved gilding shop story.

As Fred walked to work each day from his home in Shelton, he would call in at the shop and ask how things were and he would often pick up a small repair or cleaning job which he could do at the factory, either during his lunch break or after working hours in the evening. It was routine for Fred to use his lunch hour for repair work and he would spread out a newspaper on which he would dismantle the watch or clock preparatory to working on it. If he was interrupted while carrying out this delicate work he would fold over the newspaper and safely cover up all the parts.

One day he received a message from the lodge at the factory gates that some person wanted to speak to him there. Fred carefully folded his newspaper over the watch parts he was working on and obeyed the call. Little did he know that it was a bogus summons and after he had left the room his companions switched the watch parts he had so carefully laid out with a prepared collection which looked similar but which was in fact made up of junk bits and pieces from worn out watches. When Fred returned from his futile visit to the lodge, one of the gilders carelessly and apparently accidentally knocked the newspaper off the workbench onto the floor and the bits and pieces were scattered in all directions.

Poor old Fred is said to have jumped several feet in the air when this happened and he wondered how he would explain the disaster to his partner and his customer. It must have been quite a sight to see the old man on his hands and knees scrabbling around trying to find the minute parts which were scattered over the dusty floorboards, but after a short time his colleagues owned up to the trick and gave him back his property intact, much to his relief.

One could eulogise at great length about the skill and character of such men as Fred Hulme. Examples of their work must be treasured by people all over the world who have never heard of their names, for they worked anonymously. Sometimes, though, when a dish or case is turned over to view the manufacturer's mark, some minute initials painted in small red letters are to be found: FH, in Fred Hulme's case. These were not to give the gilders credit but were applied to the ware so that the gilding was easily identifiable during the decorating process.

Fred's bench mate (for all the gilders worked two to a bench) was a gilder named Harry Boothby. He was completely opposite in personality to his partner. He was slight and small in stature, with thinning hair that was combed over his head in an endeavour to hide the bald patches. He was kindly and gentle and a deep thinker who never wasted words in idle conversation. His quiet demeanour radiated calmness and dignity, which you could always experience in his presence. He was very happily married with a son, Frank, who joined the firm as an apprentice engraver in 1932 and became, like his father, a great craftsman.

Harry was a few years younger than Fred Hulme but was equally accomplished and he was only given the best selection of fine gilding patterns to work on. Like most of the pieceworkers of this period he never wasted a minute of his time and if one asked him a question he would continue with his work while he

gave you the answer. He lived in Fenton and was a life-long friend of Arthur Perry. His son Frank has shown me a number of very fine examples of plates and plaques featuring the work of his father and Arthur Perry. These pieces were painted and gilt at the homes of the two men in their spare time. The system was to buy defective white pieces and, after completing the painting and gilding, have them fired at the factory with the blessing of the fireman and a pint of ale to be collected later at the local.

Mr Albert Thompson was another interesting member of the gilding team. He was a first-class gilder who was, I believe, even older than Fred Hulme. As a native of Wellington, it was his proud boast that it was the birthplace of Captain Webb, the first man to swim the English Channel.

I believe he received his early training and spent many years service as a gilder with the Coalport China Factory, which used to be sited at Coalbrookdale in Shropshire. About 1929, it was decided to transfer Coalport's business to the Cauldon factory in Shelton. The move seems not to have been a success and quite a number of workmen drifted away to other factories in the Potteries. The Coalport painters and gilders enjoyed a very good reputation and had little difficulty in finding new jobs with the fine china companies.

Albert Thompson had very poor sight but with the aid of spectacles he did some very fine gilding for Copeland's. He held the item very near to his nose because of his extreme short-sightedness and he sometimes wore two pairs of spectacles at the same time. He was ever hopeful of finding a pair of spectacles at Woolworth's that would help him with his sight problem. In those days, which now seems so far off, people in need of glasses often sorted through a great pile of metal-framed spectacles – all 6d. a pair – to find some suitable. Albert Thompson continued to work into his eighties and always remained a confirmed bachelor, whose pleasure was an evening stroll to the local pub to enjoy a whisky and hot water and chat with his friends in the 'gentlemen only' bar.

Mr Walter Heapy and Mr William Ball were a duo of very competent gilders who were slightly younger than the three I have described. William Ball, who was Copeland-trained, was a very tall, thin man. He had a strident voice and a forceful manner, but, even so, he was completely subjugated by his wife who was the head of the women's on-glaze painting department, known as Mrs Ball's painting shop. Her christian name was Ada and her signature was often to be seen as part of the engravings of fruit or flower centre decorations that produced the outlines subsequently filled in by the paintresses employed in her department. This practice smacked of deliberate deception to me because the customers, mainly North American, very likely assumed that they had a fully hand-painted decoration.

Walter Heapy was William Ball's bench mate and he, also, was Copeland-trained; there the similarity ended, for Walter was a huge man who must have weighed around eighteen stone. To see his backside bulging over a very low gilder's stool was a sight to be seen and ever remembered. He was a quietly spoken man with a very genial manner and a kind and helpful disposition.

Mr Percy Mallaburn and Mr Jack Stone were bosom friends together at the same bench for many years. They were almost like boys compared to the old-timers, for Percy was at least thirty years younger than they were. He served throughout the First World War without suffering any ill effects and returned after his demobilization to the gilding shop where he had served his pre-war apprenticeship. None of the older gilders had been eligible for the war service so Percy's experiences were listened to eagerly and he was held in high esteem by them.

Like Fred Hulme, he was a good watch and clock repairer and he was one of the few men I knew who, in those early days, could afford a motor car. It was only used on rare occasions and never under any circumstances driven to the factory. He also owned a beautifully maintained Sunbeam bicycle, which was heavy and old-fashioned with a reassuring traditional look to it, and, as he lived in Oakhill, just over a mile from the factory, he used it for his journey to work. He presented a very dignified picture as he pedalled along at a leisurely pace. For many years I thought Percy was a confirmed bachelor and it was a great surprise to me when he later admitted to having a girlfriend. The date and month of his birth coincided with my son's birthday, 8th April 1943, and at my invitation, he readily agreed to become his godfather. This forged a personal link between us, which was to last to the end of his days. Regrettably, they came all too soon, for he passed away on 25th March 1954, aged 58 years.

Jack Stone had the misfortune in his boyhood to lose a leg. When he first joined the factory as an apprentice gilder he was befriended by Percy Mallaburn. Jack was younger than Percy and looked on him as his protector and chief in all matters. Jack stood over six feet in height on his one leg and he possessed a perfect sense of balance. Although he used a primitive pole-type crutch with a padded T-end, which fitted into his armpit, he could discard this aid and hop around on one leg with tremendous agility and use his crutch to poke and prod at objects and people if he so desired. He was married and a model husband. His disability in no way prevented him from competing with any of his fellows, particularly as a gilder.

The last of the 'Severn Dwarfs', Alec Kelsall, was a very privileged young man indeed because of the decision of the old gilders to accept him as an apprentice. Alec took up his seat like a newcomer entering Parliament, all awe and wonderment. One can well imagine what the atmosphere was like for him in the midst of all these elderly men – his own grandfather was younger than several of them!

His presence was like a breath of fresh air in the room and his youthful exuberance and cheerfulness acted as a tonic on the elderly gilders. They reciprocated by making sure that he had the finest instruction it was possible to give during the whole of his training period. He became a first-class gilder and eventually head of gilding at the factory. It was a sad day for the department when Alec reported for duty as a soldier at the beginning of the Second World War. This was due to his membership of the territorial peacetime army, who were the first to be called to the colours. He was given survivor's leave after the fall of Dunkirk and from a boy soldier he had changed, overnight it seemed, into a battle-hardened veteran.

In a continuation of the gilder's room, separated from them by a huge sliding door, were other workers who were also gilders but who handled a different form of gilding, the simple finishing work, mainly decorating edges and ornamenting handles. This was a quantity operation and these men accounted for substantial amounts of ware: simple stock patterns with bands of colour with a gold edge and line finish and large quantities of richly groundlaid and gold-printed tea and coffee ware.

The employment of men in this department changed more frequently than most as some of them sought a change to a more interesting job. John Tomlinson, 'Jake', was an example. He was tired of the monotony of the job and became a milkman. After several winter stints of handling cold bottles and getting up at the crack of dawn, he returned to the factory to practise a new trade, groundlaying. He mastered this and became a most skilled exponent. Others left never to return, like Norman Goodwin. He was slightly disabled and although he wore a heavy built-up shoe, he was a very active man. He was with the company for many years but a temporary shortage of orders during the Second World War prompted him to apply for a job as a postman. This job he held down until his ultimate retirement and he was always very satisfied with his decision to change horses in midstream.

One member of this department who subsequently made a very good career for himself was Kenneth Bailey. He was a handsome, likeable young man with a mild air of superiority. He was asked by Mr Hassall to take over responsibility for the under-glaze printing department, a daunting task that he tackled with great enthusiasm. After a few months, however, he decided to try his hand in other fields and left Copeland's to join a local lithographic transfer company as a designer-salesman. He made a great success of this job and during the very early days of the war he started his own company, having his designs printed in Holland and supplying transfers to the English potters, thus helping to provide valuable exports. This was the beginning of what was to become one of the best and most highly respected litho and silk-screen companies in the pottery industry, which made Kenneth a very prosperous man. His firm flourishes to this day (2004).

In remembering the past and describing the factory's painters and gilders of many years ago, it is easy for me to forget how few people can visualise their surroundings and the conditions in which they worked. For some years past, potteries have accepted the wisdom of providing their decorating staff with good working conditions in clean, comfortable and well-lit surroundings but in the 1930s not much attention was paid to the subject. There may have been worse factories than ours in this respect but ours was pretty bad.

The men painter's department was situated on the first floor of a building, which was tacked on to the side of a hovel. The hovel housed the hard kiln, which was an enamel kiln for the firing of groundlaid colours needing a high temperature – 800-850 degrees Celsius. For a number of days each week the heat from the coal-fired kiln also heated the room through the brickwork of the hovel. In winter, this was useful additional warmth, but in the summer, the temperature was almost unbearable and far too hot for comfortable working. Such conditions would be condemned today by any factory inspector.

The main source of controllable heating was a stove-pot in the centre of the room placed on an iron tray, three feet square, because of the danger of the floorboards catching fire. The stove was lit by a labourer who came in early each morning so that it was warm enough when the artists arrived for work. Each occupant paid a small fee to him for this service

and for his prowess in augmenting the supply of coal with appropriations from the bulk supplies used for firing the ovens – a crafty operation!

In the oddly shaped room were housed a number of workbenches measuring three and a half feet wide by two and half feet which were positioned adjacent to the room's small windows. All the senior painters had a bench apiece while two apprentices shared one. This overcrowding meant that lots of chinaware had to rest on the floor beside them. The floor was of wooden boards, which were swept clean in the evenings by the night sweepers, using a liberal amount of wet sawdust to keep down the dust. The air in the room reeked of turpentine and aniseed, which was the medium used to mix the enamel colours. It permeated the clothes of all pottery artists and when they travelled home on the bus or tramcar they were instantly identifiable as painters.

The gilders had their own, separate workplace, which was on the top floor of the factory's highest building, up several flights of stairs. They were more crowded than the senior painters as all of them sat two to a bench, close to the light source. They did, however, enjoy a better light than the painters because the windows were larger. They too had a coal-fired stove-pot for warmth.

In our vast old factory, with its odd collection of buildings sprawled across several acres, bodily comfort was accorded a low priority. But the old place had its charms. Many of the buildings were dowdy, but most of them dated back to the factory's origins and there was visual variety and interest. The warren of segregated workshops, some tucked away in quiet places that enjoyed difficult access, meant that in the china-decorating process it was hard to discern anything resembling a production line. All over the factory, all day long, men and women, boys and girls, moved ware, often carrying it in baskets. They went up and down rickety stairs with it, they squeezed through narrow doorways with it, they negotiated awkward twists and turns in the corridors with it and, miraculously, they hardly ever dropped it.

Today, factories may be more convenient and comfortable but they are short of peace and quiet. At Copeland's, these precious commodities were still to be found in abundance among the gilders. When you entered their room you were immediately aware of a calm and peaceful atmosphere and felt it was incumbent upon you to walk on tiptoe and talk in whispers in an endeavour to preserve the studious silence.

Vivid pictures stay in the mind. Anyone for the first

time who came upon the gilders at work on a winter's evening had a scene to treasure forever. The room was lit by lamps of an early Anglepoise type, each fitted with a small, deep, basin-shaped metal shade. They were lowered down very close to the article being decorated and they created an extraordinary effect in the room, lighting, in the case of each gilder, just their hands, one holding the article and the other his brush, deftly applying the gold. As only these bench lights were lit in the room, the effect was dramatic, for all the world like a stage setting with a number of spotlights showing just hands and pieces of china, with ghostly faces of the gilders dimly discernible in the reflected light.

Each man, at the end of the day, would finish the piece of ware he was working on. Each, in turn, would stand, stretch his limbs, put on his hat and coat and quietly leave the room, bidding his fellows goodnight. Gradually the room would empty, until only one man remained, carrying on working until the piece he was decorating was completed and the time had come for him, too, to go home.

Retain this scene in mind for just one more gilders' shop story. One lovely old gilder, slightly hard of hearing, was sitting at his bench on his three-legged stool, with only his solitary light illuminating the large room. An unusual happening was about to occur, for, in a far-off warehouse, several hundred yards away, a man named Fred Roberts – who fancied himself as a runner – was preparing to beat his previous best time for a sprint to the gilding shop and back. To produce a fast time meant he had to take off his boots and run in his socks. His pals were encouraging him to attempt to beat his record for distance and small bets were laid on that evening's effort. With stopwatch in hand, the starter sent him off on his run. The timekeepers knew that someone would be working in the gilding shop for Fred to tap on the shoulder so that he could bear witness that Fred made the distance before he sped back to the starting point.

Unfortunately, no one had remembered to inform the solitary gilder about the attempt and when Fred, in his stockinged feet, tapped the old man on the shoulder he wondered what was happening, for when he turned round, Fred had vanished, so the gilder had not seen or heard anything. He was very startled of course, but he shrugged his shoulders and carried on with his gilding, thinking that he had imagined things. In the meantime, Fred reckoned that he could improve his time after a short rest, and he then repeated the exercise. This was to prove too much for the old man and he hastily put on his coat and hat and rushed off home. The next day, he told his fellows of the strange happenings of the previous evening. He was sure that the place was haunted and he never stayed late on his own again. What is more, his fellow workers never told him the truth of what had happened that night!

One of the many sets of worn steps on the Spode factory.

DESIGNS OF NOTE 1934–1943

With supervisory duties, strictly laid down by Mr T. Hassall, which occupied a large percentage of my working hours, the opportunities to create new designs and decorations were limited, but this did not prevent me from using design prowess from time to time. Mr Hassall would tell me what type of ware needed to be decorated, usually in answer to requests from agents and customers. One such occasion was his suggestion that I should produce an idea or two for our stone china range known as Lowestoft. This was a shape of oriental style in a grey stoneware type of body, which was very popular with the American customers. We had a very distinctive range of patterns selling regularly, but new ideas were called for to give added interest and variety to the shape.

A few books of reference were available at the factory and one which I thought might be of interest and stimulus was the history of Delft tiles. I was attracted to the simple treatment of birds used in their composition and this inspired me to produce one or two sketches for, I hoped, approval by Mr Hassall. After some deliberation, he gave the OK to go ahead and paint by hand two 10in dinner plates showing the different subjects. Whereas the Delft tile studies were painted in cobalt blue on white ware, I used the grey-coloured stoneware body and with a very fine black outline to the composition, I added delicate touches of colour in a restrained manner. The resulting designs were definitely English in character with a dash of Oriental flavour.

As the British Industries Fair of 1937 was due to open in London the following week, Mr Hassall, on viewing my sample plates, decided to put them on show. This decision pleased me greatly, but in the midst of a very large display of our wares, the two plates were almost lost from view, hidden away in a corner of the stand. However, Her Majesty Queen Elizabeth, who opened the exhibition, visited the Copeland stand and, much to everyone's surprise, picked out one of the two sample plates. She remarked how charming it was and asked if it was possible for her to have a dinner set for her personal use. I don't know who said yes to her – possibly Mr Ronald Copeland – but it proved to be a very wise decision.

It meant a terrific amount of hard work for myself and the engravers. The pattern was a relatively simple composition, but I insisted on each piece having a different species of bird depicted to provide additional interest. This stretched my imagination to the limit, particularly as it was for the Queen, but, eventually, after a number of months, the job was completed to Mr Hassall's – and, more importantly – my own satisfaction. The design was christened "Queen's Bird" in honour of the first and most illustrious customer, and it has been in continuous

Queen's Bird: The Delft tile inspired design was chosen by Queen Elizabeth in 1937 and is still produced today.

A colour trial of the Christmas Tree pattern.

Rare coloured Christmas Tree patten with a puce border.

A 1938 Christmas Tree plate with modern day miniature items.

Christmas Tree tile.

Original pattern book entry and backstamp with 1938 Christmas greeting that was recalled. Note the greeting crossed out on the pattern book, courtesy of Spode Museum Trust, copyright Spode.

Gold version presented to Harold on his retirement.

production, selling in vast quantities all over the world, for fifty years or more.

Each year in early spring we used to have a visit from our American agent, Mr Sydney Thompson, a Canadian of Scottish descent, living in America, who had set up a business with Mr Ronald Copeland as his partner. The company known as Copeland and Thompson Inc. was based in Fifth Avenue, New York. The partnership lasted for some years and then Mr Thompson became the sole owner. He was stockily built, of medium height and a taciturn man of few words, but he was nevertheless a brilliant sales executive.

His stay was usually of about three weeks' duration and in that time he would organise over a hundred new decorations to be produced for testing in the US market. He spent most of his time during the visit closeted with Mr Hassall and between them various ideas were planned. The two men would sit side by side in Mr Hassall's office, the air filled with dense fumes from Mr Thompson's large pipe, as they pored over the old pattern books, making notes of what they required.

Each artist was given instructions to produce ideas on different themes as soon as possible. I carried out very little supervision of the decorating departments during Thompson's visit! We, that is Harry Hammersley, Charles Deaville and myself, were harried and badgered into producing samples for Mr Thompson to comment on. The sequence of events was as follows: the artist would place in the hands of Mr Hassall his sketch or piece of ware showing the design suggestion. Without comment he would hand it over to Mr Thompson who in turn would either nod his approval or shake his head if the artist's effort was not to his liking. If the latter gesture was made, Mr Hassall then told the artist, in very forceful language, to go back and try again and "not waste valuable time". If on your next attempt to gain approval for your work, Mr Thompson's head nodded, Mr Hassall would then comment, "Why in Hell's name didn't you do it like that in the first place?" After this the artist left the room with instructions to produce further ideas for appraisal.

It was on such a day in the spring of 1938 that I was sent for and told to work on ideas for a Christmas plate. All sorts of ideas came to mind and I eventually settled on a Christmas Tree as a central motif for my design. The tree occupied the main area of the plate centre and was profusely decorated with gifts, baubles and tinsel adorning the fronds of the tree. The artistic detailing of the tree fronds was composed of small-scale brush strokes, which conveyed a new concept of treatment. The plate, which measured 10.5in diameter, was finished with a green border.

After completion, I showed it to Mr Hassall, who handed it to Mr Thompson for his appraisal. He studied the design carefully and then informed me that, in America, Christmas gifts, wrapped in gaily-coloured paper and tied with ribbon, were placed at the foot of the tree. I accepted this with good grace and amended my design to accommodate his suggestion. This alteration improved the general balance of the design by giving a greater weight of pattern at the base of the tree. When Mr Thompson saw the amended version, he nodded his head, accepting the idea as suitable for samples to be prepared for his salesmen.

In later years I learnt that when he viewed the samples on arrival in New York, he almost had second thoughts about selling the plate, because it was an obvious giftware item and it was his firm opinion that the selling of giftware was not good policy. However, the youthful members of his sales staff pleaded with him that they should be allowed to sell the item to their customers. On completion of their first trip, every member of the sales force reported an excellent reception for the plate and substantial orders for early delivery. The first orders were quickly sold out and the retailers sent urgent requests for more supplies. In anticipation of large orders for the following year and the advent of the Second World War, great efforts were made to increase production because exports were to be of even more importance. Ships bringing valuable arms, planes, tanks, guns and food supplies from North America were loaded for their return journey with our pottery exports which, when packed in casks, provided the perfect form of ballast.

The following year, a decision was taken to increase the range of items of Christmas Tree, so a teacup and saucer was added, to be followed later by the production of a complete dinner, tea and coffee ware range. The moral, of course, is that although the decoration started life as a giftware item, it became the largest selling pattern, in the greatest number of items, ever to have been produced at the Copeland Spode factory in its entire history. The fact that Christmas Tree became such a best-seller did not fail to be appreciated by rival factories; throughout the life of the Copeland pattern many attempts have been made to copy the theme, but for some strange reason they never quite made it. It has always amazed me that the decoration should have such appeal, because when I first created it I was not at all hopeful that it would have any real chance of success!

Another most successful design that I created prior

The original 1938 Christmas Tree pencil design sketch is badly stained from lying around the engraving depatment for several years. Although this is one of Spode's most successful patterns, Harold did not really like the design as the triangular tree does not fit well on a circular plate. Spode estimates that Christmas Tree pattern is in 10 million US households.

to the war, which gave me great satisfaction, was titled 'Strathmere'. At the time of its inception, the factory was experiencing a particularly bad spell of 'spit-out' on earthenware – the dreaded sandpaper-like textured glaze fault, which only appears after an enamel decorating fire. One of the reasons given for this deadly fault was attributed to hard-fired biscuit ware, so it was decided to separate the hard-fired ware from the normally fired and try and develop new appealing decoration which could be applied underglaze.

Enamel decoration on-glaze was always of a much brighter appearance than underglaze decorations. Because of the inability of the colour manufacturers to produce bright colours for underglaze painting, this became a limiting factor for the designers who were ever hopeful of obtaining a more colourful palette for use in the production of their designs. A slight breakthrough, however, was made by one of the leading colour manufacturers when they managed to produce a distinctly brighter tone of red, which they named Coraline. Although it was not as vivid as the lower temperature reds, it was, nevertheless, a very useful addition to the underglaze colour range. It had a terracotta semblance and I decided to try out the colour on my new design because I felt sure that it would enhance the overall colour effect.

The shape used for the decoration was called Hamburg which had a shaped edge divided into six sections or panels. The design consisted of three differing Chinese-style floral groups interspersed with three small separating sprigs between two borders, one at the edge and one on the shoulder of the rim. The pattern was hand-engraved, printed in a pleasant chrome green and hand-painted in a variety of colours. The glaze chosen was known as Jasmine, which gave a delicate honey-coloured effect.

As the pattern was to be hand-engraved, I decided to compose the spray arrangements on each item in a different form to give a more interesting overall effect. This meant a lot more work for me; ringing the changes for each set of sprays turned out to be quite a test of patience. As my artwork was executed much more quickly than the time taken to process the engraving, on reflection, I think that the extra endeavour on my part was fully justified when the finished service was viewed and praised by the customers.

Strathmere was sold mainly in the home, Australian and South African markets. The USA and continental customers considered the overall effect too delicate to be termed a Spode pattern and consequently these markets did not have much success with it. Sales were temporarily reduced during the war when decorated goods were not permitted for sale in the United Kingdom, but the pattern resumed good sales after the end of the war, particularly in the home market. It had, in fact, a very successful rebirth and remained a firm favourite for many years.

The acceptance of my designs for general production continued, particularly for the home and Commonwealth markets, and one that met with great favour was a decoration called 'Lauriston'. My fondness for Chinese decorations inspired me to make use of the style once again, following the success of Strathmere. Lauriston featured oriental groups of flower arrangements placed between framing borders. The choice of using the White Crown earthenware body, with the sprays gaily painted in bright enamel colours and trimmed with a blue-green edge, provided an effect that was cheerful and soon captured the imagination of the buying public. Such was the popularity of the pattern on earthenware dinner ware that at a later date the decoration was introduced as a china tea ware production and resulted in equal sales success.

One of the last designs I produced during the reign of Mr Hassall was named 'Audley'. This design, which proved to be the most popular, used Chinese-style sprays set between a narrow bead at the edge and a wider border on the shoulder, printed in sepia. The decoration on earthenware with Jasmine glaze was enamelled on-glaze in gay colours with a turquoise edge finish. As with Lauriston, Audley was also produced on china tea ware and coffee ware with equal success.

I have a continuing faith in and admiration of the great skills of the oriental ceramic masters who were such a wonderful inspiration to designers in the West. I will always feel a personal debt and deep admiration of the fine example they set and the high standards they achieved.

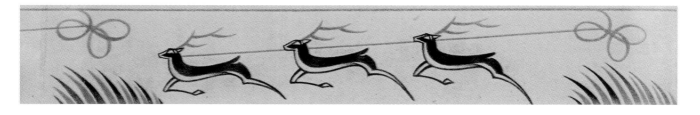

Above: Sales leaflet of Berkeley designed by Harold in 1938.
Right: Sales leaflet of Lauiston.
Below: Sales leaflets of Audley (left) and Strathmere (right).

Below: Photos courtesy of Spode Museum Trust; copyright Spode.

Right: Tournai. Pages from Spode's on-glaze subject book. Designed by HH in 1939, influenced by Delftware tiles. HH writes: "Mr T. Hassall, accompanied by Mr Ronald Copeland, paid a visit to Holland and suggested I might find some inspiration for a new design from a ceramic book on Tournai ware. The design was accepted by the USA market and was a good seller. In later years it became known as Fisherman and Fly."

Reindeer: Harold nicknamed this pattern "Three reindeers and a bow bow" with reference to the two bows. Harold designed the pattern but some early pieces, such as the cover dish, have backstamps bearing T. Hassall's name. 1936. Courtesy of Spode Museum Trust.

Early Commemorative Wares

My first experience of commemorative ware design was the occasion of the Silver Jubilee of their Majesties King George V and Queen Mary, which was to be celebrated on 6th May 1935. The British Pottery Manufacturers Federation promoted a competition for designs of suitable items for the event, and W.T. Copeland's were honoured by the acceptance of Mr T Hassall's beaker shape as the best submitted design. A prize was also given for the best applied decoration, which was won by a company other than W.T. Copeland & Sons. Orders for these official items were in great demand by the general public, particularly the Education Authorities who presented every schoolboy and girl with the official item to mark the Jubilee occasion, as was the accepted custom at the time.

All members of the Federation were allocated a proportional share of orders depending on the production capacity of each firm, which provided full order books for many months. In addition to the Federation items, most firms produced a variety of pieces for their normal retailers' needs, and also provided a number of inexpensive pieces, which in my opinion were of little merit. The most important piece produced by Copeland's was a three-handled loving mug, commissioned by Messrs Thomas Goode and Company of London. Goode's, who had a resident artist, provided us with rough drawings of the design requirements, following clearly the suggestions of Her Majesty Queen Mary. It was decided to produce a small limited edition with the No. 1 specimen specially finished for Her Majesty, which she graciously accepted. Mr Hassall called upon all his designers and artists to play a part in the creating of the finished artwork – these included Mr Harry Hammersley, Mr Fred Micklewright, Mr Joe Fenn, Mr Charles Deaville and myself.

The design consisted of three panels, one showing silver-framed medallion portraits of their Majesties, while the other two panels showed the Royal residences of Windsor Castle and Sandringham. They were painted in full colour and set within a garland of roses, with rose, thistle, shamrock and leek sprays in each corner of the decorated area. On the rim was an inscription and at the base a wreath of oak leaves set on a silver background. This was a very ambitious and over-elaborate design fraught with many production difficulties, which, however, were eventually overcome. For me this exercise was a disappointing experience and I realised that I had much to learn in this particular field, but I hoped that I would be able to enhance the reputation of both the firm and myself when the next occasion presented itself.

In January 1936, the finest examples of Chinese art gathered from the world's greatest collections – including priceless specimens from the Republic of China – were on exhibition at the Victoria and Albert Museum in London. I pleaded with Mr Hassall to be allowed to visit this once-in-a-lifetime display, for I believed then, and still do today, that no period in the history of art will ever compare with the artistic achievements and standards set and practised by generations of Chinese artists and craftsmen – in particular their complete mastery of ceramic form and decoration. After due consideration, Mr Hassall agreed that a visit would be worthwhile, so, together with our resident modellers, Mr Max Henk and Mr Tom Barlow, the necessary arrangements were made. A date was chosen for the trip, which, sadly, happened to be the day following the death of King George V, and, as the three of us made our way to the railway station we wondered if the exhibition would be open to the public at all. As it happened the museum was open as usual. The breathtaking sight of so many treasures made me feel so very small and humble. It was a truly wonderful experience, the memory of which I shall always value and which has been a lasting influence on me throughout my artistic career.

This was my first visit to London, a London that was already in mourning for the late King, with many of the shop windows dressed to show a mark of respect. After visiting the exhibition, we spent a short time seeing the sights, and by chance, we caught a glimpse of the Prince of Wales, now Edward VIII, leaving Buckingham Palace, huddled in the back of the Royal car. The sight of his pale face brought me down to earth with the realisation of how much work was to be done to mark the occasion of his accession and future coronation.

The experience gained in the fairly recent production of the Silver Jubilee piece was very useful, particularly in the avoidance of elementary pitfalls. The creation of Coronation souvenirs is quite a rare occurrence in the career lifetime of a design artist, so I was singularly happy when Mr Hassall invited me to submit ideas for the occasion.

It was the intention for the firm to produce a number of items, some expensive and elaborate, others simpler in character and cost. Firstly, a small earthenware mug was modelled with a lion-headed handle to instructions laid down by Messrs Thomas Goode of London, which, although it appeared to me to be a little incongruous, was nevertheless the customer's choice and it was my task to create a suitable applied design. This was quite a challenge and a chance for me to show just what I could do. I hoped that, instead of the usual medallion bearing a portrait, I could at least create something that would be different and more suitable to the occasion. After some research of possible subject matter, I decided to show the Prince of Wales at his investiture in Caernarvon, surrounded by achievements of the British nation.

The workmanship I displayed in the design was almost miniature in dimension and would be a tremendous challenge to whoever was given the task of reproducing the scene. We were congratulated on the finished artwork by Thomas Goode's, who gave the go-ahead to proceed with the production of samples. The lithograph company who produced the transfer for the decoration from the motifs did a fine job of reproducing my design from the original artwork, and the resultant samples submitted to Goode's were approved in readiness for quantity production.

Unfortunately, the news of the King's impending troubles, first rumoured and then confirmed, resulted in the decision to delay production. Several designs were being produced concurrently, using portraits and other themes, but the small mug was the only one that could not be adapted to the revised designs that had to be made following the King's abdication on 10th December 1936.

However, the acceptance of my design for the small mug encouraged Mr Hassall to invite me to submit ideas for the three-handled loving cup decoration. The shape was of good traditional style with nice handles. The straight sides were well proportioned and ideally suited for the reception of design motifs. I was excited at the prospect of creating something attractive, because this was to be the prestige item in the company's Coronation range. Patience was not a facet of Mr Hassall's character and I knew that he would be very keen to know how I would cope with the assignment. He was not disappointed, however, for by chance and good fortune, I hit on a theme that appealed to him, so he insisted that I complete the artwork as quickly as possible.

The central panel originally consisted of a portrait of HM King Edward VIII in military uniform, set in an oval frame of the Royal Garter and surmounted by the Royal Crown. This was supported by two knights in armour holding staffs bearing flags of Saint George, with a background of rose, thistle, shamrock and oak leaves and with a ribbon carrying the motto 'Dieu et mon Droit' at the base. The cup was finished with a green band and descriptive lettering at the top and a stylised wreath of laurel on the flanged foot. The second panel showed the full Royal arms supported by crowned staffs with entwined ribbons bearing the names of six of the principal nations of the Empire. The third panel, set within a framed oval, bore the seated figure of Britannia against a background of British achievements on land, sea and in the air. The panels were painted in full colour. When the cup was shown to our customers, it was well received and, although the abdication upset the initial sales arrangements, all we had to do was to insert a double portrait in the Garter panel and change the names to Their Majesties King George VI and Queen Elizabeth.

To complete my personal contribution to the Coronation items produced in 1936–7 I was asked to create a special design for Sir Francis Joseph, the leading businessman in the city of Stoke-on-Trent. As president of Stoke City Football Club, he decided to present a loving cup to each club in the First Division of the Football League. It was to be richly decorated to commemorate the event, and the recipients were

Design for a three-handled loving cup for King Edward VIII's Coronation that was never produced but altered for King George VI and Queen Elizabeth's Coronation.

to toast the health of the monarch at the first home match of the new year.

The shape to be used was the same as the traditional one used for general production but with a changed design of handle – these were to be shaped in the form of the Staffordshire Knot. Whether this was specially requested I do not know, but to me it was a mistake and spoiled an otherwise beautiful shape. But, as a junior, I had no say in what should or should not be, and I accepted the shape, knotted handles and all. Although the edition was relatively small – thirty pieces – the value of the order was substantial and proved to be a very satisfying experience for me.

For this cup I used the Royal Arms as depicted on the standard Coronation loving cup and created two new panel designs incorporating a football scene on one, while the other, against a background of stylised national flowers, had a shield with mantling, helmet and crest of the pottery thrower, as used in the coat of arms of the City of Stoke-on-Trent. Also on the shield area, in fine old English lettering was a descriptive message and the motto of Stoke-on-Trent – *'Vis Unita Fortior'* – was at the base of the design.

In addition to the special pieces I have described in detail, a number of inexpensive items were made for general sale. These were of little merit and consisted mainly of framed photo-etched family portraits and groups with a simple border at the edge and/or a descriptive panel on the reverse side. Copeland's also produced its apportioned share of the mugs and beakers of the official Pottery Manufacturers Federation version, which had quite a pleasing design.

This was my baptism in the field of commemorative design. Although I was a young man of limited experience, I realised that I still had much to learn. As the schoolmaster said: "This student must try harder!"

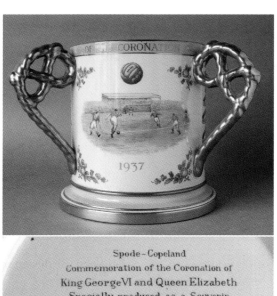

Above: Edward VIII Coronation mug with lion head handle. It was never sold.
Below: Lithographs for an Edward VIII mug that was never produced.

Left: Two views and the backstamp of the loving cup commemorating the Coronation of George VI and Elizabeth. Given by Stoke City FC to all First Division football clubs.

ENGRAVERS, ENAMELLERS AND MODELLERS

The success of any good design is dependent on the ability of the craftsmen and women, such as the engravers, enamellers and modellers whose job it is to interpret the artist's original work.

Engravers

As the majority of decorations produced by the Spode factory were self prints consisting of a simple colour with a complete variable tonal range or prints with hand enamelling, the engraving was the most important factor of the decorating process. Engraving is a most exacting craft needing great artistic ability, patience and precision. The Spode factory, by virtue of having a predominance of printed patterns, employed a large staff of engravers, each and every man carefully selected because of his specialist technical and artistic skills, which were needed to cope with the great variety of patterns.

The head of the engraving department, Mr Joseph Hassall, was the younger brother of the art director, Mr Thomas Hassall. He was a mild-mannered man of dignified bearing and completely opposite in character to that of his ebullient, extroverted brother. He obeyed without question his brother's every whim and wish, never opposing his opinion on any occasion.

The engraving shop, as it was called, was situated on the topmost floor of the china-making block, which was situated in the area known as the Terrace, and was completely isolated from the rest of the factory. A climb of forty-nine steps – which deterred casual visitors – was necessary to reach the workroom, which contained sufficient bench space to house at least twenty workmen. As with most workrooms in the early Thirties, it was heated by two large iron stove-pots, which in addition to providing heat for the room, were also used for cooking fry-ups, heating of soup as well as water for the tea-making. On entering the engraving department, one of the most noticeable aspects was the feeling of discipline and calm, for Mr Joe Hassall insisted on maintaining an atmosphere which was conducive to good workmanship so smoking, gossiping, whistling and time-wasting in general were strictly forbidden. Such conditions made life a little tedious for the younger members of the staff and the apprentices. Punctuality was also insisted upon and always maintained.

Engraving is basically a two-tooled operation – a graver to cut fine lines into the surface of the copper plate and a sharpened punch to produce the graduated tones of light and shade. The punching operation is dependent upon the craftsman's delicate striking of the head of the punch with a light hammer, which produces a constant metallic tapping sound which echoes around the room. This operation was even more intriguing when more than one operative was using the punch at the same time. It reminded me of the staccato sounds of a woodpecker with a metal beak!

The only time any engraver left his seat was for the mid-morning and afternoon break of ten minutes when there was always a concerted rush to the toilet facilities, situated in another part of the factory – usually for a quick puff or two of a cigarette or a pipe. This Victorian-like severity was quite unique and only existed in the engraving department, whereas the rest of the factory workers enjoyed a much more relaxed and leisurely approach to their work and conditions. However, Mr Joe Hassall's calm temperament stood him in good stead in facing the exigencies and heavy demands made upon him and his department.

It was important for him to choose the right craftsman for each new design to be processed and close co-operation was necessary between the designer who produced the artwork and the individual who was chosen to execute the engraving. Some of the men were more adept with specific design subjects

Paul Holdway engraving the Italian pattern using a graver to cut into the copper plate.

Engraving team, left to right.
Back row: Gerald Maudsley, Ken Scarratt, Len Potts (Jnr), Harry Webster, Stan Bedwell, Frank Boothby, George Cartlidge.
Middle row: Jack Longmore (Snr), J. Barker, Roland Littler, Joe Hassall, James Wood, Jack Longmore (Jnr).
Front row: Apprentices, Stan Clowes, Jim Dunn.

and styles of design. Most of the men employed during this period had served their apprenticeship at the factory and few, if any, ever expressed a desire to leave or work for any other pottery manufacturer. Engravers were by union standards amongst the highest paid 'worker operatives' in the industry and, as Copeland's had the greatest reputation for quality workmanship, it was no surprise that every man employed in the department was proud to be part of the team and jealously guarded the satisfaction, pleasure and security derived from their work.

The design to be engraved was usually presented to the engraver in the form of painstakingly drawn design fittings; this could mean as many as forty or fifty drawings having to be made to cover the range of items of the approved decoration.

As smoking was not allowed in the department, most of the senior engravers were inveterate snuff-takers and, as evidence of this, many oil and other stains soon appeared in the Bristol Board surfaces of the artist's drawings. By the time an engraving was completed, the artwork was almost ruined with the rough treatment it had received during the time taken to produce the finished copper plate. In later years, with the invention of Cellophane, the drawings were always covered with this transparent material. Consequently, the drawings survived their handling by the engravers, so original drawings are now carefully preserved for future use if ever the need arises for replacement engravings.

When I first joined the company, most of the engraving staff were elderly men possessing a wealth of knowledge and experience. In addition, there were a small number of young men who had in recent years qualified as journeymen, and one solitary apprentice, aged nineteen. The elder statesman of the department

was a Mr Roland Littler, who was one of the all-time characters with whom I had the good fortune to work. He was a most obstreperous character and most difficult to talk to. His ability as an engraver was absolutely par excellence and I marvelled at his skill of interpretation of any artistic work placed before him. It took many years for me to be accepted by him as a serious designer.

It was also quite natural for all younger engravers to seek the advice of Roland in his role of senior worker, rather than approach Mr Joe Hassall, their foreman. This could only mean one thing; that by comparison Roland's advice was the wiser and therefore the more sought after.

I often wondered why he was such a sad man. I was later made aware of some of the reasons for this unhappiness when I learned that he had lost his wife and was left to rear twin baby sons alone, a task which he accomplished very successfully. I remember one occasion when I saw Roland dressed to kill, in a black jacket and grey waistcoat, patent leather shoes with grey spats, winged collar and gay tie, also with rosy cheeks, in the lounge bar of the local pub – The Marquis of Granby in Penkhull. He had imbibed rather well and was in a truly happy state. On my entering the room, he immediately introduced me to all his friends and ordered drinks for me and the colleague who was with me. This was one of the rare occasions I ever saw Roland really happy and wearing a smile.

He continued as an engraver until he was over eighty years of age, and I never saw any sign of deterioration of his skills, and it was only when a troublesome knee ailment prevented him from climbing the forty-nine steps to the engraving department that he decided to call it a day and retire.

He continued to live on his own, catering for himself for a number of years, and then living with his son until his death. This son was the only one of the twins whom I met, and that was not until years later, when I was appointed art director at Spode. Details of this were published in the local newspaper, and Ronald's son contacted me and suggested that I might visit him to see if his father had left anything that might be of interest to the company. He lived in a nice semi-detached house in Meir Heath, a pleasant suburb close to Stoke-on-Trent and I paid him a visit to view his father's work.

Ronald had saved a lot of material showing his artistic versatility from different periods of his life. One fact that I learnt was that Roland had spent a number of years as a tutor at the Stoke School of Art, taking classes in the evenings in general art subjects. After careful study of the creative work he had produced in earlier years, I felt that a veil had been lifted, exposing the reasons for his unhappiness. I soon became aware that I was looking at the work of a very capable artist whose creative ability had never been recognized or made use of during his lifetime. He did however, have control of the engraving and underglaze departments for a few years during the First World War while Mr Joe Hassall was on military service, but at the end of the hostilities, Roland was demoted 'back to the bench' when Joe returned, and Roland's cup of sadness was full to the brim once again.

One of my memories of Roland Littler is connected with a pattern I created which gave me great satisfaction. It was named 'Kent' and was a bone china border decoration with finishing gold bands on the shoulder and at the edge of the plate. The idea of this design was derived from an illustration in an early Spode pattern book of a hand-painted, fully coloured depiction of an arrangement of oak leaves and acorns, dated about 1810. It was a china tea ware pattern, very elaborately decorated, which would have been far too expensive to produce today. So I set to work to try to capture the charm of this early design and eventually produced a very detailed monochrome sketch in sepia to fit the border of the plate.

Mr Thomas Hassall was quite pleased with my effort and instructed me to give the artwork to his brother Joe for a section of the design to be engraved. He in turn told me to ask Mr Littler to do the job. With a grunt and a snort he took it from me and, after a casual glance, tossed the sketch to the back of his untidy bench and proceeded to ignore me, carrying on with the work he was doing. I did not stay to offer any advice as to how the engraving should be done. No one ever did with Roland! After a fortnight or more I asked what progress had been made with my design. Brother Joe said that it had been completed and was ready for me to collect and make initial trials to see if it was OK for the production of samples. I dashed up the forty-nine steps two at a time with keen anticipation as to what sort of effort Roland had made of my design. Joe handed me the finished copper engraving, and I can only describe my reactions as ecstatic, for Roland had produced a magnificent interpretation of my design. I went to him and expressed my congratulations on his doing such a lovely job, thanking him profusely. In return, he just snorted and said: "Well, what did you expect other than a perfect job!?"

I tried out the engraving in various tints of sepia and chose one that I thought suitable to be used on the sample plate, which was produced with the gold finish. I presented it to Mr T. Hassall who thought that it was a winner! And so it turned out to be in all the world markets, though it took many weeks for me to draw out all the fittings that were required for the full range of ware and many months of work for the engravers to complete their part of the decorating process. In my opinion, the secret of its success was the brilliant standard Roland had set when he engraved the first section.

Every member of the engraving department in 1934 was an individual character in his own right. Mr Jack

Kent pattern, designed by Harold, engraved by Roland Littler. The pattern book entry for the earthenware version of Kent. Photo: Courtesy of Spode Museum Trust; copyright Spode.

53

Longmore and his son – also christened Jack – sat side by side during the whole of their working life together, which covered young Jack's apprenticeship and his journeyman days. Young Jack, being a very lively character, needed his father's restraining hand from time to time, but nevertheless he had a very thorough training and became a first-class engraver. Father and son possessed so many characteristics in common, their height (about 5ft 4in) their colouring, build and particularly the way they walked. They always arrived at work together and left together at the end of the working day. I used to think what a wonderful arrangement this was – I was very envious – because I had never experienced the close relationship of father and son – my own father having died in 1918 when I was five years of age. However, I am sure that young Jack would have liked, from time to time, a little more freedom to express himself, away from the watchful eye of his father, particularly when the young man's fancy strayed in the direction of the pretty girls.

Mr Longmore senior, was a first-class engraver and a highly respected member of the staff and was also a close friend of Mr Joe Hassall, the foreman, who often consulted him and valued his opinion when problems had to be solved. At this point, I should mention how the workload was handled and the method of distribution among the various members of the department. The work was mainly split into three categories; new designs, new replacements of existing patterns and general maintenance of current engravings which were showing signs of wear because of constant use.

The category of new design engraving was by far the most difficult and only the best workers were used for this important task. For an engraver to reproduce the artist's design, a graver and punch was used to transfer the design onto a copper plate, which was both difficult and time-taking, needing great powers of concentration to achieve a satisfactory result. The creator of the design often spent a lot of time sitting next to the engraver, making useful comments and patiently watching the slow and painstaking progress of his design taking shape on the copper plate.

The second category, that of providing new replacements for worn-out copper engravings was a process of great importance and always given to the experienced workers. The only difference between this category and that of new design work was that in this case it was solely a question of making an accurate copy of the existing engraving and not having to worry about methods of interpretation.

Lastly, the maintenance of coppers in constant use. At least a third of the engravers were engaged in this often dull and boring part of the engraving process, which was, nevertheless, a most important service for efficient production of orders. To repair a copper engraving can sometimes take several weeks, so careful planning has to be made by the printing shop foreman and adequate notice given when sets of coppers are required. The engravers who did this type of work were always envious of the more senior men in the department and hoped that Brother Joe would relent and elevate them to the more interesting and creative work.

Sitting next to Mr Hassall at a bench apart from the other engravers was a young man in his early twenties. His name: George Leslie Cartlidge, a person who was to play an important part in the future history of the company. Because of the excellent standard of the workmanship he attained during his apprenticeship and his ability to produce extremely delicate effects, he was chosen to produce the engravings of crests, coats of arms, monograms, lettering and other subjects which needed extra special care and precision. He was also accepted as the second in command when Joe was absent from the workroom for any reason. In spite of his modest youth, he possessed a very strong character and, together with his specialist skills, his authority was unquestioned by all the men of the department.

Mr James Wood – a man of gentle disposition – was another of the engravers whose work I admired, but I was a little apprehensive when Mr Joe Hassall asked me to give him the artwork I had produced as a precursor for a new series of Rhododendron Botanical Studies. My requirement was for an extremely delicate engraving that would act as a guide for the artist to colour realistically. The shades and tones that were needed in the engraving to help to give shape and form to the flowers were to be executed in a much finer and more subtle way than anything that had been attempted before and I wondered if Mr Wood – who was an elderly man – had the necessary ability to carry out the work efficiently. After careful instruction from me, he soon grasped what my requirements were and with painstaking care and true dedication he produced a masterly piece of work, which set a new standard for this range of engraving. When completed, the decoration became an all-time best seller and was in constant demand for many years.[4]

Mr Wood was one of the few engravers who had not been trained at the Spode works. His expertise had been learnt at the famous independent engraving

[4] Harold has confused this story slightly as Jack Longmore had to re-engrave this series to make them finer.

establishment owned by Mr H. Fennell, who supplied complete services of engravings to a variety of manufacturers. His workshop was situated in Hanley. Because of a temporary shortage of orders at Fennell's, Mr Wood applied for a job at Copeland's, where he spent the rest of his working life.

The remaining members of the engraving staff were also of great importance and contributed in no small way towards the making of the finest engraving team in the industry. Many changes were to take place in the not too distant future, which we could not envisage in these early days. To abandon methods and standards, which had stood the test of time for well over a hundred years, was unimaginable and the engravers held firmly to the opinion that their skills would for ever be most sought after.

Enamellers – Painting by Paintresses

Once a pattern choice had been made and a decision taken to produce the design by the print and enamel method, we then had to consider which branch of the great variety of processes would be used for the decorating of the new design and so complete the final stage. There are many variations and methods of applying decoration and to achieve this aim there were well over 50% of the total factory workforce to call upon to do this. Printers and transferrers, both underglaze and on-glaze decorations, are very important and when their part has been completed then the stage is set for the hand colouring, which is the final operation. After a lengthy apprenticeship the girls, having reached a high standard of skill, are allocated to differing categories of decorating. Usually this takes place when they reach the age of twenty-one.

One of the most capable forewomen was a Mrs F. Challoner, who served the firm for over sixty years. Married late in life to an engraver who also worked for the firm, she was responsible for the initial training of young girls straight from school. She used to say that the kids put more colour on their hands and faces than onto the ware. In addition to the training schedule, she also used to count and check the amount of work done by all the enamel paintresses. As well as this, she made out the wage sheets for the pieceworkers in all the on-glaze painting departments, which, at a guess, would be in excess of a hundred and twenty persons.

The Trimble sisters – Annie and Alice – from Trent Vale, were also to play a very important part in the training of the on-glaze paintresses. Annie was for many years in charge of a large department of girls who, having passed through the initial training department and reached the age of sixteen years, were then promoted and given more advanced types of work to paint under her supervision. Annie, in latter years, became a forewoman and was responsible for the checking and counting of all the orders in process. Annie took over the difficult job relinquished by Mrs Challoner when she retired and held this position until her own retirement.

Modelling for Tableware

A vital function at the factory is the modelling department, which in 1934, was run by Mr Louis Henk and his son Max. In addition to creating surface decorations, a competent designer is usually expected from time to time to develop ideas for new shapes

Above: Annie Trimble's decorating shop where advanced training was given.
Right: Unnamed enamel paintress.

to cover market requirements. As instructed by Mr Ronald Copeland, Mr Hassall introduced me to Mr Henk and his son, telling them both with heavy sarcasm that I was going to show them how "because I was from Art School." This was not a very nice form of introduction, but I brushed this attitude aside and soon made friends with the two men, who became most helpful.

Unfortunately, Mr Henk Senior died soon after I began my employment with the firm and, in 1935, a new face appeared – Mr Tom Barlow, a relation of Mr Hassall. He was a man of great ability, having served his apprenticeship at Josiah Wedgwood's factory at Etruria. I knew of Tom's background from an early association at the Burslem Art School, which he attended as a senior student. As Tom was the elder of the two modellers, it was decided that Max and he would have equal status, which was a disappointment to Max, but, as this was Mr Hassall's decision, this arrangement was enforced.

During my early years at the factory I did not have many opportunities to show my capabilities in this field for no new shapes of any importance were contemplated in either earthenware or china. The modellers during this period were mainly concerned with the maintenance work on existing shapes but,

on the rare occasions when a new item was to be produced, I was delighted and thrilled to see a three-dimensional form emerge from a line drawing, which I had provided. Many shapes were formed on a lathe and I spent many hours instructing the modeller where and how to apply his shaping tool so as to produce the form I desired. During my student days I had learned how to form clay on a throwing wheel, and also how to turn shapes on a lathe, either in plaster or in clay. This knowledge helped enormously if the modeller was experiencing difficulties in satisfying my requirements, and he welcomed my being able to show him what was needed by actually doing the shaping or turning myself.

Fancy Modelling

Few modellers were able to master both forms of precision and fancy modelling with equal skill. Fancy modelling was a term used to describe the more ornate parts of tableware such as handles, knobs and embossments, but in the main, the term was used in relation to the modelling of figures and animals, etc. culminating in almost lifelike floral studies, groups of flowers, single blooms, and complicated bird and flower arrangements such as those produced so

Tom Barlow with the loving cup designed for the Silver Wedding anniversary of Queen Elizabeth II and HRH The Duke of Edinburgh.

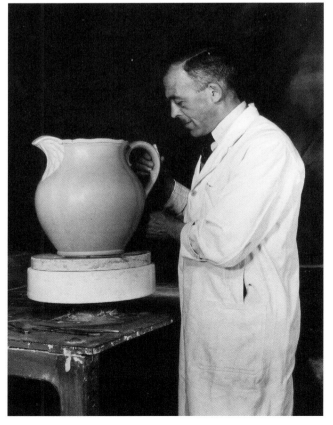

Tom Barlow

perfectly by the Royal Worcester factory which were sold at very high prices, the series of Doughty Birds being the most famous.

This practice was soon copied by other potters. The famous Boehm Company of the USA produced equally fine examples. These models were often purchased as presentation pieces and given to visiting dignitaries. The high point was reached when HM The Queen, on her visit to the USA, presented President Eisenhower with a Worcester group and the President gave The Queen a Boehm group as a departing present. This type of model form was produced in almost every imaginative subject, which included racehorses, cattle and dogs, etc. with each manufacturer striving to reach perfection.

Some of the titles given to many important processes which come under the heading of decorating include: gold printing, colour printing and transferring on-glaze and underglaze, groundlaying, freehand painting, acid etching, banding and lining, colour edging, decoration of knobs and handles etc. To describe them fully and enlarge about the skills of the personnel who were involved would take many chapters. Some of the processes were more interesting to perform than others and lots of fine characters were intimately involved and responsible for playing major roles in the production of the high quality china and earthenware for which Copeland's were so justly famed.

Unnamed enamel paintress.

Hot Words

I mentioned briefly the job of decorating knobs and handles, which reminds me of an incident when I was accompanying Mr Hassall along the Terrace towards the earthenware sorting warehouse. An attractive young woman was approaching us and as she was about to pass, Mr Hassall glanced in her direction, bidding her good morning with a broad smile, but the girl sniffed, turned her head away and, with a red face, deliberately ignored his greeting. He turned to me and said: "What on earth is the matter with her?" To which I then reminded him of an event of the previous day when on his inspection of some spoiled handle painting – of which the girl was innocent – this particular girl was sent for and severely castigated and his culminating words of criticism were: "You ought to be roasted on red hot cinders in hell!"

The reason why I have always remembered the words was because I thought, what an original statement, and one that I had never heard before, or since. "Oh dear" he said, "I wonder if she will ever forgive me?" She didn't!

The girl's name was Ada Shenton, who later married and became Mrs Gourley and was one of the finest of all handle finishers. She worked until retirement age and then acted as a guide for factory visitors.

EARLY WAR YEARS

Following the 1937 Coronation of King George VI, trade improved noticeably and full employment was experienced at most of the pottery firms. 1938 saw a similar picture – Christmas Tree pattern had been created and the first orders despatched for Christmas sale. Mr Neville Chamberlain returned from Munich, waving a piece of paper signed by Hitler and himself, promising "peace in our time." In 1939, Mr Sydney Thompson, agent for the USA market, paid his usual spring visit, when more samples and ideas than usual were despatched in an endeavour to increase sales in North America.

Hitler made his moves in Europe and on 3rd September, war was declared. This meant a complete stoppage of trade with European countries, but increased demand from other markets, particularly the USA and Canada, more than made up for the shortage. However, severe restrictions were imposed on manufacturers, and factories producing non-essential goods were gradually closed down. Recruitment for the Armed Forces and the making of munitions were quickly put under way, and applications were made for key workers to be designated as reserved occupations.

As Copeland's had such a large export trade, we did not experience too much difficulty in retaining the services of most of our workers in the early days of the war. During 1938 and 1939, an intense recruiting campaign was conducted throughout the country and many of our workers joined the ranks on a voluntary basis. Workers who had joined the Territorials and similar voluntary bodies were called up for full-time service before the war had actually been declared. I only missed a similar fate by the skin of my teeth, for in a vacant property adjacent to the works the local branch of the Royal Engineers Territorial Army put on a very impressive display in the spring of 1939. Each time I passed the display I noticed a most imposing regular Army Sergeant standing very smartly on the steps leading to the exhibition. I think my conscience was beginning to work overtime for I became aware of his gimlet eyes staring at me fixedly. I still believe that he hypnotised me, for I found myself signing a proposal form saying I wished to join the Territorial Army – it was just like a dream!

The clerk who was taking down my details said it was not certain whether I would be acceptable and that I must have a further interview at a later date. I was duly summoned a week or two later and made the journey to Tunstall (one of Bennett's Five Towns) Drill Hall. Here I was interviewed by an officer who, on being informed that I was a draughtsman – among other things – thought I would be an ideal recruit for the Engineers. He then produced a lengthy application form, on which was the stipulation that it was imperative that I spend my annual holiday, of one week in August, taking part in practical training exercises. I informed him that this was not possible for I had booked my vacation to spend a week with my girlfriend and her family at the seaside. As this was the final condition to be agreed on before I signed the application, he informed me that unless I agreed to fulfil this duty he would not be able to approve my application.

Fortunately, as it turned out, I chose to deny myself the doubtful pleasure of the training camp and opted instead for the week's holiday with my sweetheart. I did plead with the officer to overlook this slight problem, pointing out what a fine soldier-to-be he was turning down! A few months later, war was declared so I only escaped immediate call-up by a very narrow margin indeed. Phew!

The winter of 1939/40 passed slowly and we all worried about the state of what was called the 'Phoney War'. Mr Hassall was a very worried man, wondering what the future held for us all. Design requirements were few, but production of decorated goods for the American market had never been so great. I think the Americans were hoping to build up a large stock in case war action should prevent shipments of their orders. At this date, we had lost very few of our important workers and our output soared to great heights.

During the early part of 1939 a large building programme was under way to construct a new finished-enamel warehouse, an on-glaze printing shop, a super showroom and a second-floor art gallery to house Mr Ronald Copeland's collection of Spode wares and rare European examples. This project was completed before the war started and the art gallery with its contents as dedicated at a special service conducted by the Bishop of Lichfield, Dr S. Woods. After the war started, the whole of the Spode collection was packed away and stored for safety but, as no bombing took place for over six months, Mr Copeland decided that the pieces should be unpacked and placed on display again. He said that, as the gallery and collection had received a dedication from the Bishop, he would take a chance that it would never come to any harm and that at least we should have the pleasure of viewing the wonderful examples, instead of them being buried away in a bomb-proof shelter. His faith was justified, for in spite of a few raids around Stoke, we at the factory were spared.

The 'Phoney War' came to an end after the fall of France in 1940 and severe bombing raids were a nightly routine, with civilians spending long periods in the air raid shelters. All men eligible for service in the armed forces had to undergo a strict medical and I was found to be fit for service as, when and where I might be needed. I was twenty-six years of age and had been courting strongly for a number of years, so my sweetheart and I decided to get married. We were apprehensive about what the future held in store for us but, nevertheless, we decided to take a chance.

At the time, I was living with my widowed mother in a rented modern house at a place called Blurton, situated two or three miles from the factory. My mother was not too happy about my decision to marry but, as she was a comparatively young and extremely fit woman, she decided to take up a 'live-in' appointment to the widow of a doctor who herself was a qualified general practitioner and who had a schoolgirl daughter in her early teens. This turned out to be a very satisfactory and happy arrangement for all concerned.

Once this difficulty was overcome the wedding ceremony was booked for Saturday, 6th April, 1940 at the Church of St John in Trent Vale, at the earliest possible time, which was 9.30am. This very early time had been chosen because my wife-to-be was so very nervous and terrified of having to face a huge crowd of spectators from the Spode factory, and she forbade me to tell anyone of the time the ceremony was to be conducted. These safeguards kept the crowds down but, with lots of relatives and close friends in attendance, all went very smoothly. Wartime weddings were not the posh affairs of today – I was dressed in an ordinary lounge suit and my bride in a very smart two-piece suit with a fox-fur draped round her shoulders and carrying a small bouquet of anemones. We did, however, manage to hire an old vintage car for the journey of the bride to the church and back to the reception, which was held at her parent's home. After drinks and a wedding breakfast, my lovely new wife and I went for a walk to the house we were renting, to see if everything was shipshape. The house was situated in the Clayton area of Newcastle-under-Lyme, about two miles from my wife's home. When we arrived back at her parent's house for afternoon tea, my wife's father had decided that all the guests and ourselves would be taken to see the evening performance of the great comedian, Sid Field's Road Show at the Theatre Royal in Hanley. I thought that this was a lovely gesture and we all had a wonderful evening's entertainment.

My wife's father was a very successful art dealer, picture restorer and frame maker, and was one of the most highly respected businessmen in the Potteries. I was always a little nervous that I would not be able to provide the high standard of living that my wife had

Greetings cards drawn by Harold for Betty.
Above: Birthday 1939.
Right: Christmas 1934.

Sketch of young fiancé, Betty, 1935.

Wedding Day: 6th April 1940.

been accustomed to all her life, but as the motto says, 'love is blind', and in our case this axiom proved to be completely true. My weekly wage at this time was £3.7s.6d. and I mentioned to Mrs Hilda Beech, Mr Hassall's confidante, that I wondered if Mr Hassall would consider giving me an increase because of my forthcoming marriage. She dutifully informed him, and when I received my wages on the Friday afternoon I found that I was 5s. better off! I was now earning the princely amount of £3.12s.6d. Unfortunately, I could not thank Mr Hassall that day, because he was in hospital with a serious complaint, which was causing great concern.

When my honeymoon of two days was over, I arrived at the factory at my usual time of 8.30am, only to find that my office was dressed up like a Christmas tree with balloons, streamers, placards with pert messages, baby dolls (some black, some white), confetti and shoals of greetings cards. It took weeks to remove every trace of the disorder.

Shortly after my arrival for work I received a summons to the office of Mr Ted Hewitt, our managing director. He then gave me the sad news of Mr Thomas Hassall's death, which had taken place suddenly in hospital during Sunday, 7th April 1940. It was quite a shock and I was quite stunned, with my thoughts all of a jumble. Mr Hewitt informed me that he was expecting me to take over Mr Hassall's duties as soon as possible and that he would see me later in the week to discuss details after meeting his fellow directors.

The funeral service of Mr Hassall was held at Penkhull Church, which was full to overflowing with mourners from all parts of the country and many workpeople from the factory. Friends and customers from all over the world paid numerous glowing tributes to him. He certainly received a handsome send-off! In spite of his many faults, his presence and ability would be sadly missed and I hoped that I, in my own way, would play an equally successful role in my future with the Copeland company.

As promised, I was sent for by Mr Hewitt and he asked me to accept the job of decorating manager in addition to that of chief designer. He stated that I should be a senior staff member and receive a salary of £6 per week, to be paid into the bank each month. Unfortunately, I called this an 'Irishman's rise', because I had to work for four weeks without pay, as salaries were paid in arrears. Mr Hewitt did offer to lend me some money to tide me over, which I could repay at a later date. This offer I turned down with thanks – a case of false pride!

My new-found responsibility took some getting used to and putting into effect some of the theories and principles in which I sincerely believed was, I soon realised, going to be more difficult and take a longer time than I had envisaged. The onus of providing an efficient design function rested on my shoulders and became a matter of great importance and urgency. Steps had to be taken to augment our depleted staff. For many months I managed to maintain a reasonable amount of creative work, largely by my own efforts. Although the war was by now well under way, and all decorated ware vetoed for sale in the UK, we were still producing great quantities of wares for the USA market. Most of the orders were for well established patterns and it was incumbent upon us to take advantage of this state of affairs and attempt to set up a first-class design team able to produce shapes and decorations which would be acceptable after the war, in both the home and overseas markets.

After Mr Hassall's death, the title of art director ceased to be used. I could only imagine that this was a decision made by Mr Ronald Copeland; also Mr Hassall's office was emptied and used as a waiting room. This was a disappointment to me, for I had hoped that as chief designer I might have been considered as the successor to the title.[5]

At that time, my studio was a well-partitioned-off section of a small warehouse, well lit but with rough-hewn tables made by the works' joiner. The table surfaces were tongue and grooved floorboarding and the usual covering was a sheet of brown wrapping paper. Bare boards were the norm, well worn and dust-laden. A wooden bench ran parallel to the partition, which also contained three shelves for the display of plates and designs. Originally the room had had a stove-pot, but this had been replaced and steam pipes fitted. Washing facilities were non-existent and the only cleaning that was done had to be done by the occupants. It was a most frugal arrangement! So, I asked to have a first-class studio erected for my staff and myself.

Permission was granted and I chose the dingy room that had previously housed Mr Hammersley and Mr Deaville. It was quite a large room situated at the north end of the so-called Terrace, built over an archway which led to the enamel kilns and adjacent to the new showroom and art gallery which was built in 1939. The room was completely stripped – new windows, newly plastered walls instead of whitewashed bricks, new floorboards covered with ship's lino and polished, with the services of a "Mrs Mopp" to "do for us" each day.

The drawing and work tables were made to my own specifications together with very efficient lighting. In the north wall, set on storage cupboards stood a display case that housed a personally selected collection of fine Spode and Copeland pieces loaned from the factory museum. These showed the standard of design and craftsmanship achieved by the workpeople

in years past. Without a doubt it was a room that called for the utmost respect from the artists who would spend so many hours creating designs.

The years following the death of Mr Thomas Hassall were fully occupied on my part with an attempt to create an efficient design team, and in addition, to maintain good management of the decorating departments. It was, of necessity, a gradual and time-taking process, but slowly and surely progress was made and the first members of the design team were assembled to work in the newly appointed studio. The initial occupants of the new studio were to be three designers and myself. This arrangement proved to be a great success and during the following years a number of very capable creative artists produced many fine examples of pottery design during the time they spent working in the studio.

I was anxious to set a personal example by my own performance and to build a team of skilled creative designers who would enjoy freedom of expression and receive individual credit for successful work. They would also receive financial reward commensurate with their skills. It was also my intention to seek artists who possessed natural creative talent and then they would be given finesse training in an endeavour to maintain the Spode high standard of workmanship that had been achieved by the great craftsmen of the past.

One is entitled to think that such ambitious plans were merely pipe dreams, particularly when heavy investment was always needed for the development of new ideas; and as new goods would only exacerbate the order delivery problem, it was deemed to be unnecessary to spend too much of the artist's time creating new designs which stood little chance of being produced in the foreseeable future. I did, however, continue to experiment with the production of new ideas from time to time so that we should be ready if and when new decorations were needed to stimulate trade.

One of my first moves towards building a talented and efficient staff was to make full use of the artistic talent which was already employed at the factory and make sure that they should have at least a chance to prove their worth. Like Mr Hassall, I called upon the services of the painters when I wanted to make use of their skills. The first two persons who qualified in this respect were the ex-Minton crest painter, Mr Joe Austin and Mr Geoffrey Cholerton, a painter.

I was certain that Joe Austin would become an invaluable member of my design team, for he possessed an abundance of untapped skill, and having

[5] Between 1940 and 1947, there was not an art director although Harold was effectively doing Thomas Hassall's job.

rescued him from the shadows of anonimity, I installed him in a studio of his own. Within a short time Joe was producing really fine pieces of artwork and had fully justified my faith and judgement of his artistic skills. From the very start of this new venture he showed great enthusiasm and willingness to co-operate fully with my wishes. He also continued to execute the orders for crest painting on the few services that were still being produced in the early days of the war; this was vetoed later when all decorated goods were banned from the home market.

As Mr Joe Austin was approaching middle age I appointed two young Art School students to serve an apprenticeship with him to learn the skill of crest painting. One of the two students was a Mr Roy Trigg – who had had a Junior Art Department Scholarship training at the Burslem School of Art from 1937 to 1940. This was a similar scholarship to the one I was awarded years previously and so he had no excuse for not being 'good'! Subsequent events proved that this appointment was to turn out to be one of the finest I ever made. He never let me down – and contributed enormously to my own success.

Roy Trigg joined the company in December 1940. He was the brightest of all the budding young men who had been chosen for an artistic career at Copeland's. After a short term with the young apprentice painters, whom he outshone with ease in all the exercises he practised, I decided to place him with Mr Joe Austin, who by now was doing a lot of the follow-up drawings of my designs. Roy sought mastery of every facet of pottery design and decorating techniques and soaked up essential knowledge like a sponge. Within a short time he was helping Joe with the decorating of expensive services

and from time to time I gave him small creative design jobs. All was set fair for him to enjoy a great artistic future with the company, but, unfortunately, the time was looming up for him to be called upon for service in the armed forces.

I was ever hopeful that the war would soon be over; but it wasn't to be and in June 1943, Mr Roy Trigg joined the army as a topographical draughtsman and, after a lengthy training spell at Ruabon in North Wales, Roy spent the rest of the war in the Far Eastern war zone, where he served with distinction. Joe Austin was also heartbroken at losing yet another star junior – a young man named Fred Buxton, who was in the course of training when the war broke out, and as a reservist, was called up at the beginning of the hostilities.

Joe Austin then joined me in my studio, together with Joe Hackley, an ex-ceramic artist. During this period it was quite a battle to maintain a settled design policy and it seemed that every time things were running smoothly events would take place, which upset the level tenor of the department.

Like Mr Hassall I called upon the services of the painters when I wanted to make use of their skills. I used Mr Geoffrey Cholerton's painting services when I was producing new design prototypes, and for convenience he used my spare bench, at my invitation. As the painting of the sample is the last process to be used to complete the decoration, Geoffrey was very happy to show his painting to visitors to my room. This I accepted with equanimity because Geoffrey was a close friend and I was sure that he would not take advantage of the situation and claim credit for another person's work. To give him due credit, he certainly knew how to handle colour and I was always

Above: Crest painting, unknown artist. Photograph: Norman Jones.

Right: Roy Trigg, designer who joined the art department in 1940.

very pleased with his interpretation of my work. As the Secret Service Society for design development was no longer in existence and designs were being more openly displayed, new reputations were being created and sometimes a false picture presented to the beholder.

My skills as a designer were accepted by the directors who put in full time at the factory and took the opportunity of checking the details of their staff's output and were always loud in their praise of my contribution. But as Mr Ronald Copeland rarely visited me or had anything to say about the design work I was doing, I really began to wonder if he was aware of the true situation. I admit that this became an obsession with me for I often wondered what more I could do to convince him of my real value as a creative designer. But until the opportunity presented itself I decided to be patient and hope all would come right.

Mr A.E. Hewitt was always aware of the rivalry that existed between Geoffrey Cholerton and myself, for Mr Ronald Copeland was definitely showing a distinct leaning towards Geoffrey and often extolling at great length the virtues of his artistic skills to his fellow directors. Such was Mr Ronald's powerful personality that everyone nodded their heads in agreement. Mr Hewitt, who was of stronger character, was most sympathetic concerning my unhappiness with this state of affairs, and after a lengthy discussion with me, he said he had to have concrete proof as to who was the person with the genuine creative ability.[6]

With this in mind, he then suggested that each of the designers should be given the opportunity to show what creative skills they possessed. He instructed Eric Olsen, Geoffrey Cholerton and myself to produce an idea or ideas for an underglaze print and enamel dinner ware decoration for the home market. At long last here was my opportunity to shine! The one condition was that the design work must be handed to him in a fortnight. Eric Olsen, who was a fine modeller and sculptor but possessed only slight experience in pattern design had his studio well apart from my own workroom, while Geoffrey Cholerton made use of his workbench in the men's painting department, also away from my workroom.

The spirit of competition caused the adrenalin to course through my fingers and within a fortnight I had completed two first-class designs, which I knew in my own mind, could not be beaten by anything the other two could come up with. At the end of the fourteen days, I handed my designs, nicely mounted and presented, to Mr Hewitt. He was doubtful as to whom he should consult when making the decision on whose work was the best. However, this did not present any problem at all, because neither Eric Olsen nor Geoffrey Cholerton had made any attempt at creating a design of any kind. Their excuse for not submitting designs was that they did not have the time to complete the requirements.

Mr Hewitt informed me of the situation, and although he was disgusted by the lack of competitive spirit on the part of the other two, he was completely stymied by having a 'no contest' result. Although he was convinced that I was the one truly creative designer, he just did not have any real evidence to support my case. And so the 'status quo' was unchanged and we would hope to give battle another day! This was not quite the end of the story, however, because the two designs I had submitted were both

Merville, a result of Mr Hewitt's competition.

A sales leaflet for Ellesmere.

[6] It is unclear how a ceramic painter who both Harold and Thomas Hassall had given the opportunity to do some design work had had chance to influence Ronald Copeland to such an extent. This competition must have taken place between 1940 and 1943.

produced in full ranges of earthenware and were named 'Merville' and 'Ellesmere'. Both were printed and painted underglaze and proved to be successful and very popular for a number of years.

Shortly after the new studio was finished, Mr Ronald Copeland had decided, much to everyone's surprise, to elevate Mr Geoffrey Cholerton to a senior position in the creative field and, although the term art director was not mentioned, he was invited to install himself in the office of the late Mr T. Hassall![7] This was a decision made solely by Mr Ronald without any acquiescence from the other directors of the company. I was at the time most upset and Geoffrey, who was a close friend, never gave any hint of the likelihood. Possibly it was a surprise to him also!

History was once again repeating itself, for all too fresh in my mind and memory was the picture of the late departed Mr Hassall – art director – sitting in this self-same office, without pencil and paper, watercolour or brushes, drawing board or any semblance of any other artistic accoutrements to be seen or at any time used. Maybe my conception of what constituted the term art director was totally wrong, but for now, for the second time in my career, I was to witness a repeat performance. And so it turned out to be. With hindsight, perhaps Mr Ronald had questioned who could fulfil the role Tom Hassall had played, and here in Geoffrey Cholerton was a man of similar background who would fill the vacant position.

Notwithstanding Mr Ronald's decision to elevate Geoffrey's position to a more important role in the scheme of things, the general running of the Art Department and the production of the decorated goods showed very little change of direction. I soon realised that Geoffrey did not intend to participate in the actual creating of any form of design work. Whether this was by choice or recognition of his own limited ability to perform well in this field I did not know, but he obviously preferred to follow the methods used by Mr Hassall, but with a significant difference – I did not, in any way, at any time, allow him to utter criticism of any design work I personally created. This unspoken condition he readily accepted and never to the best of my knowledge did he ever deviate from this unwritten law. As we were still friends, he was only too willing to accept the responsibility of supervising the decorating departments. This was a roving commission covering all parts of the factory. On occasion, he would join me for discussions when production problems arose; these were many and varied due to the wartime labour conditions.

During these early war years, we gradually lost the services of a number of important members of the workforce. Many were craftsmen or women, whose skills and abilities were greatly missed. The old-time painters, who included Mr Micklewright, Mr Joe Fenn, Mr Jesse Savage, and Mr Harry Wakefield, were among those who were left because of ill health

Geoffrey Cholerton discussing Lady Blessington pattern with Harold c.1954.

7. The precise date when Geoffrey assumed the senior position is between 1940 and 1943 but he was officially made "art director" on 28.02.47 after the war. Nor is it clear who was in charge of the department between 1940 and 1947.

or old age. Both senior modellers left; Mr Max Henk joined the RAF and Mr Tom Barlow was conscripted to be a munitions engineer. Eric Olsen, the Norwegian modeller–designer, volunteered to join his country's service as a camouflage expert. Ian Forse, our tunnel design expert, joined the Navy, Billy Eccles the Army, Arthur Gaskell the Royal Air Force and Eric Bate chose to work for Doulton.

Geoffrey Cholerton and I were designated as being in reserved occupations but could be called on without any notice to serve if needed for war service. Two artists who were given employment after the departure of the aforementioned were a Mr Benbow, an elderly man, and Mr Leslie Shillito, who was much younger. These two artists managed to cope with the decoration orders for Herring Hunting Scene, which was still in demand overseas.

Another of our worries was how could we increase the output of Billingsley Rose pattern on the Jewel Embossed shape. The orders from the USA and Canada were an embarrassment and Mr Ted Hewitt invited some method study experts to do a work analysis. They submitted a report detailing methods that would increase output by 10%. This action was most hurtful, and Geoffrey and I suggested that we should be allowed to introduce a scheme of our own and, if ours was the better plan, then we would turn down the experts' solution to the problem, and avoid paying out a substantial fee for their services.

There was one slight problem, however, for the Billingsley Rose pattern was always painted by the men painters, because of the intricacy of painting the rose flower in a specialised manner. In addition to the rose there was leafage and other small flowers that had to be coloured. This part of the process was less difficult to do, but our plan was to have the men, who were four in number, paint solely the rose, while girls would be paid to paint the rest of the spray. The price for painting remained the same in total wages, but the output was double for duty. We managed to train three or four senior women artists to paint the rose motif, which enabled the company to maintain the normal production level and so satisfy the market trends.

Another solution to increase the output of the decorating department was to sometimes invite selected young students attending the Stoke School of Art evening classes to become apprentice painters.

They were given a month's trial and if their work proved to be satisfactory they were then offered an apprenticeship of five years to receive expert tuition in ceramic painting by the senior artists. This practice proved to be a great investment, particularly when increased artistic labour was required after the war ended.

The year 1943 was to prove very eventful. The fairy-tale story of Geoffrey Cholerton's rise to fame and his influence on Mr Ronald was almost unique in the history of the Copeland factory. By now, Geoffrey was using the title of art director, which to me was the greatest of misnomers, particularly as no pencil or brush was ever applied by him onto paper or pot. We were, within certain limits, still great friends, which was a very wise and sensible policy to pursue, for as long as a steady stream of creative designs was forthcoming, as art director, he basked in the glory. I am sure that Mr Ronald thought that Geoffrey inspired me with ideas by some subtle thought transference method. Although he used to give credit to me when he was viewing my work, I am sure that, in his opinion, it was only a talented form of labouring, by comparison with Geoffrey's intuitive gift. I used to think, "How can an intelligent man be so blinkered and so easily fooled?" Surely one day the penny would drop and the sun would shine again. I did consider a change of employment during this traumatic period, and then decided that the time was not propitious and I had to learn to be patient.

Geoffrey's influence continued to increase at the factory. When Mr Ronald made one of his rare visits to Spode, his first stop on arrival was at Geoffrey's office. For over an hour he would listen to all the thoughts, ideas, plans and plots, and general gossip of the happenings of the recent past, including the behaviour of the board members and senior management. The other directors were aware of the situation and treated Geoffrey with great respect. It was almost a Rasputin type of situation and most unsatisfactory. Because of his power behind the throne, Geoffrey was completely contemptuous of any form of criticism levelled at him by the directors from time to time. I often used to warn him not to overplay his hand, because if anything should happen to Mr Ronald, he would have a struggle to find friends. Time would tell!

Job Descriptions

Art Director: Mr G Cholerton

On top of work entailed as art director – also have to supervise:-

1. Arrange for the proper flow of orders through departments to ensure that all people are fully occupied; that is work for edgers, gilders, liners, etc.
2. To supervise the fair distribution of work.
3. Maintain a constant supply of colours, turpentine, aniseed, phenol, etc
4. See to general cleanliness and tidiness of the decorating departments.

Designer: Mr Harold Holdway

On top of designing:-

1. Arrange to have all finished work from the decorating departments constantly moved to the kiln   to enable the kilns to be well filled with continual flow of ware.
2. See that the trials are made of all colours, underglaze and on-glaze for china and earthenware, as you did in the past for Mr Gresham, including the seeing of colour manufacturers' reps.
3. Count and settle with decorators who are now settled for by Eric Bate and Joe Austin.

Harold with some of his designs behind him.

Harold posing like Marlon Brando with his Leica camera.

EARLY WAR YEARS: 2

The war continued in a relentless fashion but the famous names in the pottery industry were encouraged to produce more and more valuable exports for the North American markets. By this time, America was sending legions of men and great quantities of food and war materials in an effort to help defeat the enemy in Europe and the Far East. In spite of this, the British housewife had to endure many privations caused by shortages, necessitating rationing and many hours of standing in queues. The nightly visits to air raid shelters was tiresome and tiring, but somehow the workers managed to maintain maximum output even though the numbers employed in many factories were slowly being eroded owing to increasingly heavier demand for skilled workers in munitions factories.

Despite the restrictions on decorated ware for the home market, I continued to produce quite a lot of designs for the USA markets. One series of dessert ware centres on china turned out to be quite an important milestone in pattern trends. This was my first attempt at creating a botanical style of design and the subject was 'popular fruits'. I decided to use an arrangement of fruits and include the blossom as part of the design. At the time this was a novel approach, which I don't think had been attempted by other local pottery manufacturers. After a lot of research, I made a set of drawings of eleven different varieties of fruit but could not think of a suitable twelfth subject. Then, with fingers crossed, I chose a tomato; I think it used to be called a 'love apple'! This choice turned out to be completely successful.

The twelve subjects which I had created were what I would call rough drawings and, instead of making finished drawings, which would have been painstaking and time-consuming, I asked Joe Austin

if he felt sufficiently confident to attempt the job of producing the finished artwork. In my own mind I had no doubts that he would succeed because the standard of workmanship he showed when producing crests and monograms etc. was sheer perfection. He was a little hesitant at first but completed a finished drawing and asked me if I thought it was satisfactory. It was a lovely piece of artistry and I asked how soon I could expect to have the remainder of the sketches. I used this method of working often, particularly when my own time was filled by my many other duties.

There were many occasions when I would create a small section of a border pattern, hand it to Joe and he would complete the pattern round the rim of the plate – a job which I would have found very boring – and present me with the finished design. What was most remarkable was that he enjoyed doing this type of repetitive work. Maybe this patience was developed during the repetition of scores of identical crests and motifs, which he applied to the large

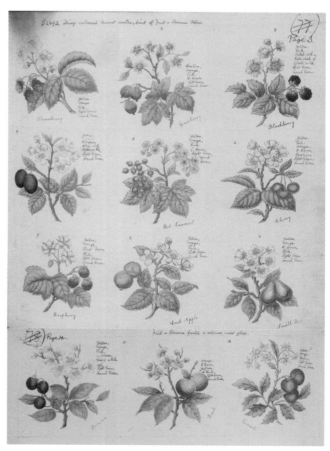

Fruit and Blossom designed by Harold and finished by Joe Austin. Pictured from Spode's underglaze subject book. Photo courtesy of Spode Museum Trust; copyright Spode.

'A Class' wartime decoration for the home market.

services he had decorated in his earlier days as a crest painter.

My twelve designs were named 'Fruit and Blossom' and the pattern became a bestseller on china dessert ware. Also, a set of engravings was made for tea ware – of a smaller size – and lastly it was produced as an underglaze earthenware painted decoration, which sold in large quantities overseas. Following the success of the Fruit and Blossom decoration in the USA market, a further request was made for a new design in a similar vein. In the summer of 1942 our US agent, Sydney Thompson, asked if it would be possible to create a botanical type series of English flowers, and if it could take the form of a simple flower arrangement of six or more varieties.

I supplied him with sample dessert plates, hand-painted prototypes with each of the following subjects: rose, iris and rhododendron. They were finished with a simple gold band at the edge and when completed looked attractive. On receipt, Mr Thompson and his staff liked them very much, and he was loud in his praise, but as he could have only one subject he chose the rhododendron. Mr Ronald Copeland was very pleased with Mr Thompson's choice and set about providing me with examples of blooms of infinite variety. It so happened that the rhododendron was Mr Copeland's favourite flower. He had many varieties of the lovely flower in his gardens at Colwich and at Trelissick in Cornwall, so he decided to bring to the works specimens that he thought would be suitable subjects and might be used in the series.

The first example he brought was, in my opinion, the most exquisite of the many varieties in existence. The name of the species was *Dalhousiae*, a lily-like cluster with large cream flowers, two or three in number, with a simple surround of sage-green leaves. One of the secrets of drawing from nature is that the artist should capture the living quality of the flower as quickly as possible and follow on with the drawing of the leafage. Mr Copeland personally delivered the bloom to me as soon as he arrived at the factory and left me to get on with the drawing. I grabbed a receptacle in haste, filled it with water and with all speed made three sketches of the small spray. One viewpoint turned out to be better than the others and so was chosen to be coloured. First thing after lunch, Mr Ronald came to see what progress I had made with the recording of his precious bloom; in my opinion the drawings I had made were very good.

Instead of a word of congratulation on my skill

in capturing the fragile beauty of the bloom, he just 'blew his top'! I had committed a cardinal sin in his eyes for I had placed his prized bloom in a glass jam jar filled with water! To him this was a sacrilegious act and he ordered me to take the flower group out of the 'filthy jar' at once and find a suitable china vase for its display. He never even glanced at my sketches and I don't think he ever forgave me for perpetrating such an irreligious act. Over the next six weeks I completed the initial six arrangements of the series and I am still positive that the finest study I made, and one that contributed most towards the success and abundance of orders that followed, was the jam jar arrangement of the *Dalhousiae* specimen!

As the rhododendron bloom lasts for only a short time in late April and May, Mr Copeland insisted on the whole of the Art Department staff spending as much time as possible producing factual studies of the many varieties he was so familiar with. He indulged in this ritual each year into the 1950s, even after the series was completed.[8] He also organised visits to all the famous rhododendron growers in the country. One such trip was arranged during the spring days of 1951, which I think is worthy of mention here.

Our North of England representative, Mr Charles Audley, a very capable and able salesman, had built up a goodly number of accounts and clients, many of which were situated in and around Wales, often in noted beauty spots and seaside resorts. Mr Ronald decided to accompany him on this particular Welsh spring trip, together with his two artists, Geoffrey Cholerton and myself. Charles drove a large Humber car and at this time of year the gorse and the rhododendrons were in full bloom. A packed lunch of quality, prepared in the director's kitchen, was eaten in a deserted picnic spot in the Welsh hills and a tot or two of whisky imbibed as liquid refreshment – dear Charles as the driver had to forgo this. It was a divine situation, birds singing, hardly any traffic on the roads and, after a short siesta, we completed our journey to Betws-y-Coed, where we had been booked into the best hotel for the night. A fine meal with good wine chosen by Mr Ronald, who was a connoisseur, and the world seemed a better place.

Up bright and early next morning, a brisk walk, good breakfast and then a drive to Bodnant Gardens to study the rhododendrons and photograph in black and white and colour the lovely blossoms with Lord Aberconway, who was at that time President of the Royal Horticultural Society. Geoffrey Cholerton cried off, saying he had developed a cold – I think it was

[8] This must have been redone as the 1942 pattern number Y6638 Rhododendron pattern was engraved in 1950 by Jack Longmore.

cold feet! Mr Ronald and myself, after a preliminary reconnoitre round the gardens, arrived back at the house and had lunch with the noble lord in his fine dining room – Charles Audley had in the meantime been despatched to visit customers. After partaking of an excellent meal, Mr Ronald and I, armed with tripods, cameras and two umbrellas – for it had started to rain – tramped round the gardens taking pictures of the flowers – they were breathtaking!

Ronald was a real hero, for he acted as the labourer, fetching and carrying for the whole exercise. I think we were out in the rain for about three hours but such was his interest in everything that was happening that I don't think that he noticed the weather at all. Back to the house, off with our wet coats, a big thank you to the noble lord and into the car which the faithful Charles had standing by ready to whisk us back to the hotel we had left so many hours before. After another fine dinner, Mr Ronald decided to go to bed early – he said he was a little tired and no wonder for he had had a hard day and wasn't exactly a young man.

Next day after breakfast, we went to Harlech and booked in at the Royal St David's Hotel. After unpacking, we had a walk along the deserted beach where we were the only people to be seen. Because Mr Ronald had a slight difficulty in walking, we took it in turns to amble slowly at his pace and I vividly remember him saying to me: "Harold, I would give anything for a new pair of feet." I really did feel sorry for him and I was quite ashamed of being so active and youthful. Good health is more important than riches – how true this maxim is.

In the afternoon, we journeyed to Portmeirion Gardens, owned by Mr Clough Williams-Ellis, the noted architect who had built the exotic Italianate village complex which, although controversial, was quite unique. Mr Ronald, from earlier days, knew the old gardener who used to tend the rhododendrons on the estate. Now he was retired so we called at his home and he gave us a conducted tour, showing us the changes that had taken place since the new owners moved in. Sadly, they had completely neglected any cultivation of the rare rhododendron species. Even so, they thrived in this almost wild environment.

Afterwards, we had afternoon tea in the hotel overlooking the sea, which, after our strenuous wanderings round the estate, was a welcome relief. But, no peace for the wicked, as my mother used to say, for in the middle of the dining room was a huge tab-handled jug, embossed with a low relief group of flowers at the front and back, holding a colossal arrangement of rhododendrons, which was most striking. Mr Ronald for once was not admiring the flowers, but he thought that the jug was just what the factory needed and ordered me to make an accurate sketch there and then on the back of an envelope so that on my return to the factory I could have it modelled immediately. My lord and master had issued an order and it was to be obeyed! The large jug was added to our Velamour range, which had a matt-glazed cream finish and the resultant sales more than paid for the expenses of our research trip to North Wales. After a good lunch at the Harlech Hotel we packed our bags in readiness for the journey on the morrow, which was accomplished with ease, arriving at the factory at lunchtime.

At this time the whole of the design staff were living and dreaming about rhododendrons and had more than enough material to complete any future requirements. Briefly, the method of applying studies onto the china was as follows: firstly a fine drawing was produced from the original watercolour sketches. This drawing was then skilfully engraved onto copper plates and transfer printed onto the surface of the

Visit to Portmeirion to view rhododendrons: Retired gardener, Charles Audley, Geoffrey Cholerton.

Rhododendron plate being painted. Photograph: Norman Jones.

No. 1 *Dalhousiae* rhododendron plate.

Dalhousiae engraving by James Wood and Jack Longmore (Jnr).

Rhododendron research trip to Portmeirion, North Wales, 1954. Left to right: Harold, retired gardener, Charles Audley, Geoffrey Cholerton.

Pattern book entry for No. 4 *Augustini*, 1942. Courtesy of Spode Museum Trust; copyright Spode.

chinaware. After the prints were fired they were then painted in ceramic colours to match the natural tones depicted in the original artwork. This was only undertaken by Spode's finest artists. The named varieties used in the first six plate centres were: No. 1 *Dalhousiae*, No. 2 *Batemanii*, No. 3 *Gwilt King*, No. 4 *Augustinii*, No. 5 *Hodgsonii*, No. 6 *Fortuneii*.

The ultimate in rhododendron painting on china was when Mr Ronald had a special dessert service produced for Lord Aberconway as a token gift in appreciation of the help he had given in making our project possible. The subjects chosen for the service were quite different both in species and arrangement from the commercial version. The service was completely hand-painted by Mr Cyril Ball, and the quality of the painting reached the acme of perfection of rhododendron painting on

china. This exercise was repeated for Sir Hector Bolitho, also as a token of appreciation for his help in providing splendid floral examples, and lastly, after Mr Ronald's death in 1959, a further set was produced for his widow, Mrs Ida Copeland, for her personal use, which she greatly treasured. As these sets were special commissions there is no pictorial record of the subjects in the factory pattern books, which seems a great pity.

Following the success of the six dinner plate centres, I was permitted to increase the range of items so as to include smaller-sized plates, teacups and saucers, coffee cups and saucers. Mr Ronald suggested that I used the smaller type of species for these extra items, which to me was a good idea. I chose six subjects for the teacups, six smaller subjects for the saucers but with different arrangements and composition of

Audubon Bird No. 3 Canada Jay.

Audubon Bird No. 1 Western Tanager.

Engraving of Western Tanager by Jack Longmore (Jnr).

Original watercolour of Western Tanager.

the floral motifs.[9] When finished they looked very attractive and a little later I called on the services of a new artist-cum-designer, Mr Joseph Hackley, whom I had recently engaged, to provide suitable artwork to decorate the 7in tea plates. As we had lots of reference studies he welcomed the challenge. Joseph was middle-aged and a First World War veteran, a very fine draughtsman and quite expert in floral arrangement designs. As he had my original artwork to act as a standard he made a first-class job of this important assignment. I believe he gained a lot from his experience and skill while employed as the senior designer of a textile company.

The next design request was: would it be possible to produce a series of centres of the quality of the rhododendron decoration but using American birds instead of flowers? This of course presents problems to an Englishman, whose knowledge of American birds is slight. Many of the American birds, although possessing the same popular names as ours, in fact are quite different in size and colouring to their English counterpart. This meant intense study on my part.

The finest of the English bird painters was Thorburn, but no American customer would be able to recognize his depictions. However, it happened that Sydney Thompson had given Mr Ronald a rather

[9] Later, customers asked for a series of 12 rhododendron plates, but instead of drawing and engraving another 6, the original 6 were painted in different colours – a practice Harold did not approve of.

71

comprehensive book on the work of Audubon, the great American bird illustrator and naturalist. It was profusely illustrated with all the known examples of his American bird paintings and, although the reproductions of his bird studies were poorly printed, it was a comprehensive work and I chose what I considered to be a few attractive subjects as a basis for the beginning of a series.

To create a good composition of the bird subjects, with a suitable background, and to make an appealing plate centre, presented me with quite a problem that needed very careful study to be sure that the supporting background of the plant, flower, or tree form was the correct habitat of the bird depicted. I produced a sample 10in plate with a simple gold finish and despatched it to the USA for approval. Mr Thompson showed it to his salesmen and buyers from the leading New York retail stores who were very pleased with the design and I was given the go-ahead to produce the first centres.

I made the original drawings of the first few examples prior to the engravings being produced and then handed the job to Mr Joe Hackley to complete the remainder of the required drawings for the service. He also created the drawings needed to complete the enlarged range of tea and coffee ware. After the war, when the restrictions were lifted on the sale of decorated goods in the UK, large quantities of this decoration were sold by English retailers in addition to USA market requirements.

A lucrative pre-war branch of business was painted china figures. We, as a factory, were very fortunate in having in our possession the original Chelsea-Derby moulds, purchased by Alderman W.T. Copeland in 1849 at the closure of the Derby factory. There were literally thousands of pieces which took years to sort and assemble and make a collection of finished models. In 1933, Mr Ronald Copeland decided to produce a series of figures to commemorate the bicentenary of the birth of Josiah Spode the First. The whole project was a great success, so, in addition, Mr Ronald had produced a series of Wheatley's Cries of London, modelled figures, which were beautifully coloured and most attractive. In addition to the figure models, the model-making department was kept busy producing a large selection of birds and animals. The birds were mainly popular in England, so Eric Olsen was asked to create a series of American small birds, which proved to be very well-liked in the North American markets.

Most of the model painting was done by men, but as the war progressed we were gradually able to train sufficient ladies to take the places of the men who had entered the forces and their work reached a very high standard.

For a short period I engaged the services of two real old-timers, Mr Anthony Connelly, the famous ex-Minton artist, and Mr William Birbeck, from whom I received some of my early training and who had retired from George Jones & Sons many years previously. Mr Connelly, then well into his seventies, painted Wild Ducks and Pheasants in pairs of cock and hen. His workmanship was absolutely superb and he over-painted these subjects to such a degree that his piecework wages were resultantly very low. I pleaded with him not to overdo the time spent in

Above: Fancy modelling; Arthur Steel casting Spode's 'Chelsea figures'.

Right: Polished biscuit 'Chelsea figure' mounted on a base. A trial piece.

painting the subjects in this manner because neither the company nor the customer would pay for such elaboration. It was no use, however, and he just carried on and painted to suit Anthony Connelly and refused to change, in spite of the fact that Mr Birbeck, a much milder character, painted his models according to our instructions and consequently earned more money than Mr Connelly.

Anthony Connelly – The Artist

A man larger than life, even in his advancing years his character and, above all, his powerful personality, was obvious to everyone who met him. Cultured, well-read and a brilliant conversationalist and I am almost sure that his country of origin was Ireland. His career at Minton's was very successful for he was trained by Mussel, the great French ceramic artist who was in his prime at that time. It was said by experts that Connelly was such an apt pupil that few people could tell their work apart. I had many conversations with him and was fascinated by his stories of his early career. I do not doubt that a little of the 'old blarney' crept into some of the accounts, but I put this down to his putting on a little extra colour to give more emphasis to his story.

He was a man of stocky build, not tall but almost as broad as he was high, with muscles like a weightlifter. When his sleeves were rolled up, a paintbrush held delicately in his fingers looked like a matchstick. It was obvious that his huge forearms had been developed by undertaking very strenuous manual work during his youth. He explained this by telling how he had left his pottery painting to become a navvy! He would spend his summer months working as a member of a road-making gang, and on one occasion, he had made the foreman ganger. He was given this responsibility, he said, because he could out-dig, out-last, out-swear, out-drink and out-fight any member of the gang. This I could well believe!

More often than not he would come to work in the shabbiest of clothes but, on a rare occasion, he used to wear what was once a most beautifully embroidered waistcoat. It was practically threadbare and the colours were almost faded out of existence. He told me that it was a relic of his glamorous past, for it was part of the apparel he wore when attending an audience with the Grand Duke Michael of Russia, who resided at Keele Hall. Each summer, Mr Connelly had to present his portfolio to the Grand Duke, who would make his personal choice. All this happened many, many years before I met

Jimmy Upsdell collecting an MBE from Buckingham Palace.

him, but he still painted the most beautiful floral pictures in gouache for all and sundry, mainly for 'beer money'.

At the time he worked for me at Copeland's he was living in the Salvation Army hostel. Later, he went to lodge with an old lady close by. The last I heard of Mr Connelly was when our local coroner congratulated him on his bravery when he put out the flames that enveloped the old lady, who sadly died from her injuries. I don't think I have ever met a more colourful character than Anthony Connelly and I am the proud possessor of one of these paintings, which I have always treasured. (One of the paintings is shown on page 75).

Jimmy Upsdell – Wartime Humour

A connecting door separated the art director's office from the Costing Department, which was run by Mr James W. Upsdell. He was a Londoner who, before the First World War saw service with the Merchant Fleet before joining the forces and becoming an Army paymaster stationed at Lichfield. He married a local girl and, after the war, obtained a job at Copeland's in the costing department where his position, one of great importance, meant that he had to deal with highly confidential matters. He also became invaluable to Mr Ronald, attending to his every personal need. He also became almost a godfather to Geoff and myself and was always ready to give good advice. Although in his fifties, he was very youthful and could appreciate a joke, an example of which I recall vividly.

The work's bell reinstalled over the arch. The two windows were Harold's second office.

During one of my wandering spells I discovered an old weatherworn ship's bell, not particularly large, but still capable of producing a very healthy loud ring. On enquiring about its history, I was informed that it was used for many years before to call the operatives to work at the beginning of each day. When the bell ceased ringing you were considered to be late. The doorman at the factory entrance performed this duty every day and developed with constant practice a steady rhythmic beat, to which the following words were chanted: "God bless Copeland's, damn and bugger Minton's." Such was the good-natured rivalry between these two great factories!

After rescuing the bell from its place of rest, I had it thoroughly cleaned and decided to have it placed at the apex of the archway directly below my new studio, at a point about nine or ten feet from the ground. It was always a temptation for tall young men to see if they could jump upwards and hit the clapper of the bell, thereby producing a loud ring. This happened quite often and was always a pleasure to hear.

During the wartime blackout strict observance was paid to safety and the lock-up procedure each night. Mr Upsdell, who was nicknamed Uncle, did his regular rounds of the art gallery, showroom and my studio, checking that all the doors were locked and all the lights were out. I usually departed for home before he performed this task, but one particular night, I stayed in my studio behind a locked door, having during the afternoon tied a length of strong black thread to the clapper of the bell, then passed the thread through the slightly opened window of the studio – which was directly above the bell – and into the room. After Jimmy had done his routine check I lay doggo for about half an hour, for as was his custom, Jimmy had a chat with Geoffrey and then went back to his office. Now was the time; I grabbed the thread and tolled the bell vigorously. At the sound they both dashed out into the Stygian darkness whereupon Jimmy was heard to murmur: "Geoff, old Josiah has come back to haunt us!"

They both moved slowly and nervously towards the bell which had ceased to toll – because I was creased with laughter. When I judged them to be directly underneath the bell, I once more pulled the thread. This time, the thread broke and dangled free, brushing the face of Uncle Jimmy, who then realised that it was an earthly presence which was the cause of the phenomenon, and he did not have to give much thought as to who was responsible.

The war was now increasing in intensity and the country's morale was very low with the defeat of France and the return of the British Expeditionary Force from Dunkirk. It seemed that evil was triumphing over good. This was the signal for Hitler to try and bomb Britain into submission and the civilian populace had a lot of sleepless nights and suffered terrible losses. We in Stoke-on-Trent had only a comparatively small share of the bombing raids, largely due to the fact that Hitler did not consider the city to be a target of real importance. Each night the bombers droned overhead on their death-dealing and destructive missions to Liverpool, Manchester and other northern cities, so we were lucky to have been, in the main, particularly ignored.

As the Spode factory was situated more or less in the centre of Stoke-on-Trent and close to the main railway station, our authorities considered it to be a vulnerable target and the company was instructed to provide a nightly patrol of air raid wardens and a firefighting unit. I was appointed leader of a firefighting squad of six persons, who had been fully trained by the regular City Fire Brigade. We operated on a rota system and had to spend one night per week on duty. This meant a total of six teams were formed to cover each night of the week. Our duties were to man a look-out post and patrol the works and occasionally have a practice run with the fire appliance. As we never had the occasion to use our skills for a real emergency we considered this to be a very small measure of inconvenience.

At last the dreaded summons came for me in the familiar buff-coloured envelope, staring out from the midst of a pile of early-delivered white Christmas mail. It instructed me to report on Boxing Day, 26th December 1943, for initial training and category selection in the Royal Naval Air Service at a shore-based training establishment named HMS *Gosling* near Warrington. This certainly put a dampener on that Christmas Day celebration.

Geoffrey had so far escaped the call-up so, for a short time, he was in sole charge. So short, in fact, that in the early months of 1944, he had to report for Army training at the King's Own Scottish Borderers' headquarters. In spite of the factory being robbed of its two 'leading lights', as has been proved often before and since, it managed to survive wonderfully well, mainly because good planning had provided a very fine reserve team, who took on this onerous task and coped admirably. Most of the responsibility for running the design and decorating facility was handled by my very good friend Joe Austin, in whom I had such great faith and trust. During the years of my absence, the company was really indebted to him and his excellent control and guidance under very difficult circumstances.

Mr Ted Hewitt, who had lost a son in the Royal Air Force during the early days of the war, was very kind and sympathetic to me when I gave him the news of my call-up and he paid my wife a monthly allowance for the whole of my service with the Navy, which was greatly appreciated and enabled her to enjoy a reasonable standard of living. The year 1943 was not all gloom and desperation however for, on 8th April, there was a wonderful happening when my dear wife Elizabeth presented me with a fine son, whom we christened Paul. This meant that I now had an extra responsibility, and as a proud father, I began to wonder what lay in store for him. There were no ready-made answers – I could only wish for a healthy, hopeful and peaceful world for him and for us all.

Anthony Connelly botanical painting done in his spare time for beer money.

WAR SERVICE

Christmas Day 1943 was spent quietly at home and after enjoying a fine turkey lunch with wine and a pudding enriched with brandy sauce, suffused with a feeling of blissful contentment, my wife and I sat wondering what the future held for the three of us. The following day I had to get an early train, so I decided to call at my parents-in-law's home. There I left my cycle and walked a weary mile to Stoke-on-Trent railway station to catch the train to Warrington. On arrival there, I met up with a fellow recruit who hailed from Wellington in Shropshire. Together we made a short journey by bus and then walked down a pleasant country lane to the main entrance of the Royal Naval Air Station which was to be our home for the next twelve weeks.

As HMS *Gosling* was a fully rated Naval training establishment, a concessionary tobacco and rum issue necessitated an armed guard and Customs officials on duty round the clock. The entrance was most impressive by virtue of its extremely well scrubbed appearance; even the stones marking the pathways were whitewashed. A most imposing young sailor with a rifle stood on guard ready to repel the enemy, or so it seemed to us poor ignorant civilians. We stared at him in awe, and then asked him where we should report. Without moving a muscle, through very tight lips, he muttered: "**** off back, for once you get inside these gates, you'll never get out!" What a welcome! And what a way to begin our new life.

Having reported to the guard room, where there were gathered a number of very bored-looking bestriped non-commissioned officers, we were given a knife, fork, and spoon, together with a brand-new Government issue earthenware mug emblazoned with a naval badge. As every potter does when handling any strange piece of ware, I turned it over to see who had made it and – guess who? None other than W.T. Copeland & Sons Ltd, Stoke-on-Trent! This was the first free gift of pottery I had ever received and in the circumstances I would never forget!

We were then escorted to a large Nissen hut where quite a number of new recruits were idling around looking like lost souls. By this time I was feeling quite hungry, then over the tannoy system came the announcement that the midday meal was being served on the Mess Deck. I learnt that the Navy has a special language of its own; for instance, the Mess Deck is the dining hall, the Galley is the cookhouse, the floor is the Deck, etc. on land or at sea. The Mess Deck was a huge place, full of long tables that allowed twelve ratings to sit on forms. The last two men to sit at the end of the table had to act as servers. As the room filled with a large crowd of hungry men and youths, the noise became unbearable and quite deafening, and I heard for the first time in my life, cursing, swearing, obscenities uttered casually and as every second word. It was quite a spectacle, one that had to be experienced to be believed. I thought that this could not be the normal behaviour of intelligent civilized beings but I was truly surprised to find how soon I became attuned to both the noise level and the bad language spoken in a dozen different dialects. Within a few days it became just a background noise, which did not disturb me in the slightest way.

Each intake of recruits numbered about forty men who were from then on to be referred to as ratings. At thirty years of age, I was the oldest member of the class so our instructor appointed me to be the class leader. As I was a conscripted man and not a volunteer, I had made up my mind that during my service I would not take on any real responsibility, but simply accept and obey orders. But this aim was quickly quashed by the brief authority vested in an embittered, ageing, bad-tempered petty officer instructor – a reservist who had never expected to have to serve in the wartime Naval service. It was his duty to conduct the class in squad drill, arms training, general physical exercises and most importantly, to teach the men to obey orders instantly and without question. At the end of the three months we were really quite efficient and we were armed with confidence that we could take on the enemy at any time and give a good account of ourselves.

Educational training was imperative and insisted upon, with much instruction and with many tests and examinations conducted to sort out who should be recommended for the great variety of duties. After the results of these tests were known, the educationalists, psychiatrists and psychologists conducted lengthy interviews with each rating to assess whether he should be recommended for advancement and into which category he should be placed. In my case, the WRNS officer conducting the interview for job allocation suggested that I accept an officer training appointment, which I think was largely influenced by my civilian employment record of success. Without hesitation, I turned the offer down, because of my

Harold in his sailor's unifrom with baby Paul.

firm conviction that I should not accept any serious responsibility.

The decision turned out to be the biggest mistake I made during the whole of my service career. I finally accepted as a choice of job to train as a member of an aero-maintenance crew. Then, because my pre-service occupation was that of a practising artist-designer, I would be able to opt for any of the trades that were on offer. The job descriptions were: armoury, airframes, engines, and electronics & radio, and the personnel employed were either mechanics or fitters. As I had impressed the selection board of experts, I was chosen, together with two or three other ratings, to be trained as an aircraft fitter, while the rest of the class were classified as mechanics and were given a shorter and less difficult form of training.

After these decisions had been taken at the end of our initial training, in mid-March 1944, the class were granted ten days' leave, with instructions as to where and when to report for duty. The journey home seemed endless, but I was looking forward to a great welcome! First of all, however, my baby son, aged twelve months, did not recognize me in my comic opera sailor suit and on sight of me burst into tears. It was several days before he would accept me. Fortunately, the shock was not so great for my wife and it turned out to be a very happy homecoming and reunion – I am sure absence does make the heart grow fonder. As it was the beginning of spring, the garden was looking very neglected, so for part of my leave I concentrated on preparing the greenhouse for the setting of tomato plants which I thought my wife could handle during my absence.

All too soon my leave was over and I set off once again to commence the next chapter of my war-training programme. As a member of a class of about forty ratings chosen from various Naval Air Training centres, I had to report to the Fulham Gaslight and Coke Company Ltd, situated on the banks of the River Thames in London, to receive advanced theoretical and practical engineering training. I was pitched into a remarkably intelligent group of young men whose educational standards were higher than my own. I found the task of keeping up with them to be very difficult and I had to do a lot of cramming in my spare time. However, one area where I was way ahead of the class was workshop practice. This was precision work of the highest order and, although a pencil and brush were my civilian tools, I found that I was equally at home using delicate files, micrometers and other metal-shaping tools so, in consequence, my examination results were quite outstanding.

The building in which we were housed was several stories high with spacious and well-equipped accommodation. Sleeping quarters were more than adequate, each rating having a separate bed in a large dormitory. The food was nicely cooked and hatch-served, each individual having a choice of a small selection of different dishes.

Because of the small number of ratings, only a few Naval officers were needed for supervision and to maintain discipline. Most of the instructors were civilian tradesmen, while naval instruction was given by two or three commissioned officers, including the education officer, who played a most important role. The course was scheduled for about a three-month period after which, on completion of our training, we would be allocated our trade category and in turn be sent to specialist aeronautical centres, usually Royal Air Force stations.

The war at this time had changed course and only a few short sharp raids were being made on London. Flying bombs were now being used frequently together with the V2 rocket bombs, which were quite indiscriminate and lacking in accuracy. After each raid, we used to assemble on the flat roof of our building to view the numerous fires in different parts of the city, which caused quite a lot of anguish to the lads who were natives of London, for they naturally wondered if the damaged area had been near their homes. Whenever a raid took place it was as if all hell had been let loose, for the area we were in was heavily guarded with anti-aircraft guns and searchlights, which put a tracing of lace-like patterns on the night sky. During the frequent raids, we were hustled into the shelters and in consequence lost quite a lot of sleep.

Overall I enjoyed the time I spent at Fulham and made quite a few firm friends. I even practised with a pencil when I was asked to draw portraits of the boys, so that they could send them home to their parents and girlfriends. I used to charge 2s.6d. for a half-hour sketch, and the money provided most welcome extras – Navy pay was not high!

The happenings at Fulham were far too numerous to mention them all, so I shall content myself with just one. This story actually began in 1939, when my mother and I were living in a semi-detached house in Stoke. We were asked by a friend if we could provide accommodation for an overwrought young wife with a child of about three who had been living in Wimbledon, in London. The young woman was in a tense and nervous state caused by the dread of coping with the air raids alone in the frequent absences of her husband, a commercial traveller. We had plenty of room, so we said yes and within a few days, the husband had settled his wife and child with us.

This was the period of the 'Phoney War', when for six months nothing seemed to happen. A large part of the nation was lulled into a false sense of security, which in turn caused this good lady to wonder if she had made a mistake in abandoning their home so precipitously. After about four months she decided to return to Wimbledon. She thanked us profusely for being so good to her and the child, saying that when the war was over we must go and stay with her.

So now we come back to my time in Fulham. There were many occasions when, because of shortage of funds, we had to be sparing as to how we spent our spare time. On one particular occasion I had a thought, remembering the lady from Wimbledon, and I suggested to a friend that we should pay a visit to her, saying that the least we would get would be a good meal and a taste of civilian hospitality.

It was not too far by tube train so, armed with the address which I had made a note of, we started to walk along the Wimbledon Road which I am convinced is one of the longest in Britain, which I should have guessed since the house number was in the hundreds. We eventually arrived to find what had once been a pair of semi-detached houses. One house had been completely sliced off and all that remained of the other was the gatepost bearing the number that we sought. This was the most puzzling enigma I had experienced for a long time. We asked the next-door neighbour if the person I knew was known to her and had there ever been a house on this deserted site. She said yes to both questions and added that the house

was, at that time, the only house to have been hit by a German bomb – how cruel fate can be! Naturally, we asked if the family had been injured in any way and the neighbour told us that by good fortune the house was empty at the time of the air raid because the family had gone to live in the West Country. Not quite a sad end, but two hungry sailors learnt to check in future before making optimistic decisions!

The time soon arrived when we had completed our instruction and aptitude tests and each man was told which trade they would be allocated to. By virtue of their civilian employment many of the men were given automatic allocation. For instance, Post Office engineers were graded as electrical fitters. It so happened when I was interviewed I was given the choice of categories. After a lot of thought I chose aero-engines. One reason was that I thought that learning about the intricacies of the internal combustion engine might be useful after the war; if ever I had the good fortune to own a car, then I would be able to do my own servicing. But the most important reason I chose to be trained as an engine fitter was that it meant I would be stationed at the RAF station at Hednesford, less than thirty miles from my home which, with luck, I would be able to visit at weekends when twenty-four-hour passes were granted.

Many of the close friends that I had made during this period were saddened when they learned that I had opted to train as an engine fitter, whereas they were forced to accept the electrical training courses. However, the course ended on a happy note, for, during the last week we all attended a farewell party, which included the commissioned officers and civilian instructors, at the end of which everyone was in a really happy and jovial mood.

I chose this evening to confess to a subterfuge I had practised on our education officer, following a statement made by him to the men prior to the examination for engineering theory. He proclaimed that no one had ever devised a plan for cribbing for the two-hour exam, because he was aware of every trick that had ever been used. This was a challenge that could not be refused! The only items allowed in the room were a pen, pencil and eraser. After giving the matter some little thought, I had an idea. On the six facets of the pencil, in microscopic print, I painted with brush and ink the formulae for every question that was likely to be asked. As can be imagined, this entailed a lot of very laborious work, but the overall effect was just a slight darkening of the red colour of the Royal Sovereign pencil. Very few people could read the painting with the naked eye; after testing it out with a few of the boys, I decided to give it a try.

We sat the examination with the education officer carefully watching every member of the class very closely indeed, but he never saw or suspected that anyone had escaped his eagle-eyed scrutineering. Needless to say I passed with flying colours! On making my confession to the officer, he said he did not believe me so I placed the pencil in his hand. Scarcely glancing at it, he asked why I had given it to him. I then told him that he was holding the device that had fooled him so convincingly. He needed a magnifying glass to be able to read what I had written, but after close scrutiny he expressed the view that it was a miraculous piece of artistry and that I deserved to get away with the subterfuge. Accepting the situation with good grace, he begged me to give him the pencil as a souvenir. Sadly I had to refuse, because pre-war Royal Sovereign pencils were unobtainable. It was many months later that the written words on the pencil were chipped away as I maintained a sharp point for my drawing.

The day after the party, 3rd June 1944, we bade farewell to the Naval staff and the instructors and entrained to the main Fleet Air Arm drafting station at Havant, near Portsmouth, from which we would be sent to our future training locations. The journey along the south coast was a real eye-opener, for every road leading to the seafront was simply packed solid with every type of weaponry and vehicles that one could imagine. This was obviously the big build-up of materials to be used in the impending invasion by the Allied Forces.

At the drafting station, HMS *Daedalus*, there was a great buzz of excitement and it was no surprise when, just before dawn on 6th June, we were awakened by the continuous drone of our aircraft heading for France. At last the great day had dawned and we were going back to the continent to try to end the war and free the world from the tyranny of Adolf Hitler. The following days were very exciting although real news was hard to find. It was rumour and counter-rumour, but slowly our forces had established a firm foothold on French soil. Many prayers were offered in thanks. But for us, a new phase in our training was about to begin, for, as our commanding officer informed us during a lecture in our first week, we were being trained, not for the war in Europe, but for the Far Eastern theatre of hostilities.

Within a few days, the trainees for Hednesford, of which I was one, were on our way to receive expert tuition from the Royal Air Force training personnel. The journey from Havant to Hednesford

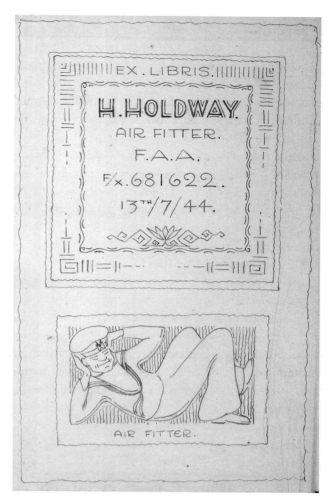

A book plate sketched by Harold in the front of his Aeronautical Engineering book.

was most pleasurable for me, because as we neared our destination, I was also getting close to my home town and my family, which, with a bit of luck, I would be able to visit at regular intervals during my training. The camp, in a rural setting on the south side of Cannock Chase near the outskirts of the mining town of Hednesford, was a huge complex, split into five complete units, each one self-contained. I was attached to Camp Three. Due to surplus facilities and lack of recruits, only three of the camps were in use when we arrived on 15th June 1944.

The course of advanced engine-fitting was to last for about six months and detailed instruction would be given in all aspects of the internal combustion engine. For some reason, the attitude of the instructors was not too friendly towards members of the Senior Service; at times they were openly hostile and punishment was handed out for the slightest misdemeanour. Gradually we overcame this state of affairs and settled down to a very interesting period of instruction. Gone were the days of squad drill, and apart from a little physical training – which was very casual – and a little guard duty, the atmosphere was more like a peacetime training course.

I derived great satisfaction from the instruction given and greatly appreciated the skill of the great aeronautical engineers who created such wonderful machines. R.J. Mitchell, of Spitfire fame, who was a local lad from Stoke-on-Trent, had become a national hero after the Battle of Britain. We in the Fleet Air Arm had a similar aeroplane called a Seafire, the only difference being that the bat-like wings folded in an upright position when they were parked in the hangars onboard aircraft carriers. Both aircraft were fitted with Rolls-Royce Merlin engines, the sight of which, when viewed after the removal from the airframe, presented an awe-inspiring object of brilliant engineering.

Because of the invasion of Europe all extended leave was severely restricted, but ratings living within close proximity to the camp could obtain 24 and sometimes 48-hour weekend passes. I availed myself of this concession whenever possible during the whole of my period at Hednesford. The bicycle was my means of transport and although the distance from the camp to my home was about twenty-five miles, with a following wind I could be home in little more than an hour and a quarter. My firm hope was that the end of the war would be declared whilst I was training at Hednesford. As I was a keen cyclist, I and several of my classmates opted for cycling as our choice of physical exercise, which meant that one afternoon each week was spent exploring the countryside and calling in at an out-of-the-way café for tea and toast, which cost 6d. per person and was a very welcome change from service routine.

The course of instruction was slow and tedious, but always of great interest, and that we were able to strip down any engine in use at that time – and there were many – and reassemble the intricate machines after only six months, training was largely due to the fine work of the instructors. I believe that, in peacetime, three years tuition was recommended as a necessary training period for a similar achievement. The time spent at Hednesford went by all too quickly and I passed out with flying colours and was granted my badge as a qualified air fitter. After taking a very pleasant end-of-course leave, which enabled me to spend Christmas at home, it was back to Havant for drafting. My thoughts that Christmas were mainly concerned with the future and what lay in store for me and how long I would have to wait for news of my assignment. Tears were shed at home because of the impossibility of spending weekends at home from such a distant station and because of not knowing where – as a fully qualified aero-fitter – I would be sent. Would it be a ship or land base, in Britain or overseas? All this, of course, was in the lap of the gods.

The journey to Havant was painfully slow and my depression increased with each mile that took me further from home. However, HMS *Daedalus*, as a fully fledged Naval Station, offered food and conditions that were a great improvement over the meagre fare provided at Hednesford. No longer were the blue-grey uniforms of the RAF to be seen and it was a pleasant change to see the commissioned officers wearing their distinctive Royal Navy blue uniforms. HMS *Daedalus* was a large station and as the war moved towards its end, the incoming and outgoing of ratings began to diminish, which meant that there were facilities and accommodation to spare. Fewer people were allocated to each Nissen hut and the Mess Decks were never overcrowded. As the contingent of which I was a member numbered about twenty ratings, we were given a Nissen hut for our quarters, which was very comfortable. Each hut was heated by a stove-pot, similar to the type used at the Spode factory at home. As we were likely to be sent to a ship or shore station at a moment's notice, the only duties we had to perform were to help with the running of the station, depending on what skills we had to offer.

First of all, we had to change our uniform because the rank of a fitter was higher than a mechanic. Mechanics wore the traditional sailor's garb known as Square Rig, with every item designed on a square shape; shirt, blouse, collar, trousers (without pockets) which had a square flap, known as a 'pigsty front', instead of flies. The fitters' uniform was what is known in Naval terms as the Fore and Aft Rig – which was to all intents and purposes a double-breasted civilian suit with white collar-attached shirts, black tie and peaked cap with naval badges. For the most part, the suit was rarely worn whilst we were at work at the station, for we were invariably clad in blue overalls and the only time we donned our suits was for parades and shore leave. Royal Navy dress was envied by all the other services, because all undergarments were white, socks were black and even blankets were made of best quality wool. Also, a clothing allowance was paid weekly to each rating which was a much-appreciated privilege.

Shortly after our arrival a notice appeared for volunteers for the jobs of barber and shoe repairer. One of the boys in our entry whom I had befriended suggested that he and I should apply for the jobs. We were duly interviewed and asked if we were qualified to do such work and without hesitation we said that we were experts. However, we insisted the

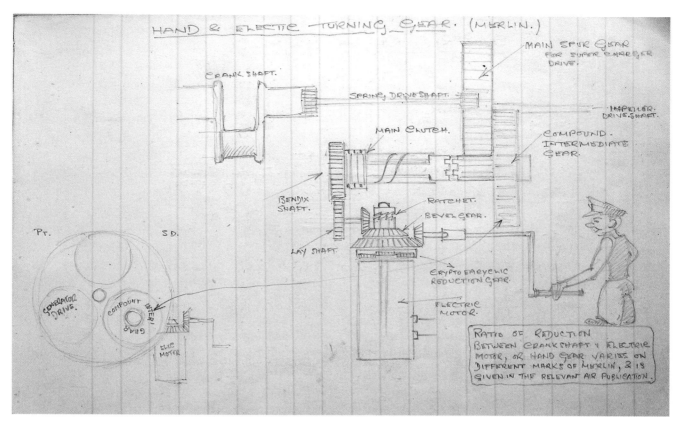

Diagrams from Harold's air-fitting notes, showing the precision he applied to even rough sketches.
Above: Hand and electric turning gear.
Left: Anchorage of a Spitfire on an aircraft carrier.
Below: An exploded drawing of the main and auxiliary drive.

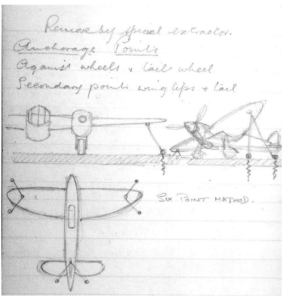

establishment must supply the two of us with the tools and materials we would need. This condition was readily agreed to, a special Nissen hut provided and an open-ended purchasing order taken out for all the items required. My friend and I then journeyed to Portsmouth where we obtained a pair of hairdresser's clippers, scissors and comb. I acquired a cobbler's last to suit the various sizes in footwear, leather hides, hammer, pincers, nails, etc.

In my early days, I had learned how to repair shoes so I did not anticipate any problems and I never did receive any complaints about my workmanship. My pal, however, had never cut any hair in his life and so

he had a mad practising session on me once he had obtained the tools of the trade. Although the early haircuts were a little amateurish, he soon overcame the snags and earned great praise for his efforts. The fact that our services were in constant demand meant that we made quite a few pounds even though our charges were very low.

The weeks continued to pass without any sign of our draft instructions being issued. We continued to improve all aspects of service life and we were even served an early lunch of our choice before the main body of men had their food in the noisy Mess Decks. As the weeks of waiting turned into months, my friend and I formed the optimistic view that maybe, because we had made ourselves so useful, the head men at the station had decided that great inconvenience would be caused if we were sent away.

However, our future was soon decided and after spending the best part of two months waiting for our posting, the dreaded day arrived when the whole of our contingent was split up and scattered to all points on both land and sea, wherever the Fleet Air Arm operated. By this time I had forgotten all that I had learned about the maintenance of our fighting planes and I hoped that I would not let the side down because of my incompetence. One thing I knew for certain – I would never have such a cushy number as the one I had had as the Cobbler of *Daedalus*. At least I had helped to keep the ratings' feet dry!

After a few days draft leave, spent in the idyllic surroundings of home, with all its creature comforts, I journeyed northwards, on 17th February 1945, to the Fleet Air Arm base at Donibristle, situated on the Forth and adjacent to the large Fleet Naval base at Rosyth. The camp, set in the vast acreage of the Earl of Murray's estate, was in a beautiful location and it was sacrilegious that an airstrip had been constructed for the take-off and landing of aircraft, but the demands of the war had to be acceded to. In addition to the Naval camp, named HMS *Merlin*, there was also a large civilian-manned aircraft maintenance unit situated on the perimeter of the naval site, where a great number of Scotsmen were gainfully employed in reserved occupations. This particular area was off limits to all Naval personnel and this rule was strictly enforced. I think that the idea was for non-fraternisation with members of the public in an endeavour to maintain security.

Conditions in the camp were excellent, with well-built quarters for the ratings, a scheduled menu for each day prepared weekly and comments invited from the men on the subject of quality and variety. Our job was to check, service and maintain every aircraft allocated to our station, which was a veritable storehouse, and to fulfil the requirements and the fitting-out of aircraft carriers and operational airfields within Fleet Air Arm command. Each day – except Sunday – after breakfast at 0800 hours, the working parties were marched to the workshops sited in the huge aircraft hangars. A compulsory physical training session was insisted upon and the ratings presented an incongruous sight bending and stretching, often in the freezing cold of a Scottish mist! This lasted for about ten minutes when everyone was thoroughly warmed up ready for work.

The servicing of each plane was carried out by a team of fitters and mechanics covering every aspect of maintenance and on completion signed for by the fitters in charge. This was a very responsible job because the lives of pilots and aircrew were dependant on efficient servicing. As we were mainly concerned with the Japanese war, our contribution to the war effort was all-important for at this time the Fleet was suffering great losses due to the fanaticism of Japanese Kamikaze pilots, which meant a constant call on our supplies of men and planes. The good news from the European theatre of operations helped to make us feel more optimistic about the ending of hostilities and also helped maintain a high morale standard.

We were always a little nervous when a ship was seen in the Firth of Forth flying the paying-off pennant after a term of war action, because this meant that the ship's company were about to be paid off. When a ship had been overhauled a new complement of men was signed on as a replacement crew. As we were situated close to the Naval Dockyard at Rosyth we were often called upon to supply last-minute replacements for men who failed to report because of sickness or some other reason.

The worries I had had as to whether I could do an efficient job as a fitter never materialised and the training we had received stood us all in good stead. Spare time activities were plentiful with picture shows every night, the film changing in midweek, as well as a tombola on most nights in the NAAFI canteen. There was also a fully operational educational block with several subjects being taught and eagerly sought after by the men. Private and peaceful study was also possible whenever a rating desired solitude. I used to avail myself of this privilege and practised my drawing skills on many occasions. I rarely visited the nearby towns of Dunfermline and Kirkcaldy, although they were quite a popular venue for the younger members of HMS *Merlin*. Edinburgh was the exception and I made quite a number of visits to this wonderful city when I had a weekend leave pass and thoroughly enjoyed the hospitality of its citizens.

The cold weather gradually faded away and spring brought forth hope to us all and, along with the daffodils and rhododendrons, came the good news that the war in Europe was drawing to a close. VE Day – Victory in Europe – 8th May 1945 – what joy! What relief! What happiness! Great celebrations everywhere! The ship's company (all personnel at HMS *Merlin*) by special dispensation spliced the mainbrace (double issue of rum) and a pal of mine who was not too keen on his rum ration handed it

1945 Birthday card to Betty.

over to me. With a good meal and four tots of rum inside me, I just passed out like a light on my bunk for four hours. This was no problem because we had all been given the day off from work so, upon my waking up from my sleep, I donned my No. 1 uniform and together with two buddies, each with a twenty-four-hour pass, went into Edinburgh to celebrate the occasion.

Hitherto I had only seen the Scottish capital in daylight and to see Princes Street with its glowing lights shinning brightly beneath the floodlit castle was a sight I shall never forget. Before we could think about how we should celebrate the great day, we were grabbed by two middle-aged ladies who had vowed to invite the first two sailors they met to a party, which was being held at their house. As long as I live I shall never forget the hospitality shown to us. The whisky they were dispensing was the result of many months of saving and of much hard bargaining with whoever could supply the scarce commodity. The home we were invited into was part of a tenement block of one-room flats, situated in one of the most poverty-stricken areas of Edinburgh – in fact it was a slum. The interior of the room had a curtained-off section which acted as a bedroom at one end and a crude sink at the other. In spite of the dilapidation of our surroundings there was a real feeling of genuine good-heartedness and kindness about the people crowded into the limited space.

The amount of food and drink provided was a veritable feast and the jollification went on for hours. The singing and carousing seemed to be interminable. At last, from sheer exhaustion, we had to call it a night and we were ushered into a vacant bed-sit room in the building, which, although sparsely furnished, had two beds that we were pleased to make use of. Unfortunately there were no bedclothes, only hard ancient mattresses which failed to relieve our discomfort. At about four o'clock in the morning

we all awoke feeling cold and stiff and painfully made our way out of the tenement. We headed towards Waverley Station, where we knew the train to Donibristle would be ready and waiting to make a start later in the morning. Lying full length on the carriage seats, we spent a few hours in real comfort, only awakening when the train started on its journey, which would deliver us back to camp. It had been a great day and night of celebration, one which none of us would ever forget.

Our thoughts for the future from now on were distinctly more optimistic and work was not so tedious. Our only worry was: would the Japanese forces decide to follow the example of the Germans? This was of course the $64,000 question and no one could give us the answer. We continued to follow the same work routine because the needs from the Far Eastern war zone were as demanding as ever, but gradually, as the weeks passed, we noticed that the workload was slowly being reduced. At this time, there was a request for craftsmen, preferably a signwriter who could paint lining and lettering on large display noticeboards, suitable to register names and titles of various subjects. Apparently complaints had been made about the poor quality of the existing signs that were being used.

I mentioned to my petty officer that I had the necessary training and professional skill to do a first-class job and he suggested that I should make an application. I then submitted a sample of my work to the lieutenant in charge and he offered me the job. He suggested that I should work in the chippies' shop (woodwork department) because the carpenter had to supply the boards that had to be used. They were firstly sprayed with matt black cellulose paint and then in white lettering I copied out whatever was required. To apply a series of 1/4" wide parallel lines covering a board 8ft x 4ft with interspaced vertical lines with headed and marginal lettering was a very time-consuming process and because my work was so much better than the previous boards I soon built up a backlog which would keep me busy for many months.

The chippies' shop was run by a time-serving petty officer, an Irishman named Mick, and a Scottish leading seaman named Andrew. Mick was an absolute craftsman, but Andy was next-door to useless. When I became tired of painting the noticeboards, or in an enforced break, I would practise using the joiners' tools, under the expert guidance of Mick, and before long I could make all sorts of objects, which were approved as satisfactory by the expert. I found this stint of painting and carpentry work most satisfying

Pen and ink sketch of Ginger with Hitler's yacht, a Woolworth Carrier and the Forth Railway Bridge in the background. 2.8.45.

and rewarding and one that stood me in good stead in later years.

During this period, too, I used to take long walks, armed with pencil and sketchbook, exploring the beautiful surroundings. Quite often I was away from the camp confines for several hours and almost out of earshot of the tannoy system that extended throughout the camp. On one occasion, after returning from one of these jaunts, I learned that I had been summoned to the guard house and that the order to report had been repeated many times. Thoroughly alarmed, I rushed to the guardroom and presented myself. After a severe drubbing by the officer of the watch, I explained to him that as an artist I had to practise my skills as often as possible. I still had my sketchbook with me, so he asked to examine my drawings. Fortunately for me he was a lover of drawing and fine painting and he dismissed me with a gentle warning and hoped he would be allowed sometime in the future to purchase an example of my work. Once again, my artistic talent had come to my rescue!

As I was interested in my daily tasks, time went by very quickly. Then, one day we heard with amazement that the first atomic bomb had been dropped on the city of Hiroshima in Japan, causing complete devastation and horrendous loss of life. The date was 6th August 1945. Three days later, on the 9th, a second atomic bomb was dropped, this time on Nagasaki. No nation could withstand such appalling punishment and, on 15th August, after losing millions of lives, the Japanese nation surrendered, signalling the end of the Second World War. VJ Day – Victory in Japan – was celebrated much more quietly than VE day; very few men on HMS *Merlin* made any real effort to make merry. I think the main thought that now occupied our minds was: how soon would it be before we would be free to return home and take up once more a normal home life?

The first step was the allocation of a demobilisation number to each rating, after which a list of names and numbers were posted on the noticeboards, giving detailed procedural instructions about release. The more important the category, the higher the release number, which meant a much longer wait for demobilisation. For instance, fitters had to wait much longer than mechanics; my own category of engine fitter was midway in the order of release. So it was just a question of trying to be very patient and waiting one's turn. It was particularly galling to see skilled hands preparing aircraft for flight. When completed, the planes were then flown to the nearest aircraft carrier and packed on board like sardines. When the ship reached mid-Atlantic, the planes were gently pushed over the side and sunk into deep water. The USA had no further use for such planes, most of which had been acquired under the Lend-Lease Act.

Many of the young sublieutenants were particularly worried because many had never had a civilian job of any kind and they wondered how their Naval training would fit them for their future civilian life. My own thoughts tended to dwell on what was happening in the potting industry, particularly my old firm of W.T. Copeland & Sons Ltd. During the course of my short period of service, I had shut my mind off completely from anything remotely connected with the production of pots, but now it was time to think of my future responsibilities. Over two years had passed by and I wondered if I had lost any of the skills that I had developed before the war. After working hours I found that I was spending more and more of my spare time in the education rooms, practising my skills. As far as I could judge, I was confident that I would be able to perform with equal skill and produce creative designs that would be completely acceptable.

My frequent presence in the education block had been noticed by several commissioned officers who were most impressed with my artistic work. This resulted in my being invited to act as a post-war rehabilitation lecturer at the camp on a full-time basis. The appointment carried a commissioned rank and I was overjoyed at being offered such a fine opportunity. However, like all good things, there was a snag. When I asked if this appointment would affect my demobilisation number and date of release, I was told that it would be so high that it would be almost out of sight and no one could give me an accurate date. The reason for the creation of the job was the need to educate and prepare ratings for their eventual release and acceptance of the vagaries of civilian working life, so obviously I would be one of the last to leave. Sadly, I had to turn down the offer – my freedom from service life was of paramount importance.

As the time passed by in the early days of 1946, frustration began to show in the mood of many of the ratings, who were well aware of the pointlessness of maintaining so many officers and men now that the war was over and industry was crying out for labour. I often gave vent to my feelings on this critical subject, particularly to the commissioned officers who often visited me. The leading hands were at their wits' end trying to keep men gainfully occupied and I remember on one occasion it was decided to clean off the black bitumastic paint, which covered all the large hangar windows. We were split up into groups of three and, armed with scrapers, had to literally scratch every last vestige of paint off the glass. Each man had to clean two windows measuring 5ft x 2ft and was given a day to finish the task. It was an arm-aching exercise and I had the idea of obtaining some paint remover from the civilian maintenance unit stores. They were glad to oblige and my team of three brushed on the remover, then waited for a few minutes until the paint formed bubbles. When dry, it only needed to be brushed off to leave a perfectly clean surface.

When the petty officer came to inspect what progress we were making, he was surprised to see three jolly sailor boys at ease smoking cigarettes and wearing smug expressions, with the job completed. The time taken was two hours to complete our six windows. After I confessed to using my initiative, he promptly put me on a charge for disobeying orders. This was the only time I was put on a charge during my service career; my punishment for the offence was confinement to camp for seven days.

Slowly the demobilisation numbers crept nearer to my own and, at the beginning of February, the great day arrived when my name was posted on the bulletin board with my release date of 6th February 1946. It was like walking on air for the next few days and it did not take me long to pack my belongings in readiness for my departure. With a little sadness I said my goodbyes to the boys on the last evening and we had a farewell drink together. With a cheery wave I said goodbye to HMS *Merlin* as I passed through the gates to travel to the Oldham Demobilisation Centre where I exchanged the Navy uniform I was wearing for my outfit of civilian clothes. As we were allowed to keep all our belongings I still had quite a heavy load to handle but eventually I arrived safely at Stoke, summoned a taxi and arrived home in style – a free man at last! What a wonderful joyous day, to be welcomed home by a happy loving wife and baby son.

No more saluting or jumping to attention when spoken to by my 'superior officers'. It was good, too, to discard my identity disc, which had had to be worn at all times, even when taking a shower, and lastly, to discard the use of the service number that was bestowed on me when I first set forth into service life. My number was F/X 681622 and has remained fresh in my memory to this very day to the exclusion of all others. I suppose that my time in the Navy must have had a strong influence on my character, but for the most part, I deeply regretted having wasted over two years of my life away from my wife and family.

HOME AGAIN!

My demobilisation leave entitlement was for a period of eight weeks and the princely sum of £33.4s.6d. After my first weekend at home I arranged to see Mr Ted Hewitt, managing director of W.T. Copeland & Sons Ltd, to announce my intention to take up full-time employment once more. Mr Ted explained at great length the facts concerning the state of affairs at the factory. He pointed out to me that after I had joined the forces in 1943, the general state of things at the factory had gone from bad to worse.

Firstly, heavy demands had been made on the factory to release more operatives to take up war work. The girls in particular, with their nimble fingers, were ideal for work in the munitions factories. The older men, also, were eagerly sought after, especially the skilled craftsmen. Tom Barlow, modeller, and Frank Boothby, head engraver, were conscripted to work at one of the local ordnance factories. The loss of such craftsmen and women made life very difficult and the demands for more and more export orders just could not be satisfied. The USA market requirements were insatiable and at the time of my demobilisation the backlog was simply increasing day by day.

Mr Hewitt pointed out that no new designs had been produced during my absence on war service and, although orders were flooding the production departments, he hoped that sufficient new ideas could be created in readiness for any fall-off in orders for the present decorations. He explained that, of all the members of the Fine China Association, we at Copeland's had the largest backlog of orders and, whilst we were doing our best to keep pace with the constant demands, the other factories were hard at work developing new ideas, particularly designs for the brides' market on the American continent. At this point I realised that the task before me was indeed a challenging one and would need a great effort on my part to help solve our difficulties.

I also learned that Geoffrey Cholerton had been granted an early release from the Army soon after the war ended as a result of an application from the firm. So once again I was passed over and made second favourite! If one was granted a special early release from the forces the person concerned had to report for work immediately after demobilisation and forgo any leave entitlement. Because of this rule, Geoffrey had been back at work for several months before my return. Mr Hewitt said that he hoped I would be able to start work the next day and was most surprised when I explained that I intended to take my full eight weeks demobilisation leave and spend it restoring my house and garden to a high standard of homeliness and comfort. Eight weeks holiday could only happen once in a lifetime and I intended to take full advantage of this unique opportunity. With a rueful smile he had to agree with my point of view and wished me the best of luck for the future.

It so happened that the weather was most kind during my leave and enabled me to complete the garden restoration and prepare the greenhouse for the future planting. A great pleasure, of course, was watching the steady growth of plants – especially when viewed from a recumbent position in a deckchair on a sunny afternoon. Nevertheless, after the garden chores had been completed, I then had to paint and decorate every room in the house and put right the things which had gone wrong while I had been away. I simply loathed having to wield the large-size brushes to cover acres of wall space and woodwork. I did, however, have a sense of pride at a job well done when I surveyed the scene on completion of each task.

Lastly, I treated my bicycle – the faithful steed I used while training at Hednesford – to a complete overhaul in readiness for my daily journey to and from the factory. Bicycles, buses, trains and 'Shank's pony' were still the main forms of workers' transport and very few people were able to afford the few motor cars that were available. Even these were pre-war designed models. The large car manufacturers were desperately trying to switch from the making of war implements to the creation of newly designed models. It was sad to watch the post-war struggle for existence of many famous car manufacturers and I fervently hoped that the elite pottery producers would survive and be able to retain their individuality and superiority of design and quality. For my part, I hoped that I would be able to play a useful role in furthering the prosperity and success of the firm of W.T. Copeland & Sons Ltd.

It did not take long to familiarise myself with the routine of a peacetime civilian way of life. My first call was a visit to Geoffrey Cholerton, who was installed in the office of the late Mr Thomas Hassall, where he gave me a most comprehensive summary of the current situation at the factory, which was very helpful. He also outlined ideas and plans for increasing production, which were well-conceived and feasible. He was genuinely pleased to see me and looked forward to our harmonious working future together.

My entry to the design studio was a very emotional experience; even the worktable was clean and polished, with drawing board, pencils and watercolours laid out ready for me to use. The first man to welcome me was my very dear friend and colleague, Mr Joe Austin, the ex-Minton crest painter who had been such a tower of strength acting as my stand-in while I was in the Navy. His recounting of the many happenings and difficulties he had had to contend with and how he had overcome them were evidence of the tremendous effort he had made. Now that I had returned, he was anticipating bearing a less exhausting workload. While I had been away, Joe had had very little opportunity to practise his artistic skills and he was keenly looking forward to resumption of the friendly working relationship we had had before I joined the services.

Gradually, the factory personnel who had been involved in war service returned, thankful to have survived the horrors many had experienced. Many of them had distinguished themselves, like Cyril Allen, ceramic chemist, who served for the duration of the war and took part in the fierce battles fought in North Africa, where he was severely wounded. Spencer Copeland, John Copeland and Gordon Hewitt, elder sons of our directors, all served for the duration of the war and returned safely to take up senior management positions in the firm. One notable person I will mention is George Leslie Cartlidge, a senior engraver.

In September 1939, George was a highly qualified engraver, second in command to Mr Joe Hassall. Nevertheless as soon as the war was declared, he volunteered for war service. It so happened that engraving was classed as a reserved occupation so his application was refused. George was bitterly disappointed that he could not 'do his bit' and, at regular intervals, pleaded with the directorate for permission to enlist. Because of his importance to the contribution and furtherance of the factory's export programme, he was constantly refused permission to volunteer his services.

Being a native of Trent Vale, he decided to join a local group of the Home Guard, the training of which was in the capable hands of Mr Ashton Maskery, a Regimental Sergeant Major of the First World War, decorated with the Military Medal and other honours. Ashton Maskery held the very important position of earthenware biscuit fireman at the Spode factory. From all accounts he was a very fine but strict instructor, highly respected, and he very soon whipped the rookies into a smart and efficient force.

The highlight of the various drill procedures was rifle practise, which was eagerly looked forward to by the Home Guard members. Although rifles were hard to come by, they were sufficient for target practice and the squad journeyed to a nearby rifle range to be taught the finer points of marksmanship. The rifles were the old-fashioned Lee-Enfield .303 type as used in the First World War, but in spite of the aged design, they were a very efficient weapon. Imagine the scene of a small number of men being handed a rifle loaded with live ammunition, instructed to lie down in the prone position, take aim at the distant target and slowly but surely squeeze – not pull – the trigger. BANG!!! In spite of the fact that the men had been warned about the kickback, caused by the recoil of the rifle against the shoulder after the firing, it nevertheless gave each man a hefty jolt and often caused bruising. After the first round or two, each man gripped his rifle very tightly!

Now came the interesting part of the exercise – what had happened to the bullets that each man had fired? Away in the distance a trench had been dug beneath the targets. In the trench were stationed men known as markers who were armed with long poles with a circular disc attached. This was hoisted up to the position of each shot that had hit the target. The disc could readily be seen by the men at the firing point. Every man of course expected to have scored a bull's-eye, but many of them did not hit the target at all. On such occasions, the disc was waved across the target from side to side. The results of each man's five shots were carefully noted and George was told that he had one bull, four misses. He was very upset with this result, especially when, on his second attempt, he was adjudged to have repeated his previous score: one bull, four misses. After protestation, it was discovered that on both occasions George had hit the bull's-eye five times, each shot so close to the others that the five shots destroyed the centre of the bull's-eye. The rifle instructor was astounded at this unique exhibition and could hardly believe that George had never handled a rifle before joining the Home Guard. George, who possessed extraordinarily fine sight, developed a very steady aim, and perfect co-ordination of the two was the secret of his great skill.

In May 1942, George finally received permission to volunteer for the Royal Air Force Regiment and was immediately accepted. His two and a half years' membership of the Home Guard stood him in good

Spencer Copeland.

Gordon Hewitt. Courtesy of Spode Museum Trust.

stead. Later he became a Sergeant Sniping Instructor and was in the vanguard of the Allied Forces in Europe. To me, George was one of the real heroes of the war for, in the four years in which he served, he experienced many hazardous and dangerous situations. He was rewarded by being mentioned in dispatches and wore the cluster of oak leaves with pride. His return unscathed from his war service was a stroke of good fortune both for himself and the Copeland factory. The experiences he had absorbed were to prove to be of inestimable value for his future career responsibilities.

Because of the time the sons of the directors had spent in the services, they had a lot of lost time to make up in the hope that they would learn quickly the art of making good decisions. The field of design was for some unknown reason scarcely ever approached, but when an opportunity did arise for discussion of the subject, we soon realised that it would be a long time before the sons would be able to confidently assess the relative design merit and sales potential of any new creation. The decision as to whether a new design or shape and applied decoration should be processed or not is very important, because of the capital expense involved. A wrong choice means months of waste of highly skilled workmanship, so it is understandably the most important of all decisions which have to be taken when planning the future prosperity of a pottery company. Consultation with important retail customers by showing them prototype designs was often very helpful in making final selections for the development of new products. The final decision was, of course, the prerogative of the board of directors, who were often guided by the sound judgement of the sales manager and

the art director.

Mr Spencer Copeland spent a lengthy period studying production methods in all the important sections of the factory and also completed a course in advanced ceramic technology at the North Staffordshire Technical College, following which he was appointed head of research and development with a well-equipped laboratory where he was ably assisted by George Dabbs, an ex-Navy man, and Cyril Allen, both of whom were highly qualified chemists. Mr John Copeland helped with the management of the earthenware clay department after studying at the Technical College, while Mr Gordon Hewitt concentrated his efforts on the furthering of European trade. His knowledge of the German language was of great assistance in our dealings with Mr August Warnecke, our European agent.

At this point, I think a special mention must be made of a charismatic character named Sam Bloor, who, before joining the forces, was assistant to the earthenware clay manager, Mr John Whalley. Sam, a very lively young man full of enthusiasm and boundless energy, became an invaluable aide to Mr Whalley, who was saddened when Sam decided to join up. I am fairly sure that he volunteered for service in the Royal Marines and, although little was heard of him until the end of the war, I for one was most impressed to see him gracing a Royal Marine Captain's uniform. Mr Ted was loud in his praise of Sam's success in the forces and allowed him to take a two-year course in ceramics and pottery management. He achieved a First Class Honours degree and was also awarded the coveted Gold Medal – a rare distinction. Fortunately, Sam had received a war rehabilitation education grant to cover his family's

John Copeland holding a piece of the first consignment of goods sent from the factory to the USA by air. November 1949. Courtesy of Spode Museum Trust.

living expenses. Subsequent events show what a wise decision Sam made at the end of his war service.

Within a few weeks of my return, Mr Hewitt decided that Geoffrey and I should attended a fourteen-day design refresher course held under the auspices of the Design in Industry organisation in London. The DIA were a forward-thinking body and I am sure that the course was organised by a Mr T.A. Fennimore, who had a pre-war association with the pottery industry. The idea was that a number of designers from different pottery firms should attend lectures given by leading artists and visit a variety of factories producing carpets, glassware, textiles, wallpaper, etc. Many noted artists in private practice, such as Felix Topolski, Gordon Russell and Graham Sutherland, as well as leading architects, were visited at their studios and they very kindly gave their opinions with informal talks and displays of their original work. Advice and suggestions were freely offered but everyone agreed that a complete solution of the problems of the market needs and trends was a very difficult one, which faced all creative artists, and which had no ready-made answers.

As pottery becomes an integral part of the furnishing in the home, the choice of tableware becomes very important and should be a complementary contribution to the overall design. Interior decorators now choose suitable wares to fit into the general design theme and certain classes of customers readily accept their choice of décor. Usually this concept is a very costly operation and really only applied to a small section of the community. The taste of the various world markets varies enormously and as we endeavoured to satisfy their needs, this meant very careful design research by the design staff. The exclusive rights for the sale of our wares in North America was in the hands of Mr Sydney Thompson and his son George, the proprietors of Copeland & Thompson Inc. of New York, who purchased large quantities of popular American choice decorations, the bulk of which were on earthenware, with patterns such as Gainsborough, Indian Tree, Buttercup, Billingsley Rose and the ever-popular Christmas Tree, to name just a few. China place settings comprising 10in, 7in and 5in plates and teacup and saucers could be ordered as part of the retailers' brides register. Mr Thompson kept large stocks in his New York warehouse and orders received were despatched quickly, which proved to be a very satisfactory sales and delivery arrangement.

As a design team, we made various attempts from time to time to show Mr Thompson new ideas for future sales in the American market, knowing full well that there was very little chance of them being accepted whilst there was such a heavy demand for our regular range of decorations. Several American china manufacturers, including the famous Lenox factory in Atlantic City, were producing very fine quality feldspathic china services, which were gaining in popularity with the young brides' taste for 'modern' decorations. The price of these services was inevitably less expensive than the imported wares from the United Kingdom. Another difficulty that we were presented with was that the whole of decorating was classed as a craft process, which indeed it was, for no lithographic or silk screen transfers were used in Spode productions. Handcraft methods were claimed for our wares on all American sales literature. The fact that our handcraft methods were more costly did not affect the quantity ordered, but our handcraft methods was a much slower process which enabled other members of the fine china and earthenware groups to handle much larger qualities and give much quicker deliveries.

Other overseas markets were experiencing difficulty in selling our higher-priced goods and we had to try to produce some less expensive and simpler forms of decoration. The freight costs to Australia and New Zealand meant that our goods were very expensive and in consequence the retailers had to buy lower-priced wares from other manufacturers. Quite a number of our pre-war patterns were still quite popular, such as old-time favourites like Blue Italian, Chinese Rose, Byron Scenes, Eden, etc. As well as buying new services many customers were anxious to replace losses due to breakage. Mr August Warnecke, who was our European agent before the war and who lived in Hamburg, soon began to place orders for the traditional patterns, blue prints, Chinese Rose and other enamelled decorations. Considering that Germany had lost the war, his skill as a salesman was truly remarkable, but he insisted on marketing only 'typical English' designs on tableware; but, of course, the most important market of all was the British one, which always received our most earnest attention.

During the first year following the end of hostilities, the factory employed over eleven hundred workers, the largest number of employees in the long history of the firm. Mr Ted Hewitt explored every avenue in an endeavour to meet the heavy demands and whatever profit we made was automatically ploughed back into the firm as capital investment. He also insisted, together with his sales director, Mr Frank Thorley, on promoting the cigarette coupon gift trade and Mr Jimmy Upsdell was deputed to make every effort to obtain this lucrative business. He had his pre-war experience to draw on which helped him to persuade the cigarette companies to favour us with their orders. Among the first patterns supplied were Flemish Green self-coloured, Blue Italian, Chinese Rose and Byron Scenes, all supplied in dinner, tea, and coffee items. It was often said that if you wanted a Spode set, all you had to do was smoke yourself to death in order to collect the required number of coupons. This type of business came under the heading of contract development, and Jimmy assumed the title of manager. Another of his achievements was the obtaining of the contract to supply BOAC with specially-designed tableware for the use of first-class passengers. The order was subject to renewal after three years on condition that the quality and delivery was of the highest order.

Government contracts were eagerly sought after by many manufacturers and we were fortunate in having a very satisfactory share of this class of work. Although the profit margin was not that great, this type of work, called 'bread and butter', helped to keep the wheels turning. Legations, consulates, embassies and city companies in many countries were supplied with handsome services decorated with personalised badges, crests and monograms as in the past. The term 'export or die' was the slogan that was uppermost in our minds and all the fine china and earthenware manufacturers of repute were eager to fulfil the government's plea for more exports. In consequence very little prestigious ware was released for the home market. This export policy allowed the manufacturers of the cheaper class of goods to establish a foothold in the British retail market. Some of these post-war designs were of a very poor standard and ill-conceived and, in later years, when better shapes and decorations became available, were quickly discarded.

We at the Spode factory operated a very fair rationing system and although the retailers were often having to turn customers away, they were truly sympathetic concerning our distribution problems. I often used to visit retailers in various parts of the country, accompanied by our salesmen, in order to note what type of goods the clientele were requesting and how best we could serve their particular needs. I always found this procedure most helpful.

PRINCESS ROSEWATER BOWL

Princess rosewater bowl with design, 1949.

During 1947, an announcement of the forthcoming marriage of Princess Elizabeth to Lieutenant Philip Mountbatten, formerly Prince Philip of Greece and soon to be created Duke of Edinburgh, was greeted with great pleasure and excitement by the populace. This was to be an event of great importance and would provide a perfect opportunity to produce commemorative souvenirs. The pottery industry, in particular, looked forward with eager anticipation to being given the chance to produce suitable items which could be offered for sale.

Mr Ronald Copeland expressed a wish that our factory should seek permission to make a gift of china to Her Royal Highness to mark the occasion. He suggested that a china rosewater dish – a shallow dish 14in diameter with a narrow rim – be decorated with a Royal theme, and was granted permission to present the dish to the Princess as a wedding gift. As chief designer, I was asked to create a suitable design, which, on completion, was submitted to Her Royal Highness for her personal approval before being produced. I was wildly excited at being given the opportunity to create such an all-important design for this memorable occasion. At this time, Joe Austin, who was now occupying a seat in my studio, was doing very fine work in accordance with all my wishes. His skill as a crest painter would be put to the test if ever the design I had in mind was to be selected for production!

I decided that two designs should be submitted in sketch form, each to be hand-painted in watercolour, actual size, on card. My first design was based on a conventional stylised oak leaf and acorn arrangement in raised gold on a crimson ground, encircling the device of the Princess in full heraldic colours, and on the rim, shields bearing the arms of the nine most important members of the Commonwealth linked with swags and pendants of laurel leaves incorporating the white rose of Yorkshire, these motifs being applied on an ivory ground. The second design was a counterchange conventional oak leaf arrangement using leather green and ivory. In the centre was a single initial E for Elizabeth within a laurel leaf garland, richly gilt. This second design was my own personal preference but, because of the historic and royal content of my first design, I could well imagine that it might be the choice of Her Royal Highness.

During the course of the preliminary drawing of the designs, disaster struck in the form of Joe Austin deciding to take up a lucrative appointment with a small Longton china firm. He had been offered a directorship and firm promises of a highly successful future, so, with regret, he bade farewell to his career at the Spode factory. The loss of his creative and practical skills was a very serious blow to my plans for future design development. Fortunately, I realised the wisdom of having Joe guide the hands of Roy

Trigg, who, as a firmly established member of my design studio since his demobilisation from the army, was able to step into the breach made by the departure of the master craftsman.

My two designs, which were actually presented as highly finished artwork executed by Roy Trigg and myself, were duly sent to the Palace for the Princess to choose and approve which of the designs she thought might be appropriate for the occasion. Mr Copeland explained in his accompanying letter that the finished Rosewater Dish would take a considerable time to produce because of the intricacy of the design. The Princess chose my first design, which featured her personal device and she fully understood the reason for the delay. The wedding duly took place on 20th of November 1947 and turned out to be a magnificent spectacle and was enjoyed by millions of her admirers worldwide.

Within a few days the artwork of the designs was returned to me with the order to produce the finished piece as soon as possible. Had Joe Austin's service and skill been available, I would merely have had to supervise the decorating process, which would have been a very pleasant duty and I would have derived great satisfaction in seeing the fruits of my imagination take shape in material form. Instead, I had to undertake the most difficult task of transposing the chosen design into a ceramic reality. Fortunately Roy Trigg, now my chief assistant, was more than capable of playing a major part in the decorating process and between the two of us, the Rosewater Dish with its regal decoration began to take shape. It was an amusing sight to see the changeover of craftsmen when I was called away to attend to other matters. As one man left the seat, the other simply took up the brush loaded with colour or gold and carried on the steady sequence of brushwork being painstakingly applied to the china surface.

Weeks and months were to pass before the dish could possibly be finished and as each process was embarked upon there was always the danger of accidental damage or breakage, which would mean only one thing – starting all over again. I uttered many prayers during those months until, early in 1949, the final firing was made and, after the process of gold burnishing had been carried out, I thanked the powers above for the safe deliverance of such a beautiful piece of ceramic commemorative ware. My original design was to have been a challenge to the most skilled of craftsmen, Joe Austin, but the scheme had backfired on me!

The time taken to produce the finished piece was well over twelve months, for only a limited amount of time could be spent on the Royal Wedding present, as there were many normal duties and projects that I had to attend to. Incidentally, I call to mind an incident that gave me pleasure tinged with sadness. I invited Joe Austin to see the Rosewater Dish when it was finished. He was by now only concerned with the production of inexpensive china and would never again have an opportunity of using his great skills. As he examined the dish with his experienced and critical gaze, tears welled up in his eyes and he said that it would have been an honour for any craftsman to have been invited to produce such a fine object and he was sorry indeed that he could not claim to have been the one responsible for it.

Mr Ronald Copeland did not wish to see any of the decorating processes being applied, saying that he only wanted to see the finished piece in all its glory. Whether this thought had been suggested to him by others, I do not know; I do know that Geoffrey Cholerton had not offered any kind of help at any time during the lengthy period of production. However, when the dish was ready to be shown to Mr Ronald for his approval, it was Geoffrey who invited him to see it. A time was fixed and Mr Copeland duly appeared in my studio, accompanied by Geoffrey.

I stood to attention and uncovered the dish for Mr Ronald's inspection. He sat in my chair, with me on his left and Geoffrey on his right. I don't think he could believe what his eyes could see. He was overwhelmed, and abundant in his praise. He thanked Geoffrey profusely for being the creator of such a masterpiece and me for being responsible for the 'execution'. He thought this was a very apt comment. After a stunned silence, I waited for Geoffrey to correct the 'faux pas' that Mr Ronald had made, but he remained silent and accepted the credit with a red face. For myself, in a somewhat dumbfounded state I mumbled 'I am mine own executioner'. After eulogising further for a while, Mr Ronald and Geoffrey left my studio. Roy Trigg, whose contribution had been invaluable, was almost speechless and he was sorry to have witnessed such a travesty of justice. He hoped that I would be able to acquaint Mr Ronald with the true facts about who was really responsible for the creative work.

With my mind in a whirl as a result of this gross injustice and of the treachery of Geoffrey, I went through the motions of work for the rest of the day and eagerly went home in a very depressed state of mind. Plans were already beginning to form in my mind, and I was in a desperate hurry to discuss with my wife what the future held for me under the present circumstances. I don't think that I had much appetite for my evening meal but, at the end of the day, my wife and I made up our minds that it was time for me to resign and seek employment elsewhere. My plans would be put into motion the next day and I would indicate my intention to each of the executive directors, explaining in detail the reason for my decision to leave the employment of W.T. Copeland & Sons Ltd.

I arrived at the factory early the next day and my first call was to inform Mr Ted Hewitt, the joint managing director, of my decision to leave. Not surprisingly, he was most sympathetic, being fully aware of the bone of contention, but although he was sorry that he could not give battle with Mr Ronald, who was chairman of the board, he had his own position to consider and was in a 'no-win' situation. His final advice to me was "Harold, there are plenty more pottery ovens that smoke". Next I informed Mr Frank Thorley, the sales director, who was also fully aware of the unjust situation and was most sympathetic. Mr Gresham Copeland was, unfortunately, not at the factory and I was sorry that I could not acquaint him of my decision.

The next event was the usual early visit by Geoffrey to me in my studio, wishing me a very good morning. Without ado, I reminded him of the behaviour of Mr Ronald and himself regarding the conversation of the previous day and the fairy story nonsense that Mr Ronald believed to be the truth about who was responsible for the creation of the Rosewater Dish. Geoffrey's face drained of all colour when I informed him of my decision to leave Copeland's and that I would be informing Mr Ronald of this decision on his arrival at the factory. He obviously suffered a severe shock on learning this news for, without a word, he turned on his heel and hurried away.

To give Geoffrey full credit, he waited for Mr Ronald's arrival and informed him of the terrible harm the previous day's happenings had caused. A short time later I was summoned to Mr Ronald's office where he welcomed me with open arms and sought forgiveness for being so obtuse and ill-informed. He pleaded with me to reconsider my decision to leave and told me that I must convey to my wife his genuine regrets for his ill-judged comments and actions. After a long discussion, in which I gave vent to my feelings and he made plain his eagerness to put things right for future, I said that I would give the matter serious thought and, together with my wife, I would decide whether to change my decision and would give him my answer the following day.

Twenty-four hours is a long period when such traumatic events have taken place and my journey home, following a day of recrimination and apology with the promise of a much brighter future, had improved my state of mind almost beyond belief. But I wondered, would all the good intentions be carried out? Is there such a thing as mutual trust among men? During the evening, my wife, with some suspicion, agreed that I should accept the promises of a fairer and more rewarding future, but warned that I should be ever vigilant and, in particular, watch carefully the activities of my so-called friends.

After the rough sea of discontent had calmed, Mr Ronald's first action was to insist that I should make the presentation of the Rosewater Dish to the Princess myself. He wrote to her personal secretary, Commander Richard Colville who, in turn, fixed a date for me to present myself at Buckingham Palace on the morning of 11th March 1949. Mr Ronald also invited my wife to accompany me and enjoy a few days in London at the firm's expense.

Mr Ronald instructed me to have a special box made by the work's joiner with a screw-down lid and that I should arm myself with a screwdriver for opening the box. I had instructions by letter to present myself at the reception door on the left-hand side of the Palace. With minutes to spare I approached the outer gates guarded by police who carefully examined my credentials and directed me to the reception door. The Guards who were on duty continued to march up and down across the front of the Palace with rifles and fixed bayonets and I asked the police if it was likely that I should be challenged. They pointed out that the war was over and that, since the Guard's duties were mainly ceremonial, they would not take any notice of my passage.

The receptionist pointed me in the direction of an old-fashioned lift and gave me brief instructions on how to locate the office of Commander Colville. I had expected to be escorted by some official, but was allowed to find the commander unaided. This seemed very strange to me, for a person to be left to their own devices, wandering unaccompanied around the corridors of this truly magnificent Royal Palace. Without any trouble, I found the room to which I had been directed, tapped on the door and a charming feminine voice bade me enter. It was a beautifully furnished and decorated room with two or three elegant ladies having morning coffee and taking their ease on splendid brocade-covered chairs.

I stated my business and within a few minutes Commander Colville put in an appearance and made me welcome. I then removed the tiny screws from the lid of the box one by one and carefully unwrapped the Rosewater Dish, placing it carefully on the table. With oohs and aahs, the Commander and the ladies-in-waiting congratulated me for being responsible for the creation of such a magnificent example of British craftsmanship and they assured me that the Princess would be very pleased to accept it as a prized wedding gift. I was sorry that I was unable to make the presentation to the Princess personally, but I believe it has become a treasured possession of Her Majesty The Queen. Later the same day, I went back to the Palace to borrow the dish for the public relations firm who had laid on a press viewing and a photo session, after which I personally returned the dish to Commander Colville. It had been a very exciting day and one that I shall always remember, though my one small regret was that a handsome presentation case might have been made to house such a priceless object.

Next day there were many accounts in the press with full descriptions and photographs. On my return, I had to relate my experience in detail to Mr Ronald, who was very pleased that 'all was well that ended well'. He often commented that it was a great pity that the dish had had to leave the factory but he hoped that one day we would make a duplicate and put it on show as an example of fine design and craftsmanship. We did produce the second design which we had submitted for approval, but instead of using the Princess Elizabeth's initial E as the central motif, I substituted the arms of the city of Stoke-on-Trent. The whole of this work, which was executed by Roy Trigg, was a magnificent piece of craftsmanship and is now permanently displayed at the Spode factory in a place of honour.

The whole sequence of events was a very important turning point in my career and, looking back over the many years, I am proud to have been responsible for the production of possibly one of the finest Royal commemorative pieces ever made at the Copeland factory and, as such, its equal will never again be made.

Harold with the Princess Rosewater Bowl at the press conference. This photo caused an upset between the Palace and W.T. Copeland & Sons as the present was a private one and should not have been used for publicity.

The Princess Elizabeth's Rosewater Bowl: A Poem

I found this rather sweet poem in the *Spode Saga Christmas Number 1949* written by P.J. The author/authoress highlighted the full story of Harold presenting the bowl at the Palace for the benefit of the workers in their quarterly newsletter, which I have included below.

The firm of Spode, with publicity on mind –
For a Princess's wedding a lovely bowl designed:
It was really quite unique, very large and round,
Beautifully hand-painted upon a pale cream ground.
The acme of perfection, a paragon of Art,
Eminently suited to delight a royal heart.
Baron Holdway of Spode, a designer of repute,
Was despatched to the Palace in a topper and striped suit.
The shirt of Mr Ronald's was a little bit too tight,
But his brown boots were beautiful, and yellow tie just right.
Proudly he marched right up to the Palace,
Was met by the Queen's secretary, the Honourable Alice,
"Good-morning," said Harold, falling flat upon his face,
"Arise," said Lady Alice, "I'll present you to Her Grace."
Into the chamber crept Harold in awe,
And reverently placed the bowl upon the floor,
"This your Majesty, is the child of my brain,"
Said Harold, falling on his face again,
He scrambled to his feet once more, his face was very red,
"I don't know if I'm on me 'eels or on my blinkin' 'ead."
He skidded on the parquet floor, and tripped over the mat,
He grabbed the Royal tablecloth, and wildly clutched his hat;
His waistcoat burst open, his buttons flew wide;
With a groan like a pole-axed bullock he cried,
"Heaven 'elp a poor sailor, not long home from the sea,
Why in heaven's name did they send me!"

A slight use of poetic licence, but there is an element of truth in the poem as Harold's button did burst off as he stooped down.

Harold painting the Rosewater Dish.

Left to right: Harold's nephew, Chris Peel; son, Paul; his sister-in-law, Flossie; and wife, Betty admiring the bowl on a Sunday morning.

CHANGES IN MANAGEMENT

On 26th June 1956, Mr Sam Bloor was appointed works manager. Mr Ian Forse was to be assistant works manager and I was appointed art director. These management changes were made by the executive directors – Mr R. Spencer Copeland, managing director, Mr Gordon Hewitt, export sales director, Mr John Copeland, production director, Mr Robert Copeland, home sales director, under the chairmanship of Mr W.H. Newton.

The most important appointment was that of Mr Sam Bloor, who was promoted from earthenware clay manager to works production manager. The control of sales, design and office management was to remain unaltered. Prior to this announcement, I received a visit from Sam, who told me of the proposed changes and informed me that he was prepared to accept the work's management on condition that Geoffrey Cholerton be relieved of his position of art director and that furthermore that he hoped that I would be willing to accept the title and responsibility. Because of my personal feelings regarding the existing art directorship, I had no difficulty in acceding to his wishes. After so many years of what I considered to be a very unfair situation, out of the blue came the answers to my prayers.

Everyone congratulated me on my appointment and said that it was richly deserved. Geoffrey Cholerton was given the post of lecturer and was to help with the organising of exhibitions, which entailed quite a lot of travelling around the country. He achieved quite a high reputation as a lecturer and his artistic knowledge of Spode and Copeland decorated ware was appreciated by many collectors and customers. I am sure that Geoffrey was, in some respects, almost relieved to relinquish the responsibilities and duties of art director and the offer of the new job was to him a much more appealing and interesting proposition. He continued this way of life for quite a period but finally resigned and became a teacher of general art subjects in Scotland, which became his home. I believe he enjoyed his new-found calling, but it was to be for only a comparatively short time for, after a few years, he died, only in his mid-fifties. To me, Geoffrey's natural ability as a ceramic artist was wasted because he did not spend enough time practising his skills.

For my part, I was now responsible only to the board of directors and enjoyed a fruitful period as head of a fine design department. Ian Forse enjoyed life in his role of assistant to Sam, because for the most part each of them was a specialist in different areas. Sam's main operational skills lay in the field of 'making' and Ian's were in modern tunnel oven firing of ware by gas and electricity, so there was little chance of the clashing of ideas. The main difference between the two men was that Sam seemed to have an extra set of gears that he activated when a major effort was needed. His energy was prodigious! Whilst carrying the burden of efficient works production, his spare time interests were pursued with equal vigour.

Sam was married, with two grown-up sons. His wife was a charming and highly skilled dressmaker and was inundated with requests for her services. Both sons had spare-time jobs in addition to attending school. One of the boys had a paper-round, and if he was ever sick, Sam was the one who deputised for him and made the round before coming to the factory at eight o'clock, the time when the clay workers started. He also ran a betting book at the factory and had a large number of clients. Betting slips were handed in during lunch breaks and winnings paid out the next day. He also provided a clothing and general goods club with operatives receiving a loan of cash to be repaid on an instalment basis over a given period of weeks with interest. It was a sound business and Sam never had any bad debts.

After school, both sons helped Sam to sell 'seconds' pottery and they 'stood market' in several town centres. Sam bought seconds from a number of local factories and soon built up a thriving business. He also ran a small taxi service conveying people to and from the North Staffordshire Royal Infirmary, which was near to his home. As his interests expanded, he rented a small shop in Hartshill and he and his wife made and sold sandwiches, hot dogs and meat pies to passers-by. This venture prospered and Sam then supplied workers with their lunchtime snacks. I am sure that I must have missed out on one or two of Sam's sidelines, but I must not forget his holiday caravans in Cornwall. He had two on a very nice site, which he let to friends during the summer season. As I did not own a motor car, my wife, son and I were driven down to Cornwall at midnight on Friday, after he had closed his café, in one of his taxis. Immediately after he had delivered us to one of the caravans, without any rest, he returned to Stoke with the party who had vacated the caravan, in this case Mr and

Sam Bloor's caravans at the factory bound for Brussels, 30th March 1958. Left: Mr Makins, Centre: Sam Bloor, Right: T.Robert Copeland. Photo coutesy of Spode Museum Trust.

Mrs Ian Forse. After this holiday, I was told by Ian Forse that Sam was serving hot dogs in his café the next evening. All this after seven hundred miles of driving and no sleep! This type of activity, of course, is superhuman and not to be recommended for ordinary mortals!

A typical example of Sam's astuteness occurred on the occasion of the Brussels International Exposition in 1958. As exhibitors, we had a double-decker display stand designed by the work's sales department and constructed by the factory joiners. It was made up of a number of sections that were bolted together and assembled at the exhibition by our own staff. Members of staff took turns week by week to be on duty for the whole of the exhibition with one member on duty the whole time. A difficulty was the high cost of accommodation until Sam suggested to the sales manager that he would be willing to hire out one of his caravans. His offer was gratefully accepted and Sam smiled! Timothy, the permanent staff member, stocked the larder in the van each week with sufficient provender to cover the needs of the visitors. One week, I accompanied Sam and we managed to exist in reasonable comfort.

When the exhibition was over and the stand had been dismantled and returned to the factory, Sam had to consider bringing back the caravan. Being a busy man, he tried desperately to get someone to volunteer, but did not have any luck with his quest. However, fortune comes to those who have faith and, within a week, we received the news that vandals had set fire to the van, which was completely gutted and Sam was pleased to receive a good insurance claim for the damage. After this 'misfortune', he decided not to tempt fate too often and ceased to be a caravan owner.

Even before he was appointed production manager, Sam was always most helpful if I made any request for something new. I well remember the occasion when I asked him if it would be possible to produce

for me an earthenware plate with a Flemish Green rim and a white centre area. I suggested that we should both pay a visit to the Royal Worcester factory where I believed that they had invented an automatic rim-width slip-banding machine for their china-making and were anxious to promote it. Their engineering department had built their own machine and would be quite willing to make and sell one to us – at a price!

It was a most ingenious machine and performed very well indeed, but after inspecting the fired examples, I did not feel that the quality of finish was good enough for us. We returned sadder and wiser, but Sam said: "You shall have your green-rimmed plate, but please be patient". Within a month he produced for me an ideal example plate I wanted. I was overjoyed and asked if the cost of production was reasonable. He replied that it was known as a 'double make plate' and as the clay and labour cost was so inexpensive the effect on the final cost was negligible. Samples were shown to the directors and approval given for trial ranges to be produced.

The process of making the plate was as follows:

Firstly, a bat or slab of green clay is applied to the surface of the mould, The jigger arm and profile tool is then operated to make the plate. When the clay reaches a predetermined thickness, the maker with a sharp blade makes a cut in the clay at the shoulders of the plate. The clay in the centre is then removed, leaving the green rim adhering to the mould. The maker then applies a second bat of white clay on the mould and the jigger arm and profile presses the clay over the complete area of the plate, including the previously made green rim. After drying in the stove the two-tone clay plate is taken from the mould revealing a perfect finish, ready to receive its biscuit firing.

The introduction of this new method of rim decoration stimulated my creative instincts, the outcome of which was a small centre decoration –

Olympus: Two-tone clay.

Meadowsweet: Winner of the Silver Medal for Excellence at the Milan Triennale exhibition, 1960, sales leaflet.

a printed stylised design in black with a minimum amount of two-tones of green painting. The name of the pattern was 'Olympus' and it became an all-time best-seller. Around this time, in 1955, the Murray Curvex machine was being used for the production of flatware decorations and Olympus decoration was chosen as the first large quantity design to be processed. Because of the simplicity of the decoration, it was possible for every item of our tableware range to be printed by the Murray Curvex machine, which was a great achievement. Other coloured clay design effects were produced at a later date, consisting of a white rim and primrose centre, known as Meadow Glory, and green rim with a yellow centre, known as Meadowsweet. The latter was awarded a Silver Medal for Excellence at the Milan Triennale Exhibition, held from 16th July to 4th November 1960.

I think one of the factors that helped the directors to offer the elevated and most important post of works manager to Sam was that, in the face of competition, he was a winner. A few months before the post was offered to him, Sam entered, for fun, a competition entitled 'Be Your Own Boss' sponsored by the daily newspaper the *News Chronicle*, with a prize of £3,000 for the winner. The first test was the placing of ticks in little boxes alongside questions, which Sam thought was quite simple. A selected number from thousands of contestants were then asked to expound on some more difficult questions in written form. Finally, a smaller number were asked what sort of business they would like to invest in and what methods they would use. By this time, Sam was getting quite excited, particularly when he was chosen as one of four people who were invited to a London venue to be vetted by four illustrious people: Sir Peter Masefield of BEA, Lady Barnett of 'What's My Line?' fame and two very

astute businessmen, formed a panel to act as judges, with the whole procedure to be broadcast on BBC television on 29th March 1956.

I think Mr Peter West was the presenter and, after each man had stated his case and answered many and varied questions, Sam was declared the winner. A cheque for £2,000 was given to him, with a further £1,000 to be presented after twelve months had been spent in the furtherance of his idea. Briefly, Sam thought that he could benefit space travel and rocket propulsion by producing high-temperature resistant fittings, nose cones, tiles, etc. He would make full use of his ceramic knowledge to produce these items and as they were of small dimensions, large capital outlay was not a great factor. As not one of the panel had the foggiest idea of what Sam was talking about, they accepted his brilliant explanation of what benefits the nation would gain, if he could perfect his theories and put them to practical use. With good intentions, Sam rented a small premises and conducted certain experiments, of which, because of their secret nature, nobody saw any examples. He assured me that he was making progress with his spare-time venture. After the twelve months were up, the *News Chronicle* handed over the £1000 final payment.

Obviously, everyone, including the Copeland directorship, was very proud of Sam's success and the thought that he might resign and devote the whole of his attention to his prize-winning project must have crossed their minds as well as the fact that we could ill afford to lose his talents. So, the decision that was made to offer him the position of works manager was without doubt influenced by his competitive spirit and will to win. One of Sam's first actions after being promoted to works manager was to fill the vacancy of clay manager by appointing Mr George Dabbs from

Above: Fortuna, retail price when new 17s.6d.

Right: 1950s display featuring Soft Whispers and Petunia.

Below: Fortuna sales brochure. February 1955. 15 pieces in the range.

the research and development department, the job of chief chemist being given to Mr Cyril Allen, who filled this exacting role with great distinction for many years.

Sam's spare-time prize-winning concept gradually ground to a halt and he then used the premises for decorating and firing seconds ware for market sale. Permission was given for him to purchase seconds ware from the Copeland factory, which to me was a great mistake and should never have been allowed. The consequence was that customers complained about his activities and that the quality of his seconds was too good and affected their sales of 'best ware'. Sam continued to perform his works' duties with great energy and was praised for his success, one of which was the introduction of the new gas-fired tunnel kiln, together with Ian Forse, under the directorship of Mr Spencer Copeland, for the firing of china biscuit ware. His contribution proved to be one of his last on a major project, for after failing to achieve what he considered to be just reward for his efforts as works manager, he decided to resign and start anew as the general manager of a pottery manufactory in South Africa. Sam's period of top management at the factory of Copeland's was but a short one, a mere four years, but his 'fame' and his exploits will be remembered

for many years. On 1st July 1960, Ian Forse was appointed works production manager and, although lacking Sam's charisma, he nevertheless became a thoroughly dependable and efficient replacement.

In the early days of Sam's employment as assistant to Mr John Whalley, the earthenware clay manager, a man by the name of Jack Gibson was engaged as the head of the biscuit warehouse by Mr William Longsdale, the general manager. Mr Longsdale knew of the man's ability for, both he and Jack had been employed by Meakin's of Tunstall, an earthenware pottery that produced medium-priced wares. Jack was happily married with two lovely children and a wife who was a skilled designer of silk textiles; they lived in Macclesfield. Jack journeyed by train every day, briskly walking to and from the railway station and the factory. He was strikingly handsome and looked more like a managing director than a mere pottery warehouseman.

Sadly, his wife was suspected of stealing silk from the factory where she worked and the police, seeking to discover how she disposed of it, lay in wait for Jack on his walk to the station. Now it happened that the police station was situated on the very route that Jack used: on the day of his wife's arrest, the police in Stoke asked Jack if he would help them in their enquiries. He asked them what was wrong and they in turn, asked him if he would mind opening his attaché case. Lo and behold, nestling beneath his newspaper was a 21-piece tea set! The police then made a further search at his home and found more evidence of stolen wares. Jack was convicted and served a prison sentence, and, of course, lost his job.

All that happened before the war, but in the late Fifties a new sales manager at Copeland's received an application from a Mr Jack Gibson, an ace salesman at present working for Mason's, who also mentioned that he could be vouched for by Mr Sam Bloor as a character reference. The new sales manager checked his story with Sam and offered Jack the job at Copeland's. He turned out to be an excellent salesman and often used to present me with thoughts about future patterns. Sadly, his second term with Copeland's was relatively short, for, one day, he announced that he was going to have a voluntary health check-up. He drove himself to the hospital and parked his car. After a preliminary examination, a specialist was called in and insisted that he should have immediate treatment. Jack was admitted as a very sick man, needing intensive care. Despite every effort by the doctors, Jack died within a week or two and his car was retrieved from the hospital car park by one of the work's drivers.

We have not come to the end of the Bloor saga, however. Towards the end of 1965, Mr John Copeland, who had resigned his directorship as a member of the Copeland board some years earlier, paid me a visit. He was accompanied by his baby daughter – she was actually in a carrycot – and he informed me that he was going to South Africa to join Sam, to assist him with the management of the factory. The look on my face must have amused him, for with a wry smile, he said; "I know what you're thinking, you think I'm mad!" I nodded my head, but he assured me that he was quite happy with the working arrangements. I wished him the best of luck and hoped that my fears would be unfounded. However, his stay in South Africa did not last too long for the company was put into the hands of a receiver! Sam vanished without trace! John was asked to stay on to help straighten out some of the problems, after which he returned home, a sadder and wiser man.

Lastly, in the late Sixties, when the company was under the ownership of the Carborundum Company, Sam, on a visit from South Africa, called at the front lodge and asked if he could have a few words with one or two of his old friends. Unfortunately, the managing director, who knew Sam's past history instructed Mr Robert Copeland, of all people, to order Sam to leave the factory immediately, even though he was only standing at the entrance. This was the last occasion that I set eyes on Sam and I often wonder what became of him. I am sure of one thing, however; that, but for his actions and insistence on being granted his own conditions in his terms of engagement as production manager, I would not have realised my personal ambition and, for that reason, I am truly indebted to Sam.

Promotional photo for Flemish Green, a plain green body.

The end of Harold Holdway's memoirs.

The following chapters have been compiled and written by Ruth Holdway

DESIGNS OF THE 1950s, 1960s AND 1970s

Spode has a reputation for producing traditional wares, especially for America. The company is lucky as it has a wealth of pattern and shape books dating back to Josiah Spode I that the design department can draw on. Generally, apart from the 1930s and 1950s, the design department has relied heavily on traditional designs. Paul Wood, present managing director of Spode and once a member of Harold's art department, still feels that it is important to draw on the heritage of the factory, saying "it would be daft to ignore it." Paul sees Spode's heritage as like the pyramid of a coral reef; the bottom layers are dead but they are supporting the new growth above. As both Paul and Mike Kitt, another member of the design team, say, "Harold loved reinterpreting old 'pattern book' designs for new customers and developed the team to do so."

Two such patterns from antique painted fruit and flowers sprays were Blenheim, 1957, which used several small sprays of flowers scattered over the plate, and Rhona, taken from antique prints which uses a gold print in the centre with a crimson ground border. This pattern was named after a top sales girl at Gererds, London. For Spode's bicentenary in 1970, Harold designed Renaissance; a dinnerware that uses the antique Camilla pattern's border motif but was short-lived. Summer Palace, 1971, was a popular design that was taken directly from an antique Chinese charger. Harold and Robert Copeland were visiting Colonel Fitzhugh, a direct descendent of the person who the antique blue and white pattern, Fitzugh, was named after, when they saw a floral charger on the wall which they asked to borrow to take a design from. Harold inspired the 'original' design and Paul Wood drew it out. It is still in production today on a stone china Lowestoft shape. A blue version, Palace Gardens, was produced but it did not last long.

However, using the factory's heritage means that you cannot claim that the design is your own. For example Paul Wood 'designed' Stafford Flowers that proved to be popular but it was taken from old

Above: Renaissance pattern with Camilla pattern behind and the pattern book entry, 1970. Photograph: Norman Jones.

Above right: The Lord's Prayer painted by Harold twice on less than a third of a threepenny piece with a modern day penny for scale.

Right: An enlargement of the threepenny piece Lord's Prayer featuring 140 words and 560 letters.

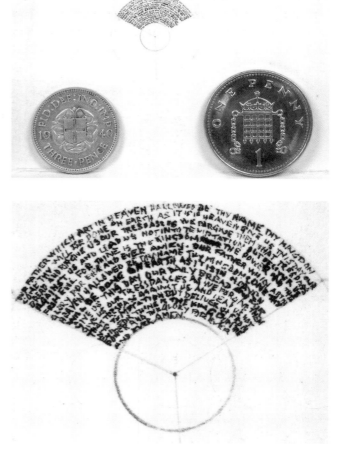

shapes and used Curtis Botanical sprays. Harold reintroduced four patterns from the Spode pattern book in 1962, which were called Delphi, Green Garland, Kensington, produced in red, and the gold version, Queen's Gate, that reminded Robert Copeland of the iron fencing surrounding Kensington Palace. Most companies with a traditional background found it difficult in the 1960s to adapt to the needs of the younger, affluent customers and Spode was no exception.

Harold said, "We can do anything today that was done years ago, within the new processes." Testing that statement Harold accepted a challenge, even though he knew this particular challenge would not be commercially successful. When Harold occupied his old studio over the arch, a request came from an insurance company for a replacement cup. A wealthy American had insured his service for replacement; he was not interested in its monetary value. A cup was broken in transit and the insurance company were asked to get a new one. The pattern was no longer in production but Harold rose to the challenge. The new finished cup was sitting on his desk when he was visited by Richard Guyatt from the Royal College of Art regarding a commission for the Goldsmiths' company . He saw the cup and said he wanted one. Harold said he couldn't have it as it was not in production, but a set did end up being made. A while later there was a complaint that the cups were cracking when coffee was being poured in. When the problem was investigated, it was found that the caterers were stacking the cups when not in use and the weight was stressing the base of the cup and

consequently the cup was cracking when hot liquid was poured in. Harold said it was a mistake to ever produce the set.

Another challenge that Harold rose to, although not actually connected with Spode designs, was to paint the Lord's Prayer on the size of a silver threepenny bit. The engraver George Cartlidge boasted that he had successfully engraved the prayer on the size of the coin, therefore Harold tried to equal, if not better, it. Using a single-haired brush he painted the prayer twice on less than a third of the coin proving that he could paint the Lord's Prayer six times on the size of a threepenny coin!

The 1950s were quite a serious time for the Copeland factory as the American market collapsed. In 1955, Joe Lee of the biscuit warehouse reported that there were a minuscule number of orders. Sydney Thompson had warned the company in the early 1950s that they needed to expand the business and production. All of a sudden the crisis struck and Harold was asked to design something for the home market urgently. Using the principle of less is more, in a matter of eight to ten minutes Harold had sketched out a simple pattern. This became known as Moondrop, three question mark-like swirls overlapping in blue, mauve and purple. The colours are frequently found in Celtic works with the scrolls apparently reflecting the symbol of Eternity and the flowers reflecting the symbol of the Trinity. It was advertised as "Spode: for everyday elegance. A Celtic pattern from the time shrouded past adds subtle grace to a modern home. Inexpensive and always replaceable." It was given the name Moondrop, as it

Moondrop, inspired by Celtic art.

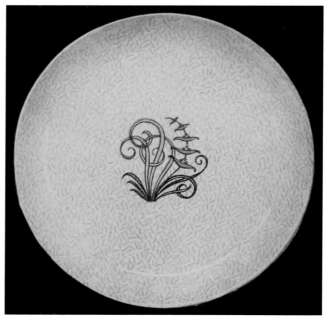

Singing Grass using the same motif as Moondrop. Sales leaflet.

Clockwise from top left: Soft Whispers, Jacinth, Montego, Petunia, Mimosa, (version to mark Royal visit to Australia, 1954, 4.5in) & Scroll.

was reminiscent of the Celt's respect for the symbol of purity, although this is more likely to be a name applied by an imaginative sales team after the pattern was designed. Moondrop was designed for the Murray Curvex printing process and experienced trouble in production as the cobalt in the colour flowed. Looking through the pattern books of this era, the same patterns are used over again trying different colours, backgrounds or combinations hoping to hit a winner. It was easy using the traditional methods to adapt the details quite easily. Most of these variations never reached the market. However, one that did was a motif from Moondrop, which was used on another pattern in 1955, Singing Grass, which had an all-over background of tiny leaves taken from an antique Spode sheet pattern. The modern pattern was marketed specifically for brides-to-be.

By 1955 W.T. Copeland & Sons had marketed eight new patterns on a new earthenware body, which was pale green and called Flemish Green ware. A full range of domestic ware was available on two shapes: Tean, a moderately contemporary shape designed by Harold, and Kaga, with a more traditional feel. Eight underglaze print and enamel patterns were designed for Flemish Ware. Sam Bloor, works manager, introduced two-tone earthenware; the centre of the plate was ivory with a green rim. On hollowware, the body of the coffee pot was ivory and the handle and the spout were green. The popular Olympus, introduced in 1955, and Soft Whispers, using a hint of gold, were produced on this body. Olympus was advertised as "Contemporary–yes! But in a restrained mood." This was very successful and a lot of ware was sold, especially since there was a promotion run by Kensitas cigarettes whereby tokens could be exchanged for Olympus ware. Harold also designed Jacinth in 1954 on a similar principle, which sold well. The name comes from the earlier word for Hyacinth, which was used in the days when these flowers had greater elegance and grace. Mystic was inspired by the Chinese technique of Sgraffito, a technique whereby a floral pattern is cut into the body to expose a different colour ground and also allows the glaze to flow into the indentations. This was liked by older people but did not sell too well.

Another pattern inspired by the Orient was Lotus. The pattern depicts an oriental summer garden looking out on to a placid lotus pool with sun-tipped hills behind. Montego was inspired by Montego Bay in West Jamaica, which is renowned for its abundant flora, particularly its ferns. The conventionalised flowers were designed from specimens sent to the factory from Montego Bay. The *Pottery Gazette and*

Oklahoma backstamp.

Glass Trade Review, May 1955, considered Scroll to be one of the most interesting designs because, "although it is smooth and rhythmic, there is no feeling of motion and restlessness. It is an entirely original abstract idea which has been given life by expert drawing and high quality engraving of the original conception." Thistle was also an abstract border decoration.

Harold's designs of this era were subtly contemporary but were in keeping with the traditional image of Copeland and Spode. Euonymous was another pattern designed for Flemish Green but it did not get produced. An eighth design was produced in 1954 specifically for the Australian market called Mimosa, which featured the yellow flowers, which have national significance in Australia. The pattern was designed to show the natural growth of the flower. A ninth design produced at a later date on Flemish Green was Petunia with a depiction of the flower in the centre in 1956. It is difficult to tell who actually designed which pattern, as unless the designer's name was used in the publicity, there is no record, not even in the pattern books, of who designed it. However, we can safely say they were all produced under Harold's guidance.

Oklahoma, introduced in 1957, on a Coupe shape sold very well, although Spring Gala, also produced in 1957 on the Tean shape did not. Harold drew his inspiration for the Oklahoma pattern from a line of lyrics of the popular musical of the day, "Oh what a beautiful morning, The corn is as high as an elephant's eye." As Harold said in a letter, "the design was created in a contemporary style to suit the youthful demands of the day." Oklahoma was one of the first water slide silk screen patterns in colour and gold, produced by Johnson Matthey incorporating

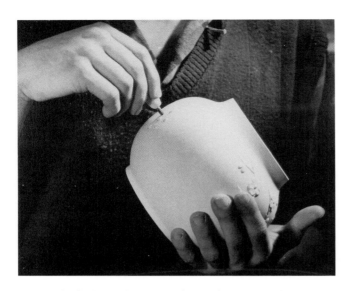

Putting the holes in the spout of a Geisha teapot. This pattern was a reverse of Prunus, blue on white. Photograph: Jones

their new covercoat process, which was supplied to the factory. There was an attempt in the 1950s to reintroduce 1930s designs or use their simplicity in new designs. One successful reintroduction was the Chinese influenced Fisherman and Fly, designed by Harold in 1937 in pastel pinks, greens and blues. It kept being reused in different colours and is now (2003) sold under the name of Pearl River. Other designs of this period attributed to Harold were Andromeda, 1950, which used a simple pattern of Pieris leaves and flowers; Melody, 1955; Chestnut using the chestnut leaves and flowers and Rannock, 1955, which features Rowan Mountain Ash in autumn colours. It was so named as the tree is prolific in this part of Scotland. These patterns were mostly for the home and commonwealth market, as the Americans did not look to Spode for modern patterns. There were very few new earthenware patterns introduced after 1966 (when the American company, Carborundum, took over WT Copeland & Sons.) The company wanted to rationalise the number of designs being used.

One design that was specifically for the British Empire and Commonwealth Games held in Perth Australia in 1962 was a crossover between commemorative and useful wares. The three-quarter-pint pale grey stoneware tankard is decorated in blue with nine different sporting motifs and the crest of the Games. As the advertisement said, "The mug is more than a souvenir, more than a means of contributing towards the cost of sending British athletes to Perth in 1962 (each mug purchased represents a contribution towards this cost) but is an article of permanent use and beauty which at the modest price of 15/11d. including its attractive gift box, is remarkably good value for money." The mug was produced for and

marketed on behalf of the United Kingdom Appeals Committee. Harold would have loved designing this mug as he was a keen lover of all sports and always followed England's successes at the big sporting events with pride.

Harold's designs were not just confined to tableware as he also designed the green and white sculptured Fortuna vases and bowls, the classical Corinthian for Velamour and the moderately successful Lincoln shape that was created especially for America, "a new coupe shape with a subtle difference." Inspired by the Chinese, Harold also designed the popular Prunus vases that were made out of pale blue earthenware with a smooth matt finish. The spring blooms were embossed in white.

One design project that Harold was really proud to be involved with was Princess Margaret's personal tea set. Harold was an ardent royalist and paid extra special attention to royal commissions. The Princess designed her own tea service using a modern but regal design. The teapot lid had a pure gold coronet for a knob. On 25th June 1957 Spencer Copeland called at Clarence House to be shown the Princess's drawings and modelled shapes. The design consists of a radial arrangement of grey and white feathers delicately flecked with gold on a background of rich royal blue. The designs for the pattern, shape and decoration were sent to the factory for modelling and apparel of feather design. The whole project was kept top secret. Princess Margaret paid a surprise visit to the factory privately to see the progress of her set on 28th November 1957 and Harold was presented to her. The whole tea set took twelve months to produce. The Princess was obviously pleased as Iris Peake, her lady-in-waiting, wrote in July 1958 to thank Spencer Copeland for the set. "Princess Margaret bids me write and say how delighted she is with the china that has arrived safely. She is most impressed by the workmanship and artistry that has been used in carrying out her designs, and I am to say how grateful she is to you for all your help and the trouble you have taken to make the set so lovely." She suggested a few modifications to some further items that she wanted. Even though Copeland's was a commercial factory, they were still able to spend the time and had the skill to personally customise ceramics to the customer's order. With the Princess's permission, the pattern was produced in dark green for her boyfriend, Peter Townsend.

Royal College Shape, or RCA for short, is one of the most celebrated designs Spode produced in the late 1950s. The shape was part of a project to celebrate the tenth anniversary of the new convention of the

Clockwise from top: Princess Margaret's tea set; Commonwealth Games mug, courtesy of Spode Museum Trust; Prunus lamp base; and prototype seaweed vase, incised grey stoneware, painted in enamel, 1947.

Five prototype designs c.1950–60, possibly ideas for a competition run by the *She* magazine, March 1957.
Bottom right: Thistledown 1952.

Royal College of Art. The principal, Robin Darwin, set up a 'House of Our Own' exhibition, three rooms from a house where the students designed everything in it. It was held at the Tea Centre in October 1958. They wanted to produce everything to a commercial standard but the only thing that they could not produce at the college was a dinner service. Spode needed a new shape so were happy for two students, Neal French and David White, to come to the Spode factory to design and discuss the practicalities of the service.

The shape was modelled by Tom Barlow and processed by the Copeland factory. The idea behind the new shape was that it would be anthropometrical, suitable for its purpose. The saucers were designed so that when the cup is lifted the teaspoon does not slide into the well, meaning that you have to move it to replace the cup. The meat dish and bread and butter plate were a rounded rectangle shape so that cooked meats or bread could be served without it being cramped at either end and they had flat rims that enabled things to be carved on them easily. The cream soup cup handles were designed so that they could be stacked in the cupboard without them rocking over. The winged knobs served as steady rests when they were placed on the table and prevented burnt fingers. Handles on cups and teapots were easy to hold and spouts were high and curved to avoid drips. The capacity of hollowware items was suitable for the number of people being served. As many pieces as possible filled a dual purpose such as cream soup bowls and stands could be used as flower bowls or open fruit saucers. Royal College shape was marketed as "The new shape for contemporary living." Both Harold and Robert Copeland agreed that RCA was not suitable for earthenware as it was far too graceful a design so a similar shape was designed for earthenware, which was called Sussex shape.

In keeping with the innovative shape, the patterns were applied by lithograph, which was a new venture for the company. Due to the urgency of producing the ware to coincide with the publicity generated by the RCA exhibition, only four designs were launched in 1958. The first very simple design was Elizabethan, a classic gold filigree band designed by RCA students. The second design was Roger Young's Golden Fern, an elegant design of a New Zealand fern leaf produced in 24-carat gold. It was described in the sales leaflet as "wind blown fern fronds, baked bronze in the sun".

Pat Albeck, a textiles student at the college, designed some of the RCA patterns including Corn Cob and Daisy in 1958, which were followed by Empire and Fruit Spray the next year. One of Pat Albeck's most popular patterns was Provence in a subtle sage green trimmed with gold inspired by the stately Regency era. David Jackson designed St John, a soft grey printed design based on a botanical study of St John's Wort. The petals and stamens are hand-coloured in pale nasturtium, while the leaves remained grey. He also designed the bold geometric Persia pattern, which was based on the motifs of a twelfth-century Persian carpet.

On a similar line, Mike Kitt's Gothic pattern used a simple gothic device taken from medieval carvings. Another strong design which Harold did was Brussels,

RCA Persia pattern designed by David Jackson.

108

an elegant geometric shape, inspired by the famous Brussels filigree lace. Delphi was a simple design in burnished gold and was inspired by an antique pattern. Another delicate simple gold and green pattern used on RCA shape was Diadem and Green Diadem which was inspired by the headband or diadem worn by royalty. Harold's Green Velvet was based on the Delphi design but had a wide band of solid green colour at the top.

Although there was a wide range of contemporary and traditional patterns, it was the plain white version that won the Duke of Edinburgh's 1960 prize for elegant design. Robert Copeland recalls that the Design Council approached Spode and asked them to produce the RCA shape in white. Robert immediately said no as it would not be profitable and would be very hard to produce as there was no pattern to hide the slight imperfections. However, when he was told that the Duke of Edinburgh wanted to give Spode his prize, but only if it was white, as the Council of Industrial Design did not think that the patterns were up to the same standard, Robert reconsidered. Robert called the set Apollo after the god of manly beauty as he felt that RCA was a manly shape that was pure and classical. The Design Centre panel described the shape in their report: "The range has a particularly English quality well rooted in our best pottery traditions, yet without in any sense copying the past."

The shape continued to sell for twenty years until 1977, although Paul Wood claims that no money was made from it as it was sold too cheaply. The company could not produce the ware cheaply enough. Paul claims that Harold was resentful of the success of RCA shape as he did not have much involvement with it, nor was he that interested in modern designs. Spencer Copeland had just become managing director and it was his personal project. He personally brought in the designers, who were kept separate from the other designers at W.T. Copeland & Sons. Harold commented on RCA in the *Newark Sunday News*, 26th July 1970.

"Interestingly enough, Holdway elaborated, although Spode's 'RC shape', a modern form, received the Duke of Edinburgh's coveted award for good contemporary design, it has not been fully accepted by Spode fans who refuse to consider it "true Spode". "People seem to want only traditional from Spode, which has always been Spode's image. To the traditionalist, 'it is either Spode or it isn't'." Yet as Holdway noted about so many elegantly subtle Spode shapes, patterns and colourings chosen by modern brides, "they represent a simple framework, a beautiful shape: what could be more contemporary?"

Two occassions during this period that Spode, along with many other factories, produced commemoratives for were HM Queen Elizabeth II's Coronation in 1953 and Churchill's death in 1965. Harold was involved in the design of both of these.

Another design of note Harold produced was a series of birds on a similar line to the Rhododendron pattern and the Audubon Bird patterns; one of the last non-commemorative designs that Harold produced was Garden Birds in 1977. The series of six presentation plates featured a blue tit, wren, green finch, robin, thrush and chaffinch.

Harold was always very proud of his designs and they were appreciated in the trade press. In an interview in *Pottery and Glass*, April 1957, Harold commented, "It is very pleasing to note the increasing appreciation of good design on the part of the manufacturers and the general public." The article summed up, "Mr Holdway himself can feel proud to know that he is a designer who, through his own good taste and ability, has helped to give the public the great pleasure of being able to use and appreciate beautiful tableware in their homes."

Trade Shows and Exhibitions

In order to gain feedback on his designs, Harold would often go to the trade shows and exhibitions to meet the customers and agents and see what they wanted. He also went on several foreign trips discerning the Continental and American tastes and also looking at different factories' production methods and training. He commented in *Pottery and Glass*, April 1957, that he thought it was very useful for designers to study the various market needs and conditions on the spot, therefore he spent some of his time away from the studio.

He worked very closely with the sales organisation, particularly with the market survey division, for he thought that it should always be borne in mind what type of pattern suited the various age groups. Douglas Hawley, foreign sales manager, went on several trips with Harold to Nuremberg and Munich attending the British Weeks. He recalls that Harold had a good sense of humour and they had some good times together. In July 1958 Harold went with Douglas to the Brussels Universal and International Exhibition. Each country had its own pavilion showing off its wares. The Spode-Copeland stand won the Gold Medal of the Diploma of Honour at the exhibition.

His Royal Highness, The Duke of Edinburgh and

Princess Margaret visited the stand and a Spode china punch bowl, made especially for the exhibition, was presented to the Duke which was to be sold to provide funds for the National Playing Fields Association of which he was the president. The bowl was designed by Harold, pressed from clay by Ken Boswell, the outline of the design applied by R. Farmer, groundlaid and stencilled by Jack Booth, the heraldic colours of the Spode/Copeland arms applied by Fred Robinson and the gilding executed by R. York which took seventy-two hours. The bowl had six oven and kiln fires before it was burnished. In total it took 430 hours to produce the finished bowl.

In July 1954, Harold, Douglas Hawley, Robert Copeland and Ian Forse went on a journey to Scandinavia, Denmark and Germany on a fact-finding mission incorporating sales, design and manufacture. They visited the Royal Copenhagen Porcelain factory and the Bing and Grondahl factory in Denmark. Harold also went on a trip to Europe with Spencer Copeland and his wife Sonia in March 1957 to Paris, Florence and Milan. Sonia was an excellent linguist and wrote Harold a basic phrase book of useful Italian words. Spode gave Harold a wonderful opportunity to travel, which he would not have otherwise experienced.

RCA period sales photos. Top: Green Velvet period place setting.

Below: left to right, Apollo, Green Velvet and Elizabethan.

Right: RCA Provence gravy boat, soup cup and stand which doubles up as a bowl, teapot, and cup and saucer.

Churchill commemorative plate and goblet celebrating his life 1874–1965.

Garden Birds: clockwise from top left: Blue Tit design work; Blue Tit plate, design and lithograph; Chaffinch lithogrpah; Chaffinch plate.

CHANGE

New Methods

Harold often despaired of short cuts in art and disliked any machines that did not produce the same high quality as older, handcrafted methods. He often lamented the weight of mass-produced modern pottery. However, Harold was not such a traditionalist that he refused to move with the times; if there was a new gadget or machine available he was often one of the first to try it out. Whilst he was at Spode, he and Geoffrey Cholerton became involved with the initial development of the first ceramic pad printing machine, the Murray Curvex machine.

Harold had already written the draft for this chapter so I have included it almost verbatim.

Murray Curvex Printing   (written by HH 26.8.90)

In the late forties the necessity for increased productivity was still the main aim and any suggestion for a speedier output was eagerly encouraged by the directorate. One such instance was of our purchasing a small printing machine for the application of backstamps.[10] Although the machine was small and portable it was capable of producing a backstamp of quality on earthenware.

Without going into the mechanical details of the machine – which was called Rejefix – it proved to be quite a labour-saving device and after a thorough testing we purchased several for various departments. The simple operation was of a ceramic colour impression taken from a brass die and being applied to a rubber-like felt pad. Then the base of the plate was pressed onto the pad thereby producing a clearly defined backstamp in a dark green colour. Our present method of printing on biscuit earthenware was a much more labour-intensive operation. There was one slight problem, however, which was that the colour supplied by the machine manufacturers was temperamental and unreliable.

By this time, other manufacturers were now using the Rejefix machine and as we were the first ceramic user, we were often approached for advice as to the best method of obtaining good quality prints, the main problem being the working properties of the colour. Geoffrey Cholerton and myself recognized that the oil used to hold the chrome oxide colour

in suspension might be improved, and after many experiments we discovered that varnish used for the production of lithograph transfers was the perfect oil, and following this discovery we ceased to use the proprietary colour which was quite expensive.

Wedgwood's and Doulton's were also experiencing difficulties with the colour and approached our company with a view to our advising them how to cure their problems. This we did and explained to them that we were willing to supply them if they so wished. The price we charged was less than the manufacturers', but still showed us a handsome profit. The demands were so heavy that we had to produce a large roller-mixing machine to supply the demand. This form of printing backstamps on our plain wares continued to be used for a lengthy period.

Thoughts were beginning to stir in our minds and we wondered whether an adaptation of the Rejefix method could be the start of a new mean's of applying a decoration.

After many experiments we finally managed to produce a simple floral decoration on a small butter pat dish, which we submitted to Mr Ted Hewitt, our managing director, for his approval. He was most interested and immediately issued a challenge: that, if we finally managed to produce a group of pieces showing a decoration of sufficient good quality then he would consult the opinion of a qualified engineer as to the possibilities of furthering the idea.

The items were produced and approved and true to his word, he engaged the services of Mr Guy Murray, a reputable consultant development engineer from Cheltenham who Mr Hewitt was personally acquainted with in his youth, when they were fellow employees at the famous engineering firm of Messrs Kerr-Stewart in Whieldon Road, Stoke.

Mr Murray, Mr Spencer Copeland and Mr Ian R. Forse carried out the development of the Murray Curvex printing process, which began in 1950, in great secrecy. The project was known as HARPS.

Mr Murray studied in great depth the many methods that had been used to produce fine prints and one that impressed him greatly was known as ceramic bat printing. The following is a brief description of this once popular method of china decoration.

Towards the end of the eighteenth century several potting firms were producing extremely fine colour

---

[10] Back stamps consisting of the company's trading name, decoration name and number, name of material, ie China, and the country of origin. Example: Spode Copeland, Bone China, England, Pattern no. Y6655, pattern name Chelsea Garden.

The Murray Curvex printing machine being demonstrated to visitors by printer Doug Burton (foreground), T. Robert Copeland (second from front) and Sam Bloor (peeping over at the back).

print decorations, mainly on china tea ware by a process known as 'bat' printing. Spode was the leading company who created a variety of decorations that proved to be very popular. This method of printing was in addition to the paper transfer process used for many earthenware patterns.

The bat printing method of applying engraved patterns on glaze was a pure craft process, requiring great skill and dexterity on the part of the transferrer. Firstly a 'bat' or flexible pad was produced by melting best quality glue together with other ingredients, which was placed into a glazed earthenware receptacle, which in turn was partly immersed into a pan of water that was brought to the boil. The resultant mixture was then poured onto a shallow glazed dish and allowed to flow over the surface to a depth of about three millimetres, which on cooling was found to be quite flexible, and at the same time retaining a true form. After cutting into flat pieces of a suitable size, the bat was then deftly, but firmly applied to the incised engraved copper plate decoration which had previously been coated with oil and polished, leaving the incision only filled with oil.

The pad, now with the oiled impression faintly visible, is next applied carefully to the desired location on the piece of ware, which on removal, the oiled

image is dusted with enamel colour applied delicately with cotton wool. Surplus colour is then cleaned off the decorated surface after which the ware is given an enamel kiln firing to fasten the colour onto the piece. The printing method of using flexible bats was studied with care and gelatine was tried as a suitable vehicle to receive the colour print from the engraving.

In late 1953, after many experiments, both mechanical and printing development, Mr Murray designed and created a working prototype machine that was fully operational. This was housed at the Spode factory behind locked doors and practical trials were conducted in great secrecy by Mr Ian Forse. I believe that the partnership of Murray and the Copelands was not a happy one, for Mr Murray had applied for a patent in his own name in 1951 and the Copeland board only learned of this when the first machine was finally completed and their own application for patent was submitted.

Mr Murray held the firm belief that he had invented the machine. Copeland insisted that it was a joint venture; they having employed Mr Murray as a consultant.

No satisfactory conclusion was reached and Copeland's decided to forgo their claim and in 1954 Mr Murray was appointed chairman and joint managing director of a company trading under the name of Murray Curvex Printing Ltd who manufactured and sold the machines to the whole of the pottery industry.

Much more could be written about this great development but I would like to state that in my opinion the Murray Curvex ceramic printing method was one of the greatest inventions of the day and it is sad that Mr Guy Murray never received his due reward for the part he played in its creation. Sadly his health failed and he died in October 1955.

Murray Curvex Ceramic Printing Machine

The Murray Curvex printing machine consists of a free-running platform onto which the hand-engraved copper plate is locked into position. Ceramic colour is then mechanically spread over the surface of the copper plate, and after the engraved decoration has been filled with colour and the surplus removed by careful scraping, the copper is traversed to a position beneath a suspended bomb-shaped flexible former, which descends, and under great pressure, flattens itself on the engraved part of the copper plate.

Pressure is then released, and the 'bomb' raised, having plucked the colour-filled patterning from the engraving. The copper plate is then traversed

Murray Curvex printing trial: the roses facing left are printed in green using the new process. The black rose facing right is possibly done using a traditional printing method.

to its former position, allowing the article, i.e. an earthenware plate, to be positioned ready to receive the downward thrust of the printed 'bomb', which under great pressure transfers the decoration onto the surface of the article. The process is controlled by one operative and produces fine quality decorations at very high speed.

A New Art Department

Although the Spode factory retains many of the original buildings with their charm and character, the factory has never stopped evolving. One of the improvements to the art department, which Harold was heavily involved with, was the construction of a new studio with big windows letting in plenty of valuable daylight. Harold was delighted to be given a whole floor dedicated to design that was self-contained and separate from the management offices. As Gordon Hewitt, former foreign sales manager, says, "Harold's art department was a law unto their own." The design department was on the top floor of the new block with the prestige department, which included the commemorative and gold printers, on the middle floor. A prestige department is staffed entirely by craftsmen who make the commemorative and special pieces that do not lend themselves to mass production. The lithograph store and the groundlayers were also in the same block on the ground floor. Unfortunately the new electric lighting was not successful, as architects planned it, not artists, and further new lighting was installed designed by the artists.

Harold, circa 1967, dutifully composed a speech to

Harold used a hands on approach. A posed photo of him designing or working out colour variations.

deliver to Mr Wendell, chairman of the group who was due to visit the factory. It contains a complete record of how to set up an art studio as well as a summary of the wares being produced at the time. Unfortunately after all Harold's thought Mr Wendel did not land; his plane flew over the Works!

Mr Wendel, Gentlemen,

I would like to take this opportunity to thank you for the fine building – empty – but soon full. With what you may ask? Artists and designers: We all know the popular idea of these temperamental creatures; it is not quite like that, and it will certainly not be filled with – just a bunch of dreamy artists – but, with a design department – which we have always had but never so well housed. I was asked to define this.

I would say that it consists of a group of people with varied skills and experience, who, working as a team are a total mechanism, for producing facts from thoughts. Before explaining this in more detail, one other important function the definition does not cover, and this is the custodian of standards; and this is not just purely artistic ones, since the line cannot be drawn – a badly made pot is an unartistic one. From thoughts, (ideas) we make facts (things.)

To do this we must at every stage work with other company departments, even such unlikely ones as finance. Now I have said that, our raw material is ideas. These come from many sources, apart from divine inspiration and natural talent; they come from sales and production and even director's wives! Its a two-way traffic as well; we throw out ideas to other departments and thus stimulate their reaction. Ideas are many and before work commences on an idea, a careful assessment is made of the validity both within and outside the department. This is most important; at every stage of work this screening and enquiring process is brought into play. Despite its new lofty location there is never any danger of the art department becoming an ivory tower.

The actual work stages are diverse. The new department houses on one floor a number of different activities, each playing an essential part in the production of artwork. In the main studio, we have the designers and draughtsmen who produce the initial ideas. When the design programme has been decided and patterns selected, the design staff, as a team, prepare the necessary artwork, shapes and fittings etc. to complete the table or giftware range of items. When completed this work is handed over to the processing departments and a new creation has started on its journey. Also in the main studio we have the artists and craftsmen who will produce individual prestige services and specialist pieces.

At the moment we have only a small staff, but this will be enlarged, year by year, as the demand for fine ceramics increases.

Also on this floor we have a standards room, which will contain perfect examples of shapes and decorations and will be available to senior staff, and management, who have to maintain the quality of our products.

In the next room will be two or three of our artists and engravers. These men are specially selected for their skills and will be carrying out the next stage in the processing of a new design.

Another important function to a creative shape designer is the opportunity to produce the idea in three-dimensional form, either in clay or plaster.

Examples here on display show two ideas for a new tableware shape. This is the only way an artist can really express his ideas without being unduly influenced by limitations of process and therefore retains freshness of approach, which is needed to move away from the orthodox.

At a later stage the factory precision modeller is consulted when slight modifications may be made to suit the various factory processes.

In addition to the areas and functions I have described, we have a well-stocked library of books of reference, an essential to every artist; a conference room and studio for myself.

This concept fulfils a perfect setting which I am sure will be conducive to the efficiency of a well-organised design department.

DESIGN POLICY

The main energies of the design department must be used to help increase the sales of bone china throughout the world markets, followed closely by fine stone china, when production has caught up with the heavy demand on the current range of patterns, and lastly earthenware which is still much sought after by several markets.

In the US market a start has been made, and a serious drive is on, for our participation and our eventual capture of the bride's market.

This is an area of stern competition and Mr George Barker with his specialised knowledge in this field of operation, together with Mr Dick De Natale have given valuable help to the design team in choosing patterns for market testing. Over 60 decorations on plates, teas and saucers have been sent to the US for appraisal, and by mid May we hope to receive the comments and selections of the patterns needed.

It is possible that six will be chosen and a firm promise has been given to have these patterns ready for sale in early 1969. This is a tall order, and will fully extend the energies of the art department.

Designers working in the new art studio with large windows, 1967.

FINE STONE

Another important line is that of fine stone china. This very beautiful shape (Lowestoft) with its traditional decorations is in ever-increasing demand and when the need arises, the art department will be ready to introduce several new decorations that will give even greater stimulus to this lucrative line. Several of these decorations are on display in this room.

EARTHENWARE

For many years experts have informed us that earthenware is on its way out, but despite these pessimistic forebodings there still seems to be a demand for our type of earthenware; this is due mainly I think to the fine range of traditional patterns that we produce.

Patterns like Tower, Camilla, Blue Italian, Indian Tree, Billingsley Rose and many others are still in great demand. And great efforts have been made by the technical development departments to produce these fine decorations by less costly methods. In this field they have proved that this can be done together with maintaining the fine quality worthy of the Spode name.

There is also a firm suggestion from overseas for the design department to produce an embossed rim decoration. Our nearest rival in the earthenware field produces this type of ware, and does a large business with two different shapes and I think serious consideration should be given to this suggestion. This would be a long-term project because of the modelling involvement, and a suitable design for this shape is already in being as a dessert plate produced many years ago.

Having stated that the brides market requirements are being explored, and conquered by the American sales force, the Spode design team has also to satisfy the ever-increasing demands from the European market. Here indeed we need to recognise the need to increase our china tableware sales.

At the moment our earthenware, printed and print and enamel tableware sales dominate the picture and the shortage of china orders leaves much to be desired.

Serious efforts are being made to improve our china sales by attempting to create designs suitable for the Continental market and at the same time sell this choice of patterns in all other markets. This can be done!!! A good example of this is our gold Fleur De Lys pattern, which was originally created for the European market and is now a worldwide favourite.

A similar state of affairs exists with our present fine stone decorations and recent new prototype designs have been judged suitable for European and American markets.

Our position in the UK market is very promising indeed, particularly with the sales of our china ware. The Royal College Shape is still a firm favourite after nearly 10 years, and for a modern shape to remain popular for such a period must reflect credit on the creators of this form. It is a great pity that the UK is practically the only market that sells this shape in quantity, and I feel we can look forward to even more sales if new decorations are added in the not too far distant future.

The bulk of our home selling is mainly concentrated around the London area and many of these orders are placed by overseas visitors. In the English provinces a reasonable business is done with our traditional patterns and the Blue Italian pattern is still No. 1 favourite after more than 170 years. This is due mainly to the vast circulation of this pattern and the constant need for replacement and additions to the original service.

The price of our earthenware decorations is considered a little high and our serious competitors have either discontinued or replaced this type of ware and are selling a less expensive translucent porcelain at a price similar to our earthenware.

The introduction of this new body has had some effect on our earthenware sales. All these innovations present a challenge in the design department; who must explore every means to establish increased sales of our products in the provincial area of the home market.

GIFTWARE AND FANCY RANGE

The intention to enlarge our giftware and fancy range is considered most important both in china and earthenware, and the decision to introduce our unique range of Chelsea-Derby figures should establish a very lucrative source of revenue.

These beautiful figures can only be obtained at the moment from collectors and antique sales and great skills are needed for the production of this fine series. It is nearly 30 years since I last saw these figures produced by the Spode factory and I eagerly look forward to their reintroduction. We are exploring many possible ideas in this field with table accessories, lamp bases, and busts of famous personalities to name only a few.

Experiments have been completed by our research chemist in an endeavour to produce a delicate ivory tinted china body. Samples have been produced with a simple gold finish and Mr George Barker will be viewing these during his forthcoming visits.

We are now acknowledged as leaders in the manufacture and sale of commemorative wares and have established a fine line of prestige plates and items, which are most profitable, and our contract manager, Mr Whiter will be giving you more information concerning this line of business.

Lastly I would like to say a few words about our prestige range, to be produced by the Spode school of painters. Examples of this type of craftsmanship are on display in the form of our recently produced Chelsea botanical series. This quality of workmanship can be applied to numerous items, with an infinite choice of subject matter, and we have a wealth of materials to be studied and drawn upon in our museum collections, which will create a challenge from the past and be reborn with our creation of the collectors' pieces of the future.

Ideas: Harold lists divine inspiration, director's wives, native talent, sales and marketing and feedback from production. Contributing to the design department's activities are: specialist studio production, drawing, 3D form, research and specialist engraving.

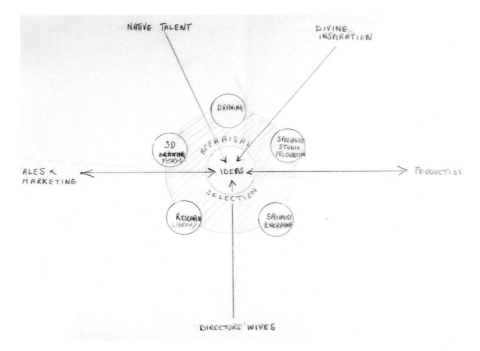

Right: Harold posing for the works' photographer.
Above: prisoner's stance pose; photo courtesy of Spode Museum Trust.

THE ART DEPARTMENT FROM 1956

Soon after Harold took over from Geoffrey Cholerton, he produced this report on 15th January 1957 on the current state of the art department.

This department has really come to life. The team are still largely doing preparatory work for the production of lines already selected. Two members are now on original work. The new member working alone and unhindered exhibits considerable originality. The principal of the ceramic section of the Royal College of Art is now finding suitable students to be trained for us. I recommend increasing the present staff of five to ten within five years. The chief designer and I will visit the studios of four independent industrial designers shortly. Their names have been submitted by the COI. The work of one of these is known and considered very good. Though our team is adequate I am satisfied we should include at least one outside designer as part of our regular policy. The recently formed design committee is a very welcome step. It is now clear that we should concentrate for a few months on gift lines to make use of fresh designs without the delay necessary with complete tea and tableware ranges.

The guidelines (opposite) issued in 1959 regarding the organisation of the art department and the roles they played is an important insight into the department's activities.

Top left: Dennis Emery.

Top right: Gillian West.

Left: John Ball modelling plaster.

Above: Roy Trigg.

Organisation of the design department
Approved by committee of management 11th March 1959

1.   The design staff are to be controlled and guided by the managing director.
2.   They will work under the chief designer, H. Holdway.
3.   The objectives of the design department are to provide new patterns and shapes to enable SPODE to be sold in all markets of the world in increasing quantities. They are to be responsible for the success (or failure) of any patterns marketed.
4.   Designers must produce designs:-
>   Which will sell within the price ranges demanded by various markets:
>   Which can be produced economically by the factory:
>   Which can uphold the reputation of the SPODE name:
>   Which fill any gaps in public demand.
5.   They must keep themselves informed of the way patterns and shapes are selling and must put forward suggestions for new   designs or modification to designs to enable slow moving or obsolete lines to be disposed of.
6.   The designers must have the courage of their convictions and must submit only those designs which they are confident will be a success. They must keep in close touch with the sales department and listen to salesmen's criticisms and suggestions, particularly those from overseas.
7.   The sales department are to submit a detailed list of their requirements and priorities to the managing director who will instruct the design department accordingly. This will normally be done through the design committee. These requirements are to be submitted as far as possible 9/12 months in advance, they must indicate style, price, range, market, colour preferred (or any colours which are not required) and any other desirable or undesirable property.
8.   A designers and sales department conference will be held quarterly or more frequently as required. At this conference the design department will submit designs in answer to 7 above and will receive criticism of them. They are not to alter these designs as a direct result of criticism unless   they are confident that the change is correct.
9.   Approximately 25% of the design staff must be kept available for contract work, preparation of special samples, etc. The sales director may communicate directly to the chief designer any questions connected with contracts or special samples, and the chief designer must use his best endeavour to satisfy these requirements quickly without employing more than 25% of his staff on them.
10.   The chief designer must run the department within the budget allotted. This budget will allow some money to enable individual designers to travel. All members of the staff must endeavour to make the department as economically productive as possible (i.e. the cost of designing each item must be kept to a minimum), and the chief designer should keep time sheets to enable the cost of each design to be calculated.
11.   The designers must keep themselves well informed of everything appertaining to sales and design both on and off the factory. They are free, and must be encouraged to submit to the design conference any design that they consider will increase the company's sales by fulfilling a public demand.
12.   The chief designer must keep his eye on the quality of finished goods and particularly must ensure that the colour, painting, etc, is in accordance with the original sample. He will report any deviation to the works manager.
13.   The proofing and ordering of lithos and silk-screen transfers must be authorised by the managing director.

The Art Department

Members of the Art Department pre-1959

Enid Seeny	Local art school trained, young designer in early design studio, now married to Bob Kelsall, an engraver. Enid went on to design the popular Homemaker pattern for Ridgways that was sold at Woolworths.
Jim Hawkins	Factory artist, junior member of the design staff.
Joe Hackley	Mature artist, fine draughtsman, local graduate of Poly Tech applied design. Left for a new job in glass.
Michael Mickleovski	Ceramic artist.

The Art Department of 1959

Christopher Boulton	Creative designer, Burslem Scool of Art trained. Left in 1963.
David Jackson	Creative designer, Royal College of Art.
Michael Kitt	Creative designer, Royal College of Art.
Roy Trigg	Ceramic artist and crest painter, born 1925, started December 1940. Forces June 1943–1947. Retired 1.4.90.
Cyril Ball	Ceramic artist, at Spode from 1946–1959.
Dennis Emery	Ceramic artist, born 1930, started 1944.
Frank Boothby	Engraver, born 1915, started 1929, died 22.1.89 aged 73.
Tom Barlow	Head modeller from 1934 until his death on 10th August 1974.
Paul Thorpe	Pattern recorder.

Additions to Art Department between 1959 and 1969

John Ball	Born 1947, started 1968. Went on to form Caverswall Pottery.
Gillian West	Born 1932, started 1962.
Paul Wood	Born 1945, started 1969, retired January 2005.
Antony Green	Sculptor, born 1947, started 1968, left 1976.
Roger Young	Graduate from RCA, started 1957.
David Walsh	Born 1946, started 1970. Locally trained. Emigrated to America in 1972 to work as a designer for Pfaltzgraft pottery.
Pauline Shone	Modeller. Produced the popular classical white figures for Spode.
Victor Reinganum	Black and white master. His most successful work for Spode was La Monde fashion pattern coasters. He was also a cartoonist. He died 29th August 1995, aged 87.
Janet O'Malley	Locally trained designer.
Lynne Joyce	Locally trained designer.
Lesley Dimkley	Born 1945, started 1965. Pattern recorder.

Art Departments of 1978

Worcester:
Staff: Mike Kitt, Peter Ewence, Stan Mitchell, Mrs Goodwin, Jannette Russell, Mrs Pat Rigby (paintress), Ken Potts, Harry Frost. Contract: Jennifer Mitchell, Neal French, James Alder, Bernard Winskill, Lorne McKcan, B. Allen & S. White – both trainees from school on twelve-month trial. Freelance: D. Brindley. Precision modeller: P. Gerter.

Spode:
Harold Holdway, Roy Trigg (aged 53), Dennis Emery (48), Patrick Howes (28), Gillian West (40), Janet O'Malley (29), David Jackson (freelance), Jack Glover, precision modeller (58) (worked at Spode for 50 years), P. Curtis – apprentice from Worcester school.

The art department of 1959 contained some talented and experienced designers. Harold had been running the department for three years and had had the chance to implement some changes. There was a mixture of formally trained designers and those that had worked their way up through the pottery industry. Roy Trigg, as already mentioned in Harold's memoirs, had been in the design department for nineteen years. He became the deputy to Harold, an expert draughtsperson and pottery artist. He progressed all the suggestions of Harold, Copeland and Thompson and other agents. He was very talented as a designer and craftsman. He sat with Joe Austin and Eddie Sutton in Harold's old office. Roy retired on 1st April 1990.

Dennis Emery had started four years after Roy in 1944. He too was a qualified pottery artist and an excellent draughtsperson and drew out patterns for processes and production. Dennis was good at designing the centres for scenic plates. He loved painting ships and asked Robert Copeland if he could have four coasters on which to paint different ships. Robert took a fancy to them, considering they would sell well. The four ships were engraved and produced as giftware. This gave George Thompson the idea to produce a similar pattern to the Chinese using American ships, as there was a demand for historical tableware. Robert Copeland insisted that at least one of the fifteen ships was British and came up with the name Trade Winds. Harold helped with the research, photographing ships at Greenwich; whilst Dennis produced the final design that Frank Boothby engraved. It was first printed in iron red and then later produced in blue only. Trade Winds, produced on stone china Lowestoft shape, sold well.

Cyril Ball was another ceramic artist who had worked his way up through the factory. He started as a Billingsley Rose painter in July 1946 after being locally trained and was employed with Spode until 1959. He became a No. 1 pottery artist who concentrated on crest work, monograms, lettering etc, general contract work and was able to work out any type of design for full-time production. Harold described him in his reference: "He is a man of good character and great ability. His talents as a free-hand painter of natural subjects could not be surpassed by any living ceramic artist and examples of his work give pride and pleasure to all who are in the good fortune to possess them. His ability as a draughtsman is excellent and he has carried out many complete design projects for full production."

A quick mention of Michael Mickleovski should be made, even though it appears, according to Harold's list, that he had left by 1959. Michael was a displaced Lithuanian artist who was recommended to Arthur Hewitt in 1946 by the camp commandant. His background was that he was a noted portrait and figure painter in his own country. He spoke very little English but Harold agreed to give him a trial and he turned out to be a very valuable member of the design staff. He was noted for his central floral designs, such as the Rembrandt pattern. His best work was the composition of the botanical drawing for the Lady Blessington pattern. Despite his talent, his wife, a transferrer, thought the job of ceramic artist was a 'sissy' job for a man and made him leave for a manual job.

Harold watching Frank Boothby engrave his loving cup design for HM Queen Elizabeth II's Silver Wedding Anniversary. Right: detail of Prince Philip.

Clockwise from top left: Lady Blessington, dish designed by Michael Mickleovski; plate by HH; prototype Walpole teapot painted by Cyril Ball, border design from pattern book, 1950; eagle in the kiln designed by Tony Green; Charles Dickens engraved by Frank Boothby; Christmas plate, designed by Gillian West, 1970.

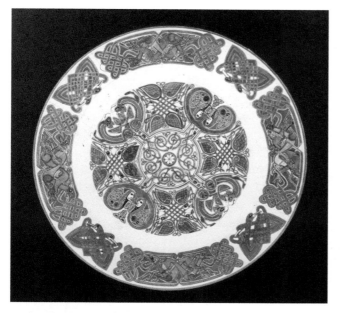

Clockwise from top left: David Jackson's design work for the Lindisfarne plate; the hand-painted Celtic plate HH designed for the Dunedin Society in Edinburgh and Glasgow, courtesy of Spode Museum Trust; a border motif from the Kells plate designed by David Jackson; and the Iona plate designed by Chistopher Boulton.

In May 1960 Harold wrote a description of the inspiration
behind David Jackson's St Chad plate.

In the centre we see the fish symbol, which in pagan times was used as the symbol of "all knowledge past and future." This motif was also used to symbolise Christianity because the first letters of the words "Jesus Christ, Son of God, saviour" in the Greek language spell 'fish'. Superimposed on the fishes are the four letters PACE in Celtic style, meaning peace in Latin. Also included is the three dot sign used frequently by the ancients to indicate respect or holiness on figures used in decorations. The fishes, pointing to the corners of the globe, are enclosed in the centre pattern of knots representing the problems of life on Earth, which are interlaced with four demons, representing the problems of life and temptation.

All these motifs are enclosed in a circle, which has long stood as a symbol of eternity. This centrepiece is a stylised Celtic or Pictish stone cross. In the four arms are placed the pictorial representations (adapted from the Book of Kells) of the four Evangelists. The winged man represents Matthew, the lion Mark, the calf – Luke, and the eagle – John, depicting Christianity being carried to the four corners of the Earth. The panels in which they rest are interwoven with the centre motif to indicate the unity of man and his spirit in everyday life, in conjunction with the animal world of the sea, land and air, as depicted by the birds and beasts enclosing the figures, and in the plaited decoration of the border.

To modern eyes the motifs will appear quaint or grotesque, but in ancient times artists were not allowed to illustrate nature literally.

Another member of the design department of note was Frank Boothby, a very talented engraver who joined the design department soon after it moved into the new studio. Engravers are not usually part of the design team but when Frank was made head of the engraving department, he could not cope with the pressures of organising the team and handed in his notice after three months. He said he was an engraver at heart and that is all he wanted to do; as a manager he no longer had enough time to engrave. It is often a mistake that when a talented person is promoted they end up not doing what they are best at. Harold was shocked and quickly offered him a place in the design department working on design development.

Frank was very happy in his new role as he was able to finish his engravings to perfection without the production line pressures. Some of his best work includes the portrait of Charles Dickens. He also re-engraved part of the Italian blue and white pattern which he did so well that it put the rest of the pieces to shame. The result was that some of the range of Italian had to be re-engraved to match. Miss Bettany recalls that Frank Boothby was the last person on the factory to raise his hat to her. Frank worked for fifty years at Spode, which duplicated his father's record at the firm. Harold and Paul Wood had wanted to mount an exhibition in Frank's memory at the museum after he had died as he considered him to be a very talented craftsman.

Christopher Boulton's work is probably some of the most recognizable design work of the department. He was trained at the Burslem School of Art. He was noted for his special edition Celtic plates, which were very popular. Harold had designed a one-off hand-painted Celtic plate for an exhibition at the Dunedin Society in Edinburgh and Glasgow, which he had displayed behind his desk. Robert Copeland, sales director, saw the bone china plate and thought that the Celtic art would sell and so Chris Boulton was asked to research and design what came to be known as the Iona plate. Harold was always interested in Celtic art and enjoyed helping with the research. He and Robert Copeland visited George Baine, the leading expert on Celtic design to discuss the idea. Harold, Robert Copeland, Eric Harris and Chris Boulton had the "tremendous privilege" of being able to privately view one of the Gospels of the Book of Kells when it was exhibited at the Royal College of Art. Harold really enjoyed that experience. The Iona plate was produced in print and paint and was engraved by Frank Boothby. This was the only Celtic plate to be print and painted, the rest were silk-screened. As can be seen by the chart in an internal memo from Robert Copeland, it was a good seller.

Special Plates in Bone China between 1958–1964

	Total Dozens	Total value at 1964 base price
Iona Plate	418	£34, 600
Passover Plate	228	6, 384
Days of Atonement	23	644

The recommendation was that another Celtic plate be designed called The Kells Plate. In total seven Celtic plates were produced, some of which David Jackson produced. The ten-inch bone china plates were very useful to the company as the design had the advantage of covering any slight faults on the body of the plates. Carborundum made the mistake of revising the Celtic plates on a cook plate with a gold band. The cheaper version did not sell well.

If there were any suitable candidates at the top art colleges Harold would approach them with the chance to work at Spode. One such time was when Harold visited the Royal College of Art in March 1957 when Harold noted: "Partridge: good draughtsman, Young: has creative ability," which resulted in Roger Young gaining a job at Spode. Professor Baker of the Royal College of Art (RCA) had close links with Harold. After a successful career at the RCA, he resigned and became the art director of Royal Worcester. His successor at the RCA was David Queensberry who completely changed Baker's policy of design training and the standard of graduates' work declined so much that Harold did not appoint any of the graduates to augment Spode's design team. When Professor Baker resigned from Royal Worcester in 1971, Michael Kitt took on the post on Harold's recommendation in July 1973.

Michael Kitt trained at the School of Ceramics at the Royal College of Art before spending five years as a designer at Spode. Mike and David Jackson first met Harold when he and Spencer Copeland visited the Royal College of Art in 1959. Mike valued his time at Spode: "I enjoyed designing at W.T. Copeland and Sons and it was an important opportunity in my career to work with the skilled craftsmen and women in every department of the factory and to learn how to interpret their capabilities into new designs." Mike thought Harold saw himself as a father figure of the family-managed company. Mike remembers, "Harold loved to debate the topic of the day and would emerge from his office/studio to join the lads for the 10 o'clock tea break in Roy Trigg's studio. Such topics as loading a dishwasher, as seen in Canada, which he thought was a waste of time, to the demise of car trafficators for the new flashing indicators, which he was very doubtful about, were discussed. He would look out at his gleaming Triumph Herald Vitesse 6-cylinder with pride, parked in a privileged position in The Yard outside, and at the end of every break would say "Well! Back to the grindstone, lads!" Each lunchtime he drove home to his wife who was not enjoying good health. He was obviously a devoted husband and family man." Mike left to become the Industrial Officer for the clay and glass industry with the Council of Industrial Design in London. Some fifteen years later when Mike was design director of Royal Worcester, the Spode and Worcester companies merged and Harold became responsible for all the design departments in the group. He visited Mike once a month to discuss the design programme and would then report back to the board. Mike comments, "Both companies had similar traditions and it appeared to be a compatible marriage at the time, but in reality both operated independently and still do. Harold did not try to create an overall design strategy, combining the strengths of the two teams, which was probably a mistake on his part, and so did not involve himself in the Worcester development programme."

David Jackson trained alongside Mike Kitt at the Royal College of Art and likewise joined Spode in 1959. He was involved in 3D prototype modelling in plaster, pattern work, engraving and gelatine printing. He travelled to Germany, Holland and Italy with design tours organised by the Council of Industrial Design to experience wider fields of modern design. Harold described his work in a reference in 1964: "He was successful in designing new shapes in earthenware together with a wide range of patterns. His designs for the more expensive market were even more successful, including two coffee pots of outstanding merit and his best-selling range of 'Persia' that is still one of our outstanding patterns." Despite Harold wanting to retain David's talents after the success of the St Galls plate, he left Spode to become an art teacher at the Elizabeth Gasket College and was awarded a BA (ed).

The art department continued to evolve through the 1960s. In 1962 the first female designer arrived in Harold's department, Gillian West. She was trained at the local college of art. Her most well-known and popular works are the limited edition dated Christmas plates, although she was not particularly proud of them. From a sales point of view the plates sold very well. The first edition of 15,000 sold out very quickly, therefore Robert Copeland decided to produce 30,000 the next year. Surprisingly, only 15,000 sold, making the first edition the rarest. She has mixed feelings about working at Spode. Although she enjoyed working for Harold, "he was nice to work for", she felt that Spode (outside of the art department) usually did not know what each individual was producing. She did not feel rewarded for her work saying the only person that ever gave her anything was Len Whiter (sales manager) who gave her a nice box of chocolates. Gill liked the new studio and was the only female in the department until Janet O'Malley and Lynne Joyce joined the team and she quite enjoyed the attention. Gill appreciated Harold's background in design and recognised that he had had a thorough training as a designer.

Although Harold was no 'walk-over', he was not an old-style draconian boss. He recognised artistic talent and rated this higher than strict productivity. He felt that Gill's design skills for the Christmas plates were invaluable even though she was notorious for dozing off during her work. He valued her Christmas plates so much that he did not mind whether or not she produced anything else during the year. Another talented artist who was not always a conscientious worker was Tony Green. Between 1968 and 1976 Tony spent many hours making very detailed sculptures of birds and was a talented ornithologist although he did have a reputation of wandering off around the factory. In 1975 he designed a Golden Eagle, the first of a new group of bird studies. Only twenty-five were made and were sold for £3,600 each.

The gates had been opened to women designers and Janet and Lynne soon followed in Gill's footsteps. The new posts were to replace John Ball and David Walsh who had recently left. Spode was the first opening for Janet once she had left Art College and it proved to be a "very enjoyable good start." Janet and Lynne did not apply to Spode at first as they had heard that Harold only wanted men; however, both got the job. Harold came up to the college to view their work but was a bit reluctant at first about employing women as there was no maternity leave so women left if they wanted a family. Janet appreciated being given the opportunity to spend time developing work and felt that she learned more at Spode than she did at college. She felt that she produced some good designs. Janet enjoyed being given the opportunity to become involved with shape work. "You could lock yourself away in the modelling room and carve away at plaster." Janet worked on developing new shapes that were based on the old Spode designs. Floral designs were her favourite work and her first pattern at Spode was Cottage Flowers. Janet enjoyed Harold's emphasis on traditional values and quality. She felt he was "a boss in the old style" as she did not see him design much; he was mostly in his office, supervising or researching, occasionally doing heraldry or commemorative work with Roy Trigg.

Lynne is still working for Spode (2006) but thinks Harold was the best boss she has ever had. He did not keep himself aloof and was friendly and approachable. He was always willing to help his young designers and give them advice. Lynne said he would support them and 'stick up' for them around the factory as they were part of his department. Harold was not restrictive and would always let them try out different media and let them develop their own ideas. Some pattern work was tedious and repetitive having to draw it out for all the different shapes, therefore Lynne enjoyed one of her early projects, a series of fish presentation plates. Although before she did not know one fish from another, she enjoyed the research. Dennis Emery painted them up afterwards. Lynne remembers Harold bringing in a telescope one day as there was a hawk nesting on the Spode chimney. She recalls he was always laughing.

Janet experienced many different art departments and ways of working, at Spode and other factories. She felt "the Americans (Carborundum) were awful" as they had a very different way of working, they wanted her to have a rationale behind everything. She did not mind working for Harold's successor, Paul Wood because at least she could talk to him but his successor was terrible as she was given very vague design briefs. Janet left to have her first child but continued freelance for Spode and had three designs accepted. Janet also worked for Doulton's "very poor quality-only interested in price" and Wedgwood's, "awful way of design, design by committee". Now, she works as a freelance designer for a Portuguese company, which is very like Spode with its emphasis on tradition and quality but gives the space for new designs. However, Janet maintains that she is a "Spode women through and through and that if you chopped my arm off it would still say Spode through it."

Perhaps the most successful careerist of present day Spode is Paul Wood who spent some of his time in Harold's art department. Paul Wood has a lot to thank Harold for in his remarkable passage up the ranks of the Spode factory from apprentice to managing director. Like Harold, Paul had very humble beginnings in Fenton and received very little education, leaving school aged 15. He liked art and attended Longton and Burslem Art Schools. His mother, a lithographic supervisor, got him a job at Spode as an apprentice engraver. Paul commented, (*The Sentinel* 23.12.98) "Spode was a peculiar place but I soon settled down. I saw engraving as being the best job in the world and by the time I was 18 I knew I wanted to be the company's design director." However, after two years he was made redundant and went to Cappers, Hanley as a junior darkroom assistant. After fifteen months he returned to Spode as a pattern safe recording artist. "The new job was fascinating, it got me everywhere in the factory recording the Spode patterns, samples and prototypes. I developed even more of a desire to become a designer at Spode. It was the whole creative process I loved."

His first career break was aged twenty when he was selected by the UK sales and marketing director to take part in the company bicentenary exhibitions in the USA and London. He was secretly being trained by the then managing director, Paul Thompson, to become the next manager of the design studio. "He recognized a talent in me I didn't recognize. I only learned about what he had done years later." From August 1977 Paul Wood was made Spode design studio manager whilst Harold continued his existing design department duties but became a member of the board.

Paul Wood respected Harold's skill and feels that he taught him to only produce quality work as he set a very high standard. Even today, he still uses Harold as a benchmark for quality, wondering whether Spode's modern products would pass his scrutiny. Harold taught Paul what not to do; he learnt by his mistakes. Whilst he was still learning, they shared some designs such as the St Leger horse racing series. Paul jokes that Harold gave him the racing commemoratives, as he did not like drawing horses. Harold used to tell the tale that he tried to work out how to draw a moving horse by running alongside it with a sketchpad, working out where each leg was placed. Before the advance of photography, most horses were depicted standing still as their movement was so hard to capture. Paul tells the amusing tale that he had finished the design for the Red Rum plate and sent the trial to the trainer. It came back with the comment, "It looks fine, except that the horse looks like its been hit up the arse with a shovel!!"

Unlike Mike Kitt, Paul felt that Harold was not really interested in the modern-day art department and that he did not outwardly show much warmth towards them; they were tolerated, including Paul when he was design manager, "I don't think he thought much of me. Harold did not engage much with the department, he was distant, and not someone you could chat to. It was as if he did not know that the modern-day people existed. He was more like a diarist and was very ordered and systematic, always recording details such as the price of gold that he plotted on a graph every week."[11] Paul said, "It was if he was measuring his life in all the detail." Paul thought he was recording and storing his experiences for some purpose, to recall on in the future. He was more interested in the characters of the Copeland era. Although never nasty, he noted people's idiosyncrasies and could mimic people and always had anecdotes to tell. The only thing Paul knew Harold was interested in was cars, as he used to like to show off about them.

Paul Wood produced Harold's retirement bowl using a scene from a plate that Harold had always admired in the Spode museum. Bill Hall painted the finished design based on the Tower of Comares attributed to Daniel Lucas Junior. On the border, groundlaid inside and outside in London stone colour is applied the raised gold design from the Renaissance pattern which Harold designed. Paul believes Harold deserved the work that went into the bowl as he had contributed so much to Spode over the years. He says Spode is "lucky" to still be able to use Harold's most popular designs.

In 1979 Paul Wood took over Harold's job as design director which rather disappointed Roy Trigg who presumed he was the natural successor. Paul describes the period following Harold's retirement as "very scary. Being Number One was very different than being Number Two as there was no one to tell you if you are doing something wrong." Paul kept the department the same for a while and did not change anything radically. Although Paul does not rate his own design skills too highly he claims that you do not have to be a good designer to be a good design manager. Conversely, Harold was not too concerned with the management side of being a director, although he did enjoy the prestige of the post. It was unusual for a designer to be on the board of directors, but the factory adapted to the different strengths and weaknesses of individuals at different times. In 1988 Spode was taken into private ownership and Paul was offered the job as managing director after being trained by Paul Thompson in business skills. Paul Wood stabilised the business, not taking a romantic view of history but using it to his advantage. Harold was pleased that, after years of mismanagement by people who did not know the pottery industry, Paul Wood, one of his own men, became the manager.

Left to right: Tony Green, Paul Wood, John Ball and Dennis Emery.

Tony Green (back) with Derek Johnson, caster/mould maker.

[11] The price of gold affected the cost of transfers, especially the commemoratives that used a lot of gold. Harold would then order the transfers when the price was low.

THE AMERICAN MARKET

Spode has had strong connections with America for a considerable length of time and still maintains strong trading links. In 1970, 76% of Spode was for the export market with half of that going to America and Canada. As Paul Wood says, the Americans have largely led the demand for new patterns, and still do today. He believed Harold enjoyed having the Americans suggesting what to do as he did not fully engage in modern design and was not too interested in setting the design brief. In a rather formal sounding design report of March 1978, Harold said, "I look forward to the forthcoming visit of our North American management team. The necessity for a carefully planned campaign to give them the 'tools' to do a good marketing job is of paramount importance. I feel there is a certain lack of communication that should be improved. It is the earnest desire of the design staff to give all help possible to solve our difficulties in the New World market place."

In 1923, Ronald Copeland decided that he wanted to expand American and Canadian trading links, therefore he appointed Sydney Thompson as Copeland's sole agent in America and W.A. Duncan in Canada. The two new trading companies were called Copeland and Thompson Inc., New York; and Copeland and Duncan, Toronto. Each year the American agents along with Thomas Goode and Daniels of London would visit the factory to discuss patterns for the coming year. George Thompson, Sydney's son and a firm friend of Harold's, defined what was wanted.

Jane Dennis decorating a Gainsborough teapot.

However, Robert Copeland, then sales director, does not believe all American design decisions were successful. George Thompson stubbornly would not accept any designs that were not hand-engraved which was a pity as none of the new designs using silk screens could be used for the American market. He was intransigent and was unwilling to accept the new designs from Spode. For example, since George Thompson did not like RCA shape, he demanded that Summerfield pattern, 1964, a spiralling floral pattern designed for the slender RCA shape, be used on the more traditional Cottage and Regimental shapes. The result was that the pattern did not suit the shape and it did not sell.

In the 1960s George Thompson had asked for a traditional scene design similar to Johnson's Friendly Village, which was selling very well. The result was Fair Haven designed by an American girl and engraved by Jack Longmore. The Americans have always preferred a scene in the centre of the plate, as they are more decorative, whereas the English would rather have just a border as it is maintained that the food on the plate is the centrepiece.

One traditional pattern that did do well in America was Gainsborough. According to Harold, it had very good decoration. It was a traditional design of English flowers in a spray in the centre of the plate. Jane Dennis, an attractive paintress, was photographed with it and it was displayed as an incentive, showing British industry throughout the UK after World War Two.

When Carborundum took over, they wanted a new shape, but not RCA. The result after three year's development in 1972 was Harmony shape and the range was called Perfect Marriage. The new shape was designed by John Ball and came in nine new patterns, some of which were designed by Harold, David Walsh and Tony Green. It was sold in both America and Britain, which was unusual, but it was a total flop, hence it was given the nickname, Perfect Divorce. Under the duress of the Americans some good patterns were produced such as Golden Galaxy, which was made up of snowflakes. Since so much of Copeland and Spode's business came from America, it was important to supply their needs because when the American market slumped, it was disastrous for the company.

As art director, it was important for Harold to ensure that the Americans were satisfied with Spode's wares as they commanded most of the market. In September 1959, Harold spent a month touring the USA and Canada. On his return, he produced a report that I have included here, as it is a very enlightening source highlighting the American market of Spode.

Report on Visit to USA September 1959 by Harold Holdway.

The main object of my trip was to judge at first hand the design trends, and requirements of the USA market. To accomplish this end my itinerary was arranged to cover as wide a field as possible, including the study of present trends in design, the types of stores, gift shops, jewellers, etc. where our goods are sold, the reactions of merchandise managers, buyers, and sales people, what advantages our competitors have if any!!! Also, the type of design recommended by leading interior decorators, who have such a tremendous influence with the buying public.

I could register only surprise at meeting such a large and efficient staff, handling our goods in New York. This was followed by a meeting with all the salesmen who were preparing their autumn programme. At our first meeting in the showroom I was a target for many queries. The outcome of which proved that Copeland and Thompson have a very strong sales force indeed. Their knowledge of the product is really excellent. They are proud to represent such a great factory and hold the firm conviction that Spode is just unbeatable. They all have long-established service with the firm of Copeland and Thompson, which is in itself quite unusual. This is due to the USA Company and the product having great stability.

Many of the other manufacturers have difficulty in retaining representatives, because of bad services, unkept promises, constant changes in policy by present companies overseas and at home. Our representatives sometimes worry what the factory at home will do next and I must admit that some of our actions here in England do seem a little strange. Some of the points raised were as follows:

- That the standard and quality of our goods must be first class. The price of Spode is really EXPENSIVE.
- Promises of delivery must be kept.
- American markets insist on a flat type rim for plates. In recent years several of our earthenware shapes have a soup plate look. This must be corrected!!! (Since my return I have checked carefully and this complaint is justified).

Stone china is one of the most sought after products in the USA. Improvements in the delivery of blue prints was noted, but the delivery of on-glaze decorations is very bad indeed. So much so that when a representative calls on a customer who has not had delivery, he most certainly does NOT get a repeat order.

The stone china Lowestoft style, shape, and patterns could quite easily be copied by other manufacturers and because the shape is a pure reproduction we could not object in any way. So far no one else is producing anything in this field and the customers are more than patient.

The glaze surface of our earthenware is quite often pitted, particularly with on-glaze decoration; if this could be improved it would be most helpful to sales. Later on during my stay I personally examined turnouts rejected by warehouse staff and customers. Glost nips, fire cracks, dirty colours, tarnishing of gold, etc. to name just a few. These complaints were justified. This indeed must be quite a small percentage of goods sent to the USA but every effort must be made at the factory to ensure good selection.

On the credit side, America is full of praise for our delivery of stock patterns, both earthenware and china. The bringing forward of delivery dates and dispatch of goods will help to overcome the delays caused by the dock strike now in force. The quality of our china and earthenware is still rated high. Great play is made by salesmen on whiteness of the china body, durability, freedom from crazing (products of recent years have been very good in this respect), sparkling glaze, brightness of underglaze colours, etc.

Buyer and customer reaction to Spode: New York

On visits to the large stores Altman, Gimbels, Macys, I was very well received by merchandise managers and buyers. The attitude to Spode is one of great respect. Quite a good number of our best traditional patterns are on display in each of the above stores, but space allotted is comparatively small. This is due to the tremendous range of goods they have to show from all the other pottery manufacturers of the world. America, Japan, Britain and all the leading European pottery manufacturers are prominently shown and English goods on display by comparison are relatively small. The goods in the pottery section virtually have to sell themselves, but the firms who are prepared to advertise on a large scale and co-operate in promotion deals do have a distinct advantage.

The sales girls are paid on a commission basis and

A design meeting with John, Gordon, Tom, Harold, Barlow, Mrs Caudwell and Harry Walles discussing RCA shape and the bridal range.

Design work and prototypes of patterns for the bridal market laid out for the American design meeting.

they just do not have the time to spend explaining the advantages of possessing high-priced quality goods from Britain. Doulton's have done well with their low-priced china decorations, particularly with the young brides who in the past would have bought earthenware but now can afford something a little more expensive. The Lenox china is a number one choice and have a very fine large display in the above stores. The quality of their china is perfect and absolutely free from blemishes and faulty potting etc. They have a large range of different designs, very refined in style, both shape and pattern, and have great appeal. When a pattern, loses popularity they do not hesitate to withdraw it, and in consequence it becomes difficult to match and replace. This is the one snag of Lenox type sales promotion and is often criticised.

Wedgwood and Worcester are represented in the large stores, also Derby. Wedgwood's plain Edme shape and other embossed earthenware patterns are great favourites. Their china patterns are all traditional in style and have an appeal similar to Spode. Where litho and silk-screen methods are used they are cheaper. Jasper fancies with variations still sell well, but the terracotta embossed range is being sold off at cut price.

Doulton earthenware patterns and shapes, because of their modern styling, are rarely seen. Worcester sells their modern china shape, Snow, at 12 dollars per place setting. Wedgwood's have now entered this field with all white china at 13 dollars. They also have an additional gold or platinum line at a very low price. How it is done for the price one can hardly imagine. The Japanese are now a force of great magnitude

Harmony shape designed for the bridal market.

Spode's designs for the American market were mostly traditional. This advertising photo shows Camilla, Blenheim, Italian, Chatham and Maritime Rose.

and using all the modern methods of decoration they are producing some very beautiful services. The American buying public do not worry much about the source of origin providing the article is of good quality and the price reasonable. Large quantities of foreign wares are sold and it is big business.

Germany is also in the above field represented by Rosenthal, Heinrich, and many others. They cater mainly for the contemporary minded customer but have lately started to introduce more traditional shapes and patterns. All their products are much cheaper than Spode, once again ideal for departmental stores who insist upon a large turnover with speedy profits. The personal touch is completely lacking in department store business and a buyer who does not choose ware that finds a ready sale is very quickly replaced. Johnson Brothers have a fine range of patterns and sell great quantities of earthenware at a very low price indeed. In consequence their goods are in great demand.

Visiting the shops of Tiffany's, Plummers and Black, Starr and Gorham, one sees a very different picture. Here Spode, Wedgwood and all high-class manufacturers have a real chance to show what can be done in the field of quality. Only the best is good enough for their customers and in consequence Spode ranks very high. The display of pottery is very artistic and table settings complete with silver and glassware etc. show off the ware to great advantage. The sales staff have intimate knowledge of each individual firm's wares and give British goods extremely high praise. This may be snob appeal but it certainly pays big dividends.

A trip with Mr John Carlin by road presented a wonderful opportunity to visit some of our customers in the New Jersey area. The cordial and enthusiastic reception accorded to us was very encouraging. They were very pleased to meet one from the Old Country and proffered many suggestions and ideas to help increase the sale of Spode. Once again the display of our wares was excellent even in the smallest of gift shops and we more than hold out own against all opposition. The jewellery shop of Mr Ralph Fava in Patterson, New Jersey (pop. 140,000) was certainly an eye opener. We certainly are well represented here and do a fine business.

A trip to Atlantic City to visit the shop of Mr Reese Palley was well worth the long journey by road. I had a lengthy discussion with Mr Palley who had many very good suggestions to offer. He was most enthusiastic over the new Derby patterns but Doulton modern earthenware patterns were being sold off at cut prices. He had a large display of Spode earthenware and china patterns shown with great taste.

A visit to the new large Lenox factory was attempted but no visitors are allowed to view the processes, which would have been most interesting. However, the showroom with all their current productions was of the greatest interest. As I have mentioned previously their tableware and fancy items are really smart. I have nothing but praise for their fine organisation and one can understand why they are so successful, particularly in the modern style of decoration, but carried out with restraint and good taste.

A journey accompanied by Mr Bill Craig Junior with the intention of visiting the Stangle earthenware factory and the small firms who produce the famous Boehm birds and figures was only partially successful.

A promotional sweet dish for a Canadian retailer.

The Stangle products we were able to view at their old factory that is now used to sell slightly substandard ware, but also has a complete display of their products currently on sale. The quality was very poor indeed with bold and very crude designs done by hand. It has, however, a popularity because of its low prices. Indeed it is good value and does fit in to schemes demanding less formality i.e. kitchen and barbecue wares. The small factory at Boehm was visited but, once again, owing to a burglary, and the illness of Mr Boehm it was not possible to see any processes. However Mrs Boehm gave a lot of her time, showing us the wonderful range of bird figures etc., which vie to some extent with the Worcester Doughty range, and are very artistic indeed, often demanding very high prices.

The visit to Philadelphia with Mr George Thompson was of great interest and a day was spent visiting the shops of Grace Lloyd Collins (Mrs Walsh) at Wilmington and Fairfax. Miss Collins is a person of excellent taste, which is reflected in her choice of the wares offered to her customers. The Spode name is very high in her estimation and her sales of our products increase each year. She made many helpful suggestions and hopes to increase still more the sale of our fine goods.

A visit to Ardmore to see Mr and Mrs Gilman was also of great interest. I was able to answer many queries concerning Spode productions and in turn received still more suggestions which were most constructive.

Philadelphia itself is a very fine city indeed with many fine buildings, stores, and superior shops etc. We visited the stores of John Wanamaker, Bailey Banks & Biddle and the fine jewellery store of J.C. Caldwell who all have a fine selection of Spode. Wanamakers were holding a very fine exhibition of Wedgwood productions, which was really extensive and created a lot of interest in New York. Everyone of note was represented but the firms who are willing to enter promotion deals and mass advertising certainly do big business.

Whilst in New York I took the opportunity to visit the Pratt Institute. I was welcomed by Associate Professor Mr Kostellon of the School of Industrial Design. I spent the whole afternoon making a tour of the design section, which was most enlightening.

The type of training was really quite advanced and there is certainly nothing to compare in England. Some of the work was almost inspired and methods of training quite unique. Altogether a very exhilarating experience and certainly gives one food for thought.

Another artistic visit of importance was to the Parsons School of Design. The outlook here was far more restrained and easier to understand and similar to the Royal College of Art type of training in London. Nevertheless many highly skilled men and women have passed through this school and have met with great success. America certainly does not lag behind in the training of future designers; I was most impressed!!!.'

A memorable occasion was the invitation to have lunch with the editor of *House Beautiful* together with the *House Furnishing* editor. This meeting was arranged by Mr Bob Inman who accompanied me. It was a wonderful experience and I derived great benefit from the stimulating views and trends forecast by such great authorities.

During my trip I was able to make a flying visit to Toronto to see the Great Canadian National Exhibition. The stand featuring Spode products was a centre of great attraction and Ian Davey, Byron Gohn, and the staff of Copeland and Duncan must be congratulated on putting up such a fine show.

The Canadian showroom display of Spode is very good and attracts many buyers. I visited the store of Eatons who carry a large number of our patterns and do a very good business. The taste of the Canadian buying public is subtly different from USA and many more English factories find a ready sale. The Longton firms are well represented and are responsible for quite substantial sales.

My stay in Canada was all too brief and I feel it would not be wise without more research to offer any criticism whatever. From what I saw Copeland and Duncan seems to be very well organised and ably led by Ian Davey and Byron Gohn.

Design

The policy of continuing with the production of traditional designs has certainly been very wise. The customer seeking British goods does not expect continental or contemporary designs from a country of such great tradition, i.e. the RCA shape is not considered to be Spode.

The designs we worked out earlier in the year were thoroughly sifted and a number of them should be considered for future development. The USA office will not commit themselves completely by saying which of the designs will be winners and possibly small sample ranges might be market tested. Many suggestions were made to me by our salesmen and buyers and I hope in the near future to make full use of this knowledge.

The future of Spode sales in the USA and Canada is indeed very optimistic and whilst we are at the top, only hard work and good service will keep us there.

Whilst Harold was enjoying many new and exciting experiences in America his wife and son were left at home preparing to move into the family bungalow the following month. In a series of touching letters, his wife Betty wrote, "I suppose by now the USA is beginning to feel like a second home?" "What a country America must be and how well you are being treated! – My! What a comeback to smokey old Stoke."

In November 1966, Harold returned, with Spencer Copeland, to America and Canada for a further two weeks. It was the first trip after the takeover by Carborundum. They were mainly visiting stores that sold Spode, looking at their accounts and visiting various trade shows.

When Carborundum took over Spode in 1966, the links with America were even stronger. Paul Wood feels that they did not do much to develop the factory directly apart from silly grand designs. They pursued massive advertising campaigns in America, creating a huge demand that the company could not meet. They invested a lot of money promoting the 1970 bicentenary and the mini Spode Niagara Falls factory. By creating the demand, they actually altered the factory. In December 1967, George Thompson of Copeland and Thompson, W.T. Copeland and Sons' American counterpart, resigned and a new company took over and was known as Spode Inc. George Barker from Stoke became head of the new business.

COMMEMORATIVES

During Harold's later years at Spode he became renowned for his detailed commemorative designs. He used to enjoy carefully researching his subjects, whether visiting cathedrals all over the country, liaising with royalty, or meeting generals at their barracks. Designing commemoratives gave him many enjoyable opportunities to leave the studio and travel over the country recording potential inspiration with his beloved camera. He was very meticulous with his research and used to spend a considerable amount of time on it. He would incorporate selected features from a particular abbey or building such as the heraldry, stone or woodcarving or ceiling bosses to use as ornamentation. Harold's commemorative works were not like the usual souvenirs, as Douglas Hawley (sales manager) said: "These plates were more outstanding than the 'scenes' that were generally produced by other factories."

Paul Wood, a designer in Harold's department, who rose to managing director, believes the success of the commemoratives was due to three factors: one, Harold was brilliant at heraldry and had excellent graphic skills; two, Len Whiter was excellent at selling and promoting the finished designs; and three, the Spode factory could easily produce a surplus of ten-inch plates which were ideal for commemoratives. Despite the slight decrease in Spode's limited edition market in the late 1970s due to growing competition from other factories, Harold's designs were still a rich source of income.

Paul Wood noted that Harold enjoyed the commemorative commissions as they were interesting projects, not mundane and were one-offs so they did not have to be repeated. Harold liked the prestige of meeting important people and all the pomp and ceremony that accompanied the commemoratives which appealed to Harold's ego. Harold demanded perfection in his designs as he said in his design review of 1978: "To be successful, the design has to be just perfect and the event or occasion of sufficient importance to justify the work involvement and cost." I believe the commemorative designs were some of Harold's most satisfying and rewarding work at Spode.

Gordon Hewitt, then foreign sales director, initiated Harold's successful run of commemorative designs for Spode. In 1965 Gordon's son, a chorister at Westminster Abbey, told his father of the impending 900th anniversary celebrations and that the abbey were looking to produce high-quality souvenirs to mark the event. Spode submitted Harold's St Edward design that was successful. Harold was delighted to mark such a significant and prestigious event.

Following a research and photography trip to the abbey, Harold used the west side of the abbey choir screen, which had been redesigned by Blore in 1831, as the basis for the border of his Westminster Abbey Plate and St Edward's plate. Harold was lucky in that he recalled that there was a copper plate in the factory archives, engraved in the 1830s, which used

Left: Limited edition St Edward plate to celebrate Westminster Abbey's 900th anniversary. Right: Westminster Abbey plate.

Some of Holdway's Commemorative Designs

Cathedrals

Westminster Abbey	1965
St Edward plate (Westminster)	1965
Selby	1969
Tewkesbury	1971
York	1972
Ripon	1972
Coventry	1972
Lichfield	1972
St Pauls	1973
Ely	1973
Salisbury	1974
Chichester	1975
Hereford	1976
St Albans	1977
St David's	1981

Regiments

Royal Regiment of Artillery	1966
Royal Air Force	1968
Duke of Wellington's	1973
Cheshire	1973
Green Howards	1973
Gloucestershire	1974
Parachute	1974
The Royal Welsh Fusiliers	1974
King's Own Scottish Borderers	1975
The Black Watch	1975
Royal Navy Submarine Service	1976
The Gordon Highlanders	1977
Argyll and Sutherland Highlanders	1977
The Royal Scots	1978
Royal Hampshire	1978

Top: The Royal Welsh Fusiliers.
Centre: St George.
Above: Design work for the City of London plate.
Left: A children's set made for Prince Charles, 1961.

Other

Churchill (plate and goblet)	1965
England (St George)	1965
Prince of Wales Investiture	1969
First National City Bank	1969
Cutty Sark	1969
Charles Dickens	1970
Mayflower	1970
Imperial Plate of Persia	1971
St Leger (with Paul Wood)	1971, 1972, 1973
Royal Silver Wedding loving cup	1972
Preston Guild vase	1972
European Community	1973
Royal Canadian Mounted Police	1973
Bristol Charter	1973
Order of Bath	1975
London Metropolitan Borough	1976
Wimbledon Centenary	1977
Silver Jubilee	1977
St John Ambulance	1977
Silver Jubilee loving cup	1977
Royal Rotary of Croydon, Australia	1980

Non Spode

(MH = Mulberry Hall Bone China)

St Peter's School (MH)	1977
Silver Jubilee ER beakers and mug (MH)	1977
Silver Jubilee plate – (Minton)	1977
Heraldic Beasts – (Minton)	1977
Winchester Cathedral plate, mug, thimble (MH)	1979
Marlborough College (MH)	1979
Charterhouse (MH)	1979
Queen Mother plate and glass goblet (MH)	1980
Institute of Chartered Accountants plate, mug, thimble (MH)	1981
Charles and Diana's wedding goblet and loving mug (Coalport)	1981
Charles and Diana's wedding (Minton)	1981
Charles and Diana's wedding, heraldic beasts (Minton)	1981
Prince William of Wales' birth (Minton)	1982
Wells Cathedral (MH)	1982
Prince Andrew's Wedding (MH)	1986

Goblet design for Queen Mother's 80th birthday, 1980.

Artwork for Chartered Accountants emblem drawn on the back of a menu. 1981.

Artwork for Prince Charles and Lady Diana's wedding used on the commemorative plate box.

the Blore screen to fit a dinner plate which he used thus saving the engraver approximately eight weeks' work. He fitted into the border three sets of arms of monarchs associated with the Abbey. The border was printed by hand in gold. In the centre was the Royal coat of arms in full heraldic colour by permission of the Queen. The final design, which was approved by Her Majesty The Queen, caused tremendous interest.

The Central Office of Information sent a camera team to the factory to film the plate being made.

An unlimited version of the plate was also produced which was sold in the abbey's bookshop to visitors; this was called the Westminster Abbey plate. The Westminster Abbey plate shares the same Blore-screen border, but instead features the arms of the present collegiate church, the arms of John Islip, the Abbot

Harold designing the Royal Artillery plate from the regimental banner, 1966.

of Westminster from 1500 to 1532, and the arms of the Very Reverend Eric Symes Abbott who was Dean of Westminster from 1959 to 1974. In the centre it has the abbey's great seal, the first time it had been depicted in the abbey's history. The chief modeller, Tom Barlow, was sent to the abbey to make a cast from the silver seal. This was then used as a basis for the engraving of an exact reproduction, which included a grammatical Latin error.

The plates proved to be very successful and received much praise: "...The workmanship is superb, the colours glowing and the staff of your firm who are responsible for the design and manufacture of this plate deserve the highest of praise." ".... Very fitting commemorative items ..... and the Dean and Chapter would like to let you know of their complete satisfaction." The quality of presentation of the two Westminster plates set the standard for further commemorative designs. The Westminster plates were so popular that an American offered £500 for one of the twenty faulty plates produced. However, the plates had to be destroyed and a plate smashing ceremony took place on 11th January 1967 in the Lord Mayor's Parlour, Stoke, in the presence of the press and television.

Gordon Hewitt also provided the connection for the first of the regimental series of commemoratives, the Royal Regiment of Artillery's 250th anniversary in 1966, as he himself had been a gunner. Harold began his search for material in the Royal Artillery Museum, Woolwich, where he was delighted to find

three pieces of ceramic, two of which were produced by the Spode factory. Harold also found an old Artillery drum banner, which bore a fine and unusual representation of the familiar regimental device. The finished design uses in the centre the device, badge and motto of the regiment and incorporates a victor's wreath of laurel and oak.

It was essential to receive approval for the design from the Queen, the regiment's Captain-General. Time was short and Her Majesty was away on tour in the West Indies. The original artwork was flown to the Caribbean for her approval, which she gave, and was then flown back to England. Work was then able to proceed in time for the prototype plate to be shown to Her Majesty shortly after her return to Britain. Only past and present gunners could purchase a plate at £8.7s. Harold received several letters of praise regarding the plate. "I am delighted with it and do congratulate Mr Holdway on his beautiful artistic work which does great justice to the occasion..... my appreciation of a supreme example of the potter's craft."

Another prestigious celebration that Harold was asked to produce a commemorative plate for was the 1969 Selby Festival. Following the success of the Westminster Abbey plate, Spode was approached to produce a similar plate for the 900th anniversary celebrations. Harold and Leonard Whiter, home sales manager, made several research visits to Selby Abbey, which is rich in carved stonework, but lacks much interior detail. Harold used the cross above the

Selby Abbey's 900th anniversary: design work for coin and the limited edition plate.

chancel screen for the centre of the plate and used some of the many heraldic shields with which Selby's stained glass windows are decorated. These windows proved hard to photograph and Harold had to edge along the narrow gallery above the chancel in order to take detailed photographs. The limited edition of 900 plates soon sold out with over half going to the inhabitants of Selby.

As well as the plate, Harold also designed two coins for the Selby Festival using a similar design. 1,969 silver coins were produced, selling for 8 guineas, and 200 gold coins were sold for export only at 75 guineas each. On one side is the chancel cross, arms of the abbey and town and an inscription 1069–1969 Selby Abbey. The other side features the Royal Arms of King William and his son Henry I, the first King of all England, who was born in Selby. In the centre is a cluster of Yorkshire roses. The inscription around the edge is "William 1st Royal Patron 1070. Visit of Elizabeth II. 3rd April 1969."

The Leonard Whiter, Michael Sinclair and Harold Holdway trio

The commemorative market for Spode really began to take off when Harold, Len Whiter and Michael Sinclair united. The dynamic combination during the 1970s of Harold, the designer; Len, the home sales manager; and Michael, the retailer, of the Mulberry Hall ceramic and glass suppliers of York was an incredibly successful and happy relationship. Not only did the three become firm friends, but also between them they commissioned, designed and sold numerous high-quality designs for Spode.

Leonard Whiter

Len took over responsibility as London sales manager in 1960 and was then promoted to UK sales manager in 1961. Harold was very close to Len; one would not do anything without the other. As Paul Wood says, "It was as if Len woke Harold up again." Len picked

2500th anniversary of the Persian Empire: only the plate on the left was for sale to the public.

138

up on Harold's graphic skills and utilised them to the best advantage, flattering Harold's ego. After Harold became a little despondent with the changes in management after the Copeland's had left, Len "kick-started Harold into action again." Len was a very talented salesman; he found solutions where most would have given up. Despite there being very little tangible evidence to celebrate or remember a salesman by, it is widely recognised that Len played a very important role in the conception of the many Spode commemoratives. For Harold, as a designer, his works of art will live on and perpetuate his memory.

One prestigious assignment where Len and Harold's perseverance paid off was the Imperial Plate of Persia. The plate celebrates the 2,500th anniversary of the founding of the Persian Empire by Cyrus the Great. A limited edition of 10,000 was made, 2,000 of which were in a special distinctive version for the Imperial Iranian Court. The anniversary is symbolised by representing the contemporary Iranian Empire and the origins of the empire by a border inspired by Achaemenian art. The ground colour, turquoise, is Persia's imperial colour.

The 3,000 miles separating Persia and Stoke meant this design was not easy to produce. The commission came about entirely by chance. Len Whiter was visiting Persia in early 1970 to arrange a loan of the elaborate jewelled service produced by Copeland in 1857, owned by the Shah of Persia, for Spode's forthcoming bicentenary exhibition at the Royal Academy. Whilst in Isfahan it was mentioned in conversation that the following year was a spectacular celebration of the 2,500th anniversary of the founding of the Persian monarchy by Cyrus the Great. Len posed the possibility of Spode producing a commemorative

item for the event. Before his departure back to England, the British Ambassador, Sir Dennis Wright, had arranged a visit for Len to the Court who were most enthusiastic. On his return to Stoke, Len and Harold studied the slides taken during the trip for design potential, especially those of the Friday Mosque, Isfahan, which was richly decorated in dazzling gold and turquoise and had an interesting use of decorative lettering.

Harold produced a design with the help of Mr Pinder Wilson, keeper of Islamic Studies at the British Museum. The border was turquoise with an Arabic inscription taken from a piece of Persian pottery. In the centre was the coat of arms of the Pahlavi dynasty with the winged figure of Ahuramazda at the top. However, the Imperial Court did not like the design. Persia was to celebrate its Achaemenian origins, therefore its Islamic traditions, dating from the Arab invasions of the ninth century, were irrelevant. A letter from Len to Harold whilst in Persia regarding a plate for the Shah shows the lengths that Len would go to get his own way.

"Not much on the Shah's set I'm afraid, where we have encountered Persian bloody-mindedness at its worst. What you are really anxious to hear about is the PLATE and now I can tell you something, its going to be a tough one and very involved but I think it will be worth it. It really started quite badly with a suggestion that we have a picture of Persepolis in the middle of the plate! I shamed him out of that one ("Design for the medium, if you want a picture go to a print shop and buy one!"). The border was a tough one. He is emphatically against any Islamic art focus on the plate: A, because the event being commemorated is pre-Islamic and B, because it looks

Royal Artilllery's 50th anniversary. Left: popular version of the plate, 2500 produced. Right: special version, 60 produced.

Len Whiter, UK sales manager from 1961.

Arabic. (The script we used actually is Arabic I learned…God help us.) …I think he (Mr Alan the BOSS) respected my sticking to my guns quite hard and I am not dissatisfied with my results."

Len had a meeting with Her Imperial Majesty the Shahrimah to get a design brief. She and the Shah were deeply interested in the project. Len enthusiastically ended the letter:

"I am sure that ultimately there will be plenty of money in it for us (i.e. Spode!), oceans of prestige and a good chance to start a trade here in normal goods. ….PS How involved can a simple salesman get?"

Assisted by a guide from the Pahlavi University, Len visited the ancient site of Persepolis to photograph everything that might be of use to the designer. A near disaster happened during the visit as the film became unwound in the camera. Len succeeded in changing the film on his hands and knees in the darkness of an old water chamber some feet underground. The remaining problem was to locate an authentic version of the Pahlavi coat of arms, which was eventually located in one of the lesser royal palaces. Harold's final design features the coat of arms of the Pahlavi dynasty in the centre, with a border inspired by the Achaemenian art of Darius the Great's private palace at Persepolis.

However, in the design, Harold had tried to transform the weakly drawn Persian lions into a nobler English heraldic version, which was frowned upon in Persia. Nevertheless, the design proved to be very successful and proved to be an international

success. There was a great response from Britain, the United States, the West Indies and the entire edition of 10,000 sold out and many orders were turned away. Harold was praised for the Imperial Persian plate: "We would like to congratulate you on your very beautiful design. The border is truly inspired and the execution of the plate is magnificent."

The Imperial Court purchased 2,000 plates, but these were of a slightly different design. Harold admits that he made the mistake of submitting two designs for the Empress's decision, as he could not choose between two different Achaemenian motifs for the border. The court had decided to purchase a quantity of plates to give away to the many important visitors who would be attending the celebrations. It was incomprehensible that these plates be the same design as those that could be readily purchased all over the world and so a happy solution presented itself. The second design uses an Achaemenian palm tree motif for the border that was taken from a ruined staircase at Persepolis. The Imperial Court was delighted with the plate, as was the British Embassy in Tehran for it appeared to be the only involvement of a British firm with the celebrations. A dinner service was produced using the border of this plate for the Shahrimah.

Len went on to form a very successful trading relationship supplying other luxury items for the Shah. He commissioned Harold to design a set of crystal to accompany the Spode set. Two further Far East commissions followed, the Pahlavi plate in 1975 to celebrate the fiftieth anniversary of the Pahlavi dynasty, and a commemorative for the Sultan of Oman in 1976. This commission, which Harold was involved with, was through Asprey's who insisted on sending their own designer, Porteous Wood, to paint the palace, which Spode painters had to faithfully copy by hand.

Michael Sinclair

Michael Sinclair first became involved with Harold's designs for Spode after 1971. Wedgwood had just produced a successful plate featuring a view of York Minster that had sold out whilst being marketed exclusively through Mulberry Hall. Harold had designed a plate for York Minster in 1972, which was being sold through the Minster shop. The plate was struggling to sell so Len Whiter approached Michael and asked if he could have the list of people who had bought the Wedgwood Minster plate. He was told in no uncertain terms certainly not. However, Michael agreed to sell the Spode plate exclusively through

Mulberry Hall, York, part of a commemorative box label.

Mulberry Hall – and so the partnership was born.

At first Len was an intermediary between Harold and Michael but when Michael first met the designer he held an immense respect for him. Miss Bettany, Len's secretary, observed the "enormous rapport of the three relatively young men who were all going somewhere." They would travel together to look at design inspiration and sales opportunities. Harold had a natural ability to find inspiration from almost anything, even when design potential seemed completely bereft. As Michael said, "Even when faced with a real poverty of material, Harold would always come up trumps!" Cathedrals and other organisations would come to Spode with a commission and Len would subsequently come to Michael to discuss the sales issues. Researching the commemorative designs was an enjoyable period for the trio. "Those years with Harold and Len, when we went round most of the cathedrals in the country and to other interesting places and organisations were some of the most satisfying in my business life. The friendship that was formed between the three of us at that time was something special."

The partnership was successful but certain individuals at Spode became suspicious that Mulberry Hall and Spode were too close so Len dutifully tried other outlets but failed. Len became disillusioned with Spode as they were not letting him do as he wanted so he left in November 1966 to take up a new appointment as sales manager of J. Goddard & Sons Ltd, silver polish manufacturers. However, this did not fulfil his expectations and Len soon returned to Spode in 1967 as contracts and commemorative ware sales manager until 1972. He then left Spode to set up his own company, Aurum Designs, with John Sutherland-Hawes, a topographical consultant designer to Spode who had supplied the silver gilt to go alongside the Shah of Persia's service. The company focused on a similar market and also included silver goblets celebrating cathedrals. Len and Michael continued to be partners on glass and ceramics and shared the research and sales costs. Len was also able to supply Harold with further freelance opportunities.

Michael Sinclair remembers Harold as a warm and generous man. He grew to know Harold and his wife Betty more familiarly after Harold's retirement when Michael used to show him design proofs for his opinion. Michael remembers Harold as "one of the most talented and most charming men that I have met. An enormously gifted artist yet at the same time a kind, generous, humble man. Humble people usually are nice, but that quality is rare in someone with so much talent. He was always rightly proud of his work, but never arrogant."

Attention to Detail

Cathedrals

York Minster plate 1972: The commemoration has a dual significance as the Minster celebrated the 500th anniversary of its completion as well as the completion of five years' restoration work in 1972. The imminent danger to the fabric of the Minster became apparent in 1967 when it was reported that the great central tower was likely to collapse within fifteen years. In five years the foundations were replaced, the three towers reinforced, the floor relaid and the new undercroft and treasury constructed.

The cost of the restoration was over £2,000,000. The burden of the responsibility of the work fell on Dean Alan Richardson for which he was knighted. The Dean and his wife showed a great deal of personal interest in the plate and went to a tremendous amount of trouble to ensure that Harold was given the correct brief. The centre of the design is based on the fifteenth-century rose window, which is depicted in gold. The cross of St Cuthbert, the patron saint of the North is also used and is superimposed with a design of Yorkshire roses, a motif that Harold used in several of his designs.

York Minster, plate and goblet (front view). The rear has a picture of the Minster depicted in gold.

Lichfield Cathedral plate and front door. Note the metalwork which is used in the centre of the design.

St Paul's Cathedral plate and lock plate that inspired the centre of the design.

Coventry Cathedral plate.

Ripon Cathedral plate.

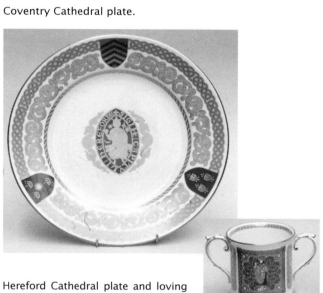

Hereford Cathedral plate and loving cup. Photo courtesy of Robert Copeland.

Royal Air Force plate.

King's Own Scottish Borderers regimental plate. (Robert Copeland)

Green Howards regimental plate.

Lichfield Cathedral 1972: The plate marked the 1,300th anniversary of the death of St Chad. The plate features the arms of the diocese that are depicted in the ornate wrought ironwork on one of the doors. The border contains the arms of three men who played an outstanding part in the successive rebuilding of the cathedral: Bishop Roger de Clinton who constructed the Norman cathedral between 1135 and 1140; Walter de Langton, Bishop from 1296 to 1321 who built the Lady Chapel; and John Hacket who helped to rebuild the war-damaged cathedral in 1662. The centre contains the arms of Lichfield Cathedral. This was the second time Harold had used these arms. As a young man in 1945 he was responsible for designing a large bowl produced for the 750th anniversary of the cathedral.

The Lichfield plate very nearly did not happen. Spode was approached at a fairly late hour, which left little time to research and develop the design. However, since Stoke lies in the diocese of Lichfield and there were strong connections between the cathedral and Spode, they were determined to overcome the problems. The cathedral was raising funds during the anniversary year to help restore the organ which had originally been presented by Josiah Spode IV. Although he was a direct descendent of the founder of the Spode factory he played no role in the business as on the death of his father he was still a minor. He later settled in Armitage in what is now known as Spode House. He had a stained glass window installed in the cathedral in memory of his wife. The certificate was signed by the Bishop of Holderness, Dean of Lichfield who visited the Spode factory to watch potters make the commemorative plates. Harold guided him round the factory.

St Paul's Cathedral 1973: This plate was designed to celebrate the 250th anniversary of the death of the cathedral's architect, Sir Christopher Wren. 2,500 plates were produced exclusively for Harrods, selling for £29.25. In the centre of the plate is the heraldic device of St Paul's, which was obtained from an ornate lock plate in a door leading off the west porch. Surrounding this is a stylized version of the saucer domes of the roof of the nave. This is superimposed on a background of red, symbolising the fire, the inspiration for which was the embroidery of an altar cloth.

Harold felt that the extent of the Victorian ornamentation in St Paul's detracts from the simplicity that Wren intended and he searched for some of the original decoration to use on the plate. He used the guilloche carving behind the west end of the nave that had escaped embellishment as it was out of sight.

The phoenix is an important symbol associated with St Paul's as the cathedral had suffered from extensive fire damage at least three times. Harold considered it essential that it should appear on the design but he searched the cathedral for a carved phoenix without success and so he sat outside in the sun contemplating his design. On returning to the factory he discovered that the phoenix installed by Wren was above the south door and that he had been sitting directly beneath it. The raised or modelled gold used in the designs since the Selby Abbey plate greatly increased the gold content of each plate, particularly so in the case of St Paul's. In the months prior to production the rapid escalation in the international price of gold added considerably to its cost and was the subject of anxious study of the *Financial Times* each day.

Coventry Cathedral 1972: The design for this plate is very different from the other cathedral plates. Spode was approached in 1970 with a view to commemorating the tenth anniversary of the new cathedral at Coventry. The decision to accept the commission was carefully considered because the anniversary was of a relatively short time. Harold was delighted at the decision to proceed as it gave him the chance to produce a design in complete contrast to his usual work. Harold was an ardent admirer of the modern cathedral which was rebuilt in 1962 following its destruction during World War Two. The strong Christian motifs impressed Harold, especially the Chapel of Christ in Gethsemene and in particular the mosaic portraying the angel that appeared to Christ in the Garden of Gethsemene. The iron screen of the Crown of Thorns framed the mosaic in a way that immediately suggested the design for the plate. The inscription, which surrounds the plate, is taken from one of the eight stone tablets in the nave.

Ripon Cathedral 1972: The plate commemorates the dedication on St. Peter's Day AD 672 by St Wilfred of Ripon Church. The Diocese of Ripon was not formed until 1836 even though some of the architecture of the cathedral dates back to the thirteenth century. Harold was inspired by the central feature of Ripon Cathedral, the seal of King James I who re-established the charter of 1604 and restored the revenues confiscated from Ripon in 1547. The Dean and Chapter agreed that the seal should have centre place, as without the seal, the cathedral would not be in existence today. The seal was badly worn and required careful examination and the help of a rare book on seals to confirm the correct wording. Harold was also impressed with the set of thirteenth-century stone bosses and was determined to use them. However, they were eighty feet up in the ceiling of the choir, the detail hardly discernable. He returned specially to Ripon, armed with a new expensive telephoto lens, and photographed the ceiling whilst lying on the floor.

Hereford Cathedral 1976: This commemorative plate celebrating the 1,300th anniversary of the founding of the Diocese, depicts St Ethlebert in the centre. The saint was Hereford's martyr and one of the cathedral's patron saints. The Bishop of Hereford, on behalf of the Queen, accepted the first edition of 679. It received a glowing review in *Tableware International*: "That doyen of Staffordshire art directors, Harold Holdway, has produced another of his delightful and successful commemorative pieces.....Mulberry Hall of York, which seems to have established a virtual monopoly of commemorative wares from several factories has been appointed official distributors."

Regiments

Royal Air Force 1968: An early regimental plate, which celebrates the 50th anniversary of the forming of the Royal Air Force. The badge of the Royal Air Force is depicted in the centre with the three badges of the organisations that can claim its parentage: the Royal Engineers who took the first step in 1911 when they formed an Air Battalion; the Royal Flying Corps; and the Royal Naval Air Service whose men and machines joined together in April 1918 to form the Royal Air Force. The linking motif of rose, thistle, shamrock and leek is inspired by the border used on all squadron standards since 1953.

The King's Own Scottish Borderers: Harold designed a series of twelve commemorative plates featuring each of the British unamalgamated infantry regiments. The King's Own Scottish Borderers plate has at the top the regiment's 'Dog and Bonnet', the Royal Crown surmounted by a lion with the regiment's motto. Surrounding this in the border is a band of the Borderer's dicing, distinguished by its inclusion of green in addition to the customary red and white. Eight of the hard-won battles are designated on the dicing. Harold was pleased when he received feedback on his designs. One such letter of approval came from Major R.G.R. Hill of the King's Own Scottish Borderers: "I have now seen and fallen in love with The King's Own Scottish Borderers Plate! All the plates in the series to date have been superb but ours is truly outstanding. I humbly offer my sincere congratulations on a magnificent design."

Green Howards: The design incorporates the badges of the four other regiments associated with the Green Howards; they were the Norwegian King's Guard, the Danish Life Regiment, the Queen's York Rangers of Canada and the Canadian Rocky Mountain Rangers. King Olav of Norway, the Colonel in Chief, who opened the Green Howard's regimental museum in Richmond, was presented with the No. 1 edition of the plate.

Other Commemorated Events

Harold designed many commemoratives for Royal occasions. Harold designed a mug for the Coronation of Queen Elizabeth II, which was selected by her for presentation to the people employed on Royal estates. He also designed a miniature tea set to celebrate the Coronation. Harold designed a two-handled loving cup for the Royal Silver Wedding in 1972 and a loving cup for the Royal Silver Jubilee in 1977. The Silver Jubilee loving cup had a rich back panel of four flora emblems, the leek, thistle, shamrock and rose. The flags of the Commonwealth surrounded the panel and were depicted in gold. The front depicts the Royal coat of arms and the border round the whole cup was of oak leaves and acorns, a symbol of England and represents the Royal Tree. Harold soon learnt to avoid using portraits on commemoratives as however accurate the engravings were, they were never quite as good as photographs. However, for the Silver Wedding loving cup it was probably dictated by one of the agents that Her Majesty The Queen and His Royal Highness The Duke of Edinburgh's portraits were used. Harold drew the profiles, which Frank Boothby expertly engraved.

Harold also designed several individual commemorative items such as retirement gifts. He was commissioned by Robert Copeland to design a 14-inch-high vase for deputy chairman, Spencer Copeland's retirement. It took six months to produce and was presented by C.R. Marsden, the general manager, in the company's showroom in October 1972, although Spencer actually retired the previous December.

Harold's designs for the European Community plate and loving cup that were commissioned by the British Council of the European Movement to mark the expanded community of nine nations were highly received. Lord Harlech, chairman of the British Council, said the plates were "truly magnificent examples of British craftsmanship. In quality and design they are worthy of the occasion."

The European Community plate was one of the

Coronation design submitted to a competition.

Coronation mug that the Queen gave to all her estate workers.

Miniature tea service to commemorate the Coronation of Elizabeth II.

Tankard marking the Silver Jubilee of Elizabeth II.

European Union.

Sailing of the Pilgrims.

Wimbledon.

Loving cup and design work commemorating HM Queen Elizabeth's Silver Jubilee, 1977.

Above and below: Silver Wedding Anniversary of HM Queen Elizabeth II and HRH Prince Philip.

most contentious commemorative plates that Spode produced. The European Movement was an official body that existed to further the progress towards a European community. It was non-political in the sense that it cut across all party divisions but the enlargement of the European Community was quite a controversial event and resulted in Spode receiving criticism from some quarters where it was least expected. The controversy was perhaps the reason why there was an almost total lack of commemorative items produced by other companies. The design for the plate presented serious problems as no common motif could be found which would link the member countries, therefore Harold richly depicted a map of Europe in the centre of the plate.

The idea was simple but was extremely ambitious in its execution as the large flat areas of colour and pure gold presented severe technical difficulties. The border has the heraldic shield of each member, separated by a drape which Harold insisted represented the raising of a new era in Europe. Each shield was submitted to each government for official approval. All were approved apart from Britain's, as it is the personal emblem of the monarch for which stringent controls are enforced. Harold devised instead, a British symbol of a stylized motif of the Union; the rose, thistle, shamrock and daffodil.

More problems were met once the engraving began the summer before the event. The European Community plate was different from the other commemorative plates in that it was a contemporary event and therefore the details were liable to change. Norway, Denmark and Eire all announced that a referendum was to be held and subsequently Norway decided not to join the Community. The design and sales teams were anxiously following the political events, monitoring the developments. The border of the plate and loving cup had to be readjusted to remove Norway's emblem and the centre map had to be completely redrawn which had the advantage of making a more compact map without Norway's long coastline.

The plates were presented to the Heads of State, including Edward Heath, at a European Movement banquet at Hampton Court Palace on 2nd January 1973. The presentation posed another new problem. To avoid causing offence, the first ten plates were unnumbered – the numbering of the edition beginning at eleven.

Sailing of the Pilgrims 1969: This plate celebrates the 350th anniversary of the pilgrims setting sail for america. The 2,500 limited editions were commis-sioned by the Sutton Harbour Improvement Company from whose tavern the pilgrims sailed. The seals of England, America and Plymouth and the first seal of the Plymouth Colony and blossoms that gave the ship its name surround the *Mayflower* ship.

Guild Merchant Vase 1972: Harold designed this 5" limited edition china vase to commemorate the guild merchants who have held a week-long celebration in Preston every twenty years since the twelfth century. It is decorated with two shields and a border of the Lancashire red rose in rich enamels using 24-carat gold on crimson ground.

Wimbledon plate 1977: A project Harold would have enjoyed was the Wimbledon Centenary plate as he was a keen lover of all sports. Harold was privileged to view the men's and ladies singles trophies at close quarters in order to capture some of the detail which features in the design. The pale blue hydrangeas, as much a part of Wimbledon fortnight as strawberries and tennis, frame the centre.

Not all commemorative designs that were submitted were successful. A competition was held to design something to commemorate the 1954 ascent of Everest. Harold's design was not picked as the winner; instead Mr R. W. Stevens was praised for being modern and innovative. This was Harold's response in a letter to Ronald Copeland: "…If this is the choice of the experts to commemorate the ascent of Everest, the losers can take heart if their efforts are termed 'old-fashioned'. To me it looks like an inverted shaving brush and Geoffrey [Cholerton] feels that there is more beauty in a cooling tower of a power station." Another commemorative commission that Harold almost succeeded on was the 1952 British Pottery Manufacturers Federation competition for Corona-tion ware. His son Paul remembers him producing the design whilst on holiday as the deadline was approaching. The winner was John Wain, a designer for Chromo-Transfer Co. Ltd, Hanley. Of the eighty entries, Harold came second with a £25 prize. He told the *Sentinel*, "I would like to congratulate Mr Wain very heartily on coming out on top." However, he was personally disappointed and declared he was never going to enter another competition.

Commemoratives for other Factories

What is very surprising is that Harold did several designs for other factories whilst he was still at Spode. Harold must have been very busy during the run-up to the Queen's Silver Jubilee, as not only did he design Spode's loving cup, but I am pretty sure he also designed a beaker for Mulberry Hall Bone China, a plate for Minton and a pair of heraldic beast candlesticks for Minton. In the same year Harold also produced a plate for St Peter's School, York that was produced by Mulberry Hall and sold out instantly. The plate celebrated the 1,350th anniversary of the school and features the school's arms. The main

border is composed of Yorkshire roses and is flanked by two supporting borders of architectural inspiration. The Minton Queen's Jubilee plate has the Royal arms in the centre. The panelled border design displays the Queen's personal cypher and ten different royal heraldic beasts. Linking them is a decorative motif inspired by the carving on the tomb of Edward the Confessor in Westminster Abbey.

R. Spencer Copeland and Harold viewing part of a 142-piece breakfast set for 24 people presented to Queen Elizabeth The Queen Mother by The British Pottery Manufacturers' Federation on the occasion of her visit to the city on 1st and 2nd November 1949. The pattern is a reproduction of an 1808 Spode design. On the back is the cipher of Queen Elizabeth's household, an E and P entwined.

1970 Bicentenary Celebrations

Princess Anne, Harold and Spencer Copeland at the Royal Banquet at the Goldsmith's Hall, London.

Perhaps the largest celebration commemorated at Spode was the 200th anniversary of Josiah Spode founding the factory in 1770. Carborundum changed the factory's name back to Spode Ltd. in October 1970. The first event of the year in March was a visit to the works for a party of American journalists who spent the afternoon and following morning on a comprehensive tour of the factory gaining material for their magazines and papers. Their itinerary also included a special bicentenary lunch at the House of Commons hosted by the three Members of Parliament for Stoke-on-Trent.

The highlight of the celebrations was a Royal Banquet at the Goldsmith's Hall, London on 14th May. The guest of honour was Her Royal Highness Princess Anne, attending her first ever official banquet. Among the distinguished guests were the ambassadors to Britain from the USA and Switzerland together with representatives of the Armed Forces, the Church, the arts, industry, trade and commerce. Other countries represented were Canada, Germany, France, Australia, the Netherlands, Portugal, Bermuda and Jamaica. Directors of Carborundum were invited, along with the entire senior management, including Harold, and the oldest employee, 70-year-old Ernest Bates, the longest-serving employee, Norman Collis, who served for 51 years, and the youngest employee, 15-year-old Diane Hough, an apprentice gilder, who had the honour of presenting Princess Anne with a bouquet.

Harold, Len and his wife and John Sutherland-Hawes, consultant graphic designer to Spode, were presented to the Princess after dinner. Princess Anne graciously accepted a Bicentenary goblet, which features Josiah Spode I and Spode/Copeland's Coat of Arms granted in 1968. It was number one of a limited edition of 200. The banquet was an overture to an exhibition of historic Spode that had been specially commissioned over the two hundred years. The exhibition was designed by John Sutherland-Hawes and displayed by Harold and Len. The majority of the modern special commissions shown were the work of Harold. Her Royal Highness Princess Margaret visited the exhibition and subsequently her Lady-in-Waiting, Juliet Smith, wrote to Spencer Copeland congratulating him and asked if it was possible to include more pieces of her set to show it to better advantage: "Princess Margaret visited the Exhibition last week and thought that it had been excellently arranged, particularly with regard to the lighting." The display was held at the Goldsmith's Hall and was open to the public from 15th May to 12th June.

Spode was again fortunate to receive further royal patronage during the bicentenary year when Her Royal Highness Princess Margaret paid a visit to the factory and revealed a plaque on a preserved bottle oven. The Princess was presented with a Bicentenary goblet by Frank Boothby who had engraved the pattern. The design was most probably executed by Harold, although his name was not used in any of the publicity. During the visit the Princess was pleasantly surprised to see the gilder Tom Lymer nervously at work on the feather pattern that she designed. The Princess had no idea that the replacement teapot she had ordered would be made whilst she was on the factory.

Harold used to recall how Princess Margaret had escaped to his office from the press for a crafty cigarette and a quick drink of whisky. David Walsh, a designer, can proudly say that he held the ashtray for Princess Margaret. Harold was a heavy smoker at the time and David remembers that his office was always clouded with smoke. Len Whiter used to recall that Harold had an antique Adams Windsor Castle blue and white dish on his wall which became heavily stained by nicotine, and every time Len came into his office he would wipe clean just the white sail of the boat on the dish.

Another celebration of the two hundred years of Spode's production was an exhibition at The Royal Academy from 8th August to 4th October. This was an honour for the company as it was the first time a craft exhibition had been held there. The wares in the exhibition were from throughout the two hundred years including modern patterns and procedures. One of the most impressive services was the Shah of Persia's service, which Len Whiter had secured the loan of. One of the modern wares on show was the Crimson Lancaster service, which showed that Spode was still able to produce wares typical of Josiah

Spode I. One section of the exhibition was devoted to the manufacture of Spode ware and visitors could follow the various processes, culminating in the ware being hand-painted by members of staff before being fired in a kiln. This kiln was of some concern to the London fire brigade who had to be convinced that it was perfectly safe.

To coincide with the event, Len Whiter produced his comprehensive volume, *Spode*, which cast much new light on the history of Spode. Harold played a big part in the photography of the book and is acknowledged: "The greatest debt of all I owe to Harold Holdway, art director of the Spode factory. Providing me with all but a few of the photographs used in this book was a task of several months, but sharing with me his vast and expert knowledge of Spode has been the patient work of years."

In July a celebration was held at Trentham Gardens, Stoke-on-Trent, for the workers and their families, when 1,530 employees and guests enjoyed an ox-roast and an evening of entertainment. The remains of the ox were to be utilised in the bone china of a commemorative bowl (it never got further than the clay stage), as was done at previous celebrations in 1834 when Copeland and Garrett took over the factory. The final celebration in the year of parties was a civic dinner celebrating the bicentenary held at Stoke's Jubilee Hall.

Above: Bicentenary celebrations for all the workers at Trentham Gardens. Robert Copeland is carving the ox.

Above right: Bicentenary commemoratives engraved by Frank Boothby.

Right: Frank Boothby presenting Princess Margaret with a goblet.

NEW MANAGEMENT

In July 1966, the Copeland pottery factory ceased to be a family-managed firm. When Carborundum, an American company specialising in grinding wheels and abrasives, took over the running of the factory, it ended a period of fraught speculation over the company's future but heralded a period of drastic and sometimes ruthless change. Despite coming at a time when earthenware and china sales were down and W.T. Copeland & Sons had a reputation for delayed deliveries, these changes affected the ambience of the factory as well as many people's work patterns. Life in the art department under Carborundum became very different from when Harold started in the 1930s.

W.T. Copeland & Sons were struggling to adapt to modern production methods and as a result orders were delivered slowly. In 1963 they were still producing ware by traditional methods and as a result prices were so high that orders were limited. Up to August 1966, only three out of a hundred or more patterns were being produced by the cheaper and quicker ways of lithograph and silk screen. As a result sales were dropping off. Alan Lowden commented in the *London Illustrated News*, 9th May 1970:

"In 1966 Spode was hardly viable. The firm was undercapitalised; the factory had insufficient capacity to produce; the cost of manufacture was too high. There was a basic management problem. There was good, though under-used middle management but insufficiently effective control at the top – financial, labour, production or technical. Cost accounting was inadequate. There was no one there who had the acumen to refuse business. It was 'sales at any price', even when the profit margins were too small to make it worthwhile."

In the early 1960s the company was beginning to run into overdraft and the bank told them they needed someone to rescue them. During 1963 there was a lot of speculation in the national and local press about Wedgwood bidding for W.T. Copeland & Sons. It is little known that Spode was under the control of Wedgwood for three months. However, at the final hour they withdrew their offer, as Wedgwood's had not signed the document and rescinded the offer. There is speculation as to why the offer did not go through. Wedgwood claimed that there was a £30,000 discrepancy between their accountant's calculation in the costing of stock and Tucker-Feltham of Spode's. It is more likely that they did not want

Managing Directors of Spode whilst Harold was there	
1932–1958	Arthur E. Hewitt and Gresham Copeland
1958–1966	Spencer Copeland
1966–1971	William J. Whatmore (resigned to become vice president of Carborudum Niagara Falls)
1971–1972	Alan Lowden and Terry Peterson (A. Lowden resigned to become MD of Barker Ellis Silver Co.
1972–1977	Paul Thompson (joined as Tablware group manager, became business director in 1973, marketing director of RWS in 1977 and appointed assistant chief executive in 1978). Around this time Lyn T. Davies was MD of Royal Worcester Spode and then became MD of both after Carborundum.
1978–1979	Roy Fraser
1979–1983	John Bullock (joined as a director and general manager in 1974, appointed marketing director in 1978)

to take on Copeland and Thompson, (the American side of the business) at a high cost. Wedgwood owned their own distribution company in the United States but Copeland had an agent, Copeland and Thompson; therefore Wedgwood's could not distribute Spode under their own banner. Copeland's had a deal that they could buy out their agents at six months, notice for ten times the average sales value over the past three years. Copeland and Thompson would have been infinitely more costly than the £600,000 that they were going to pay for Spode. Wedgwood's would have had difficulty in financing the deal. There is also speculation that a Nat West banking friend advised them against the deal. By March/April the news was out that the Wedgwood deal was off. Although this disappointed some people at the factory at the time, in retrospect, Carborundum was probably a better option, as Wedgwood could have taken over and made many cuts, if not closed the factory completely as they have done with many other factories.

Carborundum did not have a background in ceramic

Harold's sketch of the proposed layout of the Niagara Falls factory.

tableware; Spode was quite a new venture for them. Their existing products included refractories, heating elements, water resistant parts, electronic components and vitrified grinding wheels, of which, they claimed, "The technologies are just the same." They believed that their existing factory production methods could be used to modify and rationalise Spode, a factory they described as "a Congolese village with workers walking round with baskets on their shoulders and 150 small buildings scattered round a 10 acre site."[12]

Carborundum rationalised the number of patterns from 1,050 to 800, brought in more machines and rationalised the use of buildings. Alan Lowden claimed that in two and a half years they had 25% less people producing but were selling eighty percent more. These changes proved to be unpopular and not altogether successful. For example, they decided to build a conveyor belt that ran around he factory to carry finished goods. Anyone who has been to the Spode factory will know that the old buildings with their many narrow flights of stairs and varied floor levels make this type of modernisation not very practical. The conveyor belt even ran straight through the stately boardroom. Pots would often stay on the belts, going round and round the factory gathering dust until they eventually fell off. Carborundum was "very brutal" and made many redundancies; for example, cutting the number of casters and printers by half. In retrospect the Carborundum 1967 Annual Report is almost laughable but it sums up the misinformed rationale behind the changes:

"The fit of Spode with other Carborundum units has been thoroughly proven through an interchange of technology, manufacturing and inventory control. To a ceramist, the only difference between superior grinding wheels and fine china is the decoration; to a service manager, techniques used to effectively control the inventory of 300,000 types of grinding wheels are readily applicable to the effective control of a few thousand types of chinaware. The marketing vector for chinaware provides a firm base for further growth in related consumer markets."

Harold's comment in the margin is: "What a statement!"

Another failed venture of Carborundum was to build a miniature Spode factory at the company's headquarters at Niagara Falls. The Carborundum Museum of Ceramics was designed to be a tourist attraction where visitors could see selected stages of pottery production. The visitor's centre aimed to show how skilful the pottery craft was, hence they did not show any of the mechanised processes as this would be "tantamount to demonstrating that these processes are neither as difficult nor as skilful as the American public believes." The plan was to have a thrower, a turner, a printer, a transferrer, one or two painters, one or two printers and a heraldic painter. The wares produced were sold in the visitor's shop with a special backstamp. They envisaged that there would be a great demand for the heraldic painter: "His work, being entirely freehand, would be extremely expensive, but it is quite possible that the demand would soon exceed the supply and this could be used to advantage."

The company were optimistic of the museum's success and they also envisaged that the design studio there would eventually host a student awarded a

[12] Terry Maher of Carborundum 3.5.68.

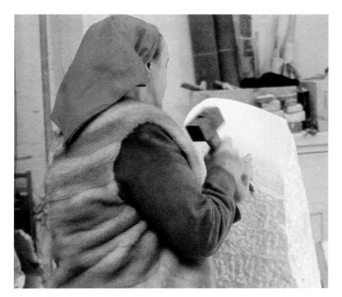

Barbara Hepworth, sculptor, at work in St Ives where she produced a sculpture for the Niagara Falls factory, pictured right.

"Carborundum Ceramic Design Scholarship". There was a celebratory send-off for a bus full of Spode workers who moved out to the States to work at the miniature factory. To accompany the production line was a museum of ceramic history which included many contemporary pieces. In 1971 Harold was involved in commissioning Barbara Hepworth, a prominent sculptor living in St Ives, Cornwall, to produce a piece of sculpture for the museum. However, the Niagara Falls factory was not a success as it was on the 'wrong' side of the river and missed out by all the tourists and soon closed.

By 1975 Carborundum had realised that you cannot market fine china like grinding wheels. In 1975 the Spode group, which included Hammersley China, Palissy and Barthmann, a German lead crystal manufacturer, was once more up for sale to a responsible buyer. Wedgwood once again showed some interest and withdrew. A year later a partnership with Royal Worcester and Carborundum was drawn up and from 1977 the company became known as Royal Worcester Spode, making it the third largest group in the English fine china industry.

Harold became disillusioned with Spode's management as he felt people who did not know the industry were running it. There was a quick succession of managers, some of whom were using Spode as a stepping-stone to further their own career. Spode was a real family business, it was more than just a job, it was not something that could be run by a 'career's manager.' Harold, like Douglas Hawley, a sales manager, became disillusioned with the management who were using their powers like "little Hitlers", ordering things they did not know about and interfering. Miss Bettany used to find it amusing to watch the managing director, Alan Lowden, strutting

through the factory with his retinue of managers in hierarchical order behind him. One example of additional bureaucracy is illustrated in a memo from Lyn T. Davies, chairman of the Royal Worcester Group, to the management board:

"I have always been used to being fully informed by everybody who reports to me about activities for which they are responsible. In this respect I want you to give some thought to a monthly report to be received in my office by Friday following the end of the month."

As Douglas Hawley said, "the Spode factory seemed to have lost much of the pleasant atmosphere…due to the changes in the administration, and the harmony and general efficiency was being affected." This led Douglas, along with other employees, to resign and move to Wedgwood. As Jean Copeland, Spencer's second wife, commented about the factory, "It was such a happy place, as far as I can judge. The whole atmosphere changed with the takeover. I don't think Spencer will ever fully recover from the takeover and the events that followed."

In the design department, the new American way of working was not liked. They wanted the designers to have a rationale behind everything. They wanted to know 'what made them tick'. Gone were the pre-war days when designers had to keep producing designs until one satisfied the director, as already described in the Christmas Tree plate story. L.T. Davies sent this memo to Harold in March 1978.

"In formulating product design, pricing and product launch, I think a great amount of progress has been made in the last six months. I now wish to take that progress to its logical conclusion by asking you to devise a system whereby I can see products one month before the date at which we spend substantial money so that if necessary I can direct that we should have an outside opinion as to whether or not the design is likely to succeed."

L.T. Davies was insulting Harold's experience as a ceramic designer and art director by offering this unoriginal piece of advice:

"The type of decorations likely to succeed are mainly traditional in feeling and also have an appearance of good value with an obvious thoroughness of design content and a particular flavour which is recognisable. Trend patterns may gain one a medal or a possible acceptance by the Council of Industrial Design but usually the life of such a creation is very short lived."

Harold had maintained the stance for years that good solid design would win every time! Harold was primarily an artist and he wanted the freedom to design without interference. His desire to pursue a limited amount of freelance work and his disheartenment over the management changes led him to hand in three month's notice to John Bullock on 27th May 1976. I think the proposal shocked the senior management who came back with an offer his wife said, "was too good to refuse." Paul Thompson had envisaged that Harold would help ease through the imminent merger between the Spode and Worcester factories by becoming an overall art director of all the factories whilst retaining his responsibilities to the Spode design studio. As Harold himself described the event: "I handed in my notice of 3 months, to take early retirement with effect on 31st August 1976, which was received by John Bullock. This action was a great shock to him and he said he would have to communicate this action with Mr Paul Thompson. At the end of July, the main board decided to make an attractive offer for me to consider the withdrawal of my notice. The proposal was an increase in salary, a Spode company directorship, and a company car, which I accepted and confirmed on 9th September 1976. The car, an Austin Princess 1800 HL was delivered on 7th December 1976. On the 20th April

1977 with 4,184 miles on the clock I handed over the car to Mr Brian Jones, technical manager of Spode. I was appointed to the management board as group art director of Royal Worcester Spode 1st January 1977" Harold was then given a Ford Granada.

Royal Worcester Spode now consisted of Worcester Royal Porcelain Co. Ltd., Spode Ltd., Palissy Pottery Ltd., Hammersley China Ltd. and Barthmann Cristall. Those based at Stoke were responsible to Paul Thompson and those based in Worcester to Mr J.P. Collis. The prestige of becoming a member of the Royal Worcester Spode board of directors seems a just reward for Harold's years of perseverance and hard work at the Spode factory. It was a role he was proud to fulfil up until his retirement on 1st July 1978.

Harold's new position was not easy as it coincided with a troubled period for the Royal Worcester Spode Group. The late 1970s were not an easy time for Royal Worcester Spode. Spode was feeling the effects of a recession in America. Sales in North America were slowing down although sales in the British market were still buoyant because more middle and working class people were starting to buy more. With all the mergers and takeovers, it was no longer just a question of supplying good quality pots at a fair price. In September 1977 the *Evening News* of Worcester reported that the last six months had been "very unsatisfactory" for Spode. Despite rises in sales from £10.4m to £15.6m, profits of the Royal Worcester group had slipped from £612,000 to £510,000 in the first half of 1977. The Spode subsidiary lost £52,000 due to losses made by subsidiaries in Canada and the USA. To make matters worse, a dock strike in the USA in November 1977 severely affected the cash flow of $750,000 worth of ware in transit.

Harold had to look at the whole picture of the entire Royal Worcester Spode group and utilise his designers to the best of their ability. This meant that Spode designers spent quite a bit of time working on Palissy limited editions, which were aimed at the cheaper end of the market, such as Patrick Howse's

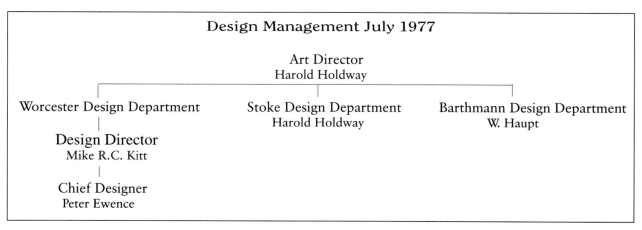

Design Management July 1977

Art Director
Harold Holdway

Worcester Design Department	Stoke Design Department	Barthmann Design Department
	Harold Holdway	W. Haupt
Design Director		
Mike R.C. Kitt		
Chief Designer		
Peter Ewence		

Water Babies in January 1978 which had "a great chance of success." Spode's monopoly of high-quality limited editions was being undermined by high quality rivals from Boehm on both quality and price. Also, Mr Bullock commented that from a marketing side, the board was not happy with Worcester bone china tableware; the design situation there was not good. The costs of introducing new patterns at Worcester between 1975–77 were too high, as even if a full manufacturing profit of 25% was made on sales, a loss of over £20,000 had been made on these patterns. New models were not being produced fast enough and the design skills were not good enough so the Stoke design team were ordered to help their Worcester counterparts out.

In November 1977, Mike Kitt produced a design management report full of woe. He bemoaned that since he joined in 1973 there had been three marketing directors and several changes in production directors leading to a lack of definition in the company's marketing position. He felt the changes in the Worcester design department sharply contrasted with Spode's department that Harold had been overseeing for forty years. "Clearly the question must be asked whether the ethic of the Worcester Company is understood by those currently programming the

design team and then approving the aesthetic results." Like Harold, he lamented that non-potters were running the company. Even though Mike Kitt refuted Paul Thompson's stringent criticism of the Worcester pattern designers performance, Harold sent two Spode designers to Worcester to design tableware patterns during 1978. Despite the troubles of the sister factories, the Spode design department was viewed optimistically. Lyn Davies hoped that the factory production capacity would be able to cope with the extra business that would be created.

Despite the prestige of being a member of the board of directors, the role left Harold with less time to design and further involved him in the problems and politics of the sister factories. As Mike Kitt says, "Harold was glad to retire, knowing that he had presided over a golden era in the company's history."

Following Harold's retirement, in order to avoid major changes and to retain the separate design environments at Worcester and Spode it was decided not to appoint a design director in place of Harold. Paul Wood became design manager in charge of Stoke Manufacturing Division, directly responsible to Roy Fraser, assistant chief executive. M.J. Batchelor was responsible for product development instead of Paul Wood.

Harold discussing designs for America with Dick De Natale, USA art director of Carborundum. 1966–1967. A Hurten flower plaque is on the wall behind.

RETIREMENT

Harold finally finished after forty-four years at Spode on 16th June 1978. The praise and congratulations Harold received on his retirement from people across the ceramic industry is testimony to his influence as an artistic designer. Several parties were held in his honour and he received many gifts including a commemorative bowl from his colleagues, which he always displayed with pride, an illuminated scroll with signatures from all who knew him at Spode, which was drawn by Roy Trigg and greatly prized, a wine cooler from Worcester and a projector amongst other things. His retirement after forty-four years at Copeland/Spode was recorded in several newspapers and announced on the local radio. Two of many letters sum up Harold's contribution to the pottery industry.

From Phillip Rayner, managing director of Thomas Goode & Co., London.

"It is difficult to find the words to express the depth of feeling that we have for such an old and valued friend who has worked with unstinting effort whenever we have had anything special for your company to produce on our behalf. Whatever ideas we may have had of our own have always been much enhanced by your magic touch and we will greatly miss this valuable asset in years to come."

From John Robinson, prestige department decorating manager.

"Having spent 25 of those [44] years with you I would like to thank you for the training and knowledge you imparted to me in that time. Some of the lessons were not easy at the time but they have proved invaluable in later years. No one who has worked with you can deny that your guidance and criticism has improved their own ability in the field of draughtsmanship and design. Your high standards have kept the company in the forefront of the industry."

Miss Bettany and several of the ladies that knew Harold had catered for a party at the Talbot pub opposite the factory. Harold used to call Miss Bettany "the lady who has two eyes but fails to use them" as he thought she did not look or notice things. However, she had always been fascinated with rooflines and had asked Harold to sketch her the rooflines visible from

Spode. Nothing materialised from this; however, on his last day he brought in a drawing from home for her. She also recalled that one of Harold's sayings was that "you're only a true potter if when you cut your vein, slip (liquid clay) pours out." Harold could not have been a more devoted potter.

What is amazing is that Harold secretly carried on after his retirement designing commemoratives for several different factories unknown to even his family! The Mulberry Hall bone china commissions he received from Michael Sinclair for the other companies' commemoratives were presumably negotiated through Len Whiter. Whereas previously the publicity material had always made use of the designer's name, these later designs do not mention a designer, therefore I am not entirely sure that I have produced a complete list of all his designs.

Harold would have been delighted to receive commissions for four major royal occasions after retirement including HRH Prince Charles and Lady Diana Spencer's wedding, HM the Queen Mother's 80th Birthday, HRH Prince Andrew and Miss Sarah Ferguson's wedding and HRH Prince William of Wales' birth. Harold was granted the right to use various royal coats of arms on several occasions, a privilege not often granted to commemorative designers. In the case of Lady Diana's wedding, Michael Sinclair received a letter from the Countess Spencer, Althorp, Northampton. "I think your designs look beautiful. We are prepared to waive restrictions in the same way as the Lord Chamberlain, for use of crests etc."

For the Royal Wedding a limited edition of 1,000 plates were produced by Minton. The sales leaflet described the plate as "a design to evoke the great occasion in pure, heraldic terms." In the centre is the shield of HRH The Prince of Wales alongside Lady Diana's arms. The arms appear in a setting of rose, thistle and shamrock, as well as oak leaves and acorns. The oak is a universal symbol of strength and in ancient times was an emblem of conjugal devotion and happiness. It has been a favourite motif among English pottery designers for wares intended either for royal use or to mark important royal events. Within the border of oak leaves are the Princess' ostrich feathers and five heraldic beasts associated with the couple. Harold also produced a loving cup using the same crests for the wedding, which was produced by Coalport and a pair of heraldic beasts

Tower of Comares retirement bowl with a Renaissance pattern border. Paul Wood designed it, Roy Trigg executed it and Bill Hall painted the centre. The bowl cost £1000s to produce and 20 china bowls had to be made to get a perfect one.

which were produced by Minton. Another splendid design, although perhaps not of the same high quality as his earlier designs, was Harold's plate for HM The Queen Mother's eightieth birthday. Her personal coat of arms stands out in the middle. The border is in delicate pastel colours and features pink English roses and petite blue forget-me-nots, which reflects her love of flowers. Elizabeth's personal cypher features at the top. This also features on a crystal goblet also retailed through Mulberry Hall. The use of the cypher was a privilege granted by the Queen Mother as its use was prohibited even during the celebratory years. She thought, "the design for the plate is charming … and that it meets with Queen Elizabeth The Queen Mother's approval."

Harold designed a further two cathedral commemoratives after he had retired; Wells and Winchester. The latter celebrated in 1979 nine hundred years since the beginning of the building of the cathedral by Bishop Walkelin. In the centre is St Swithin looking like a section of illuminated manuscript. An acanthus leaf border is separated by four coats of arms of four famous bishops. Wells Cathedral plate was produced in 1982 but does not have a specific celebration. The centre of the plate portrays the central boss of the cathedral's Lady Chapel, which features a figure of Christ in glory, supported by four angels. The red, green and gold of the central boss recaptures the spirit of the medieval colour which once adorned the whole interior of the cathedral. The plate's border is inspired by the quire. The hexagon pattern design is based on the stone tracery of the quire's vault which links together the richly coloured and gilded roof bosses. At the top of

the border are the arms of the Dean and Chapter of Wells and at the bottom is a Wells swan, holding in its beak the rope of the gatehouse bell which the swans of the palace moat had to pull when they wished to be fed.

In 1980, Harold designed a commemorative plate, mug and thimble for the Institute of Chartered Accountants in England and Wales who were celebrating their centenary. The richly decorated plate was inspired by the renaissance architecture of the Institute's hall. The centre of the plate portrays the arms of the Institute that features the figure of Economia. She holds a rod of command in one hand and is equipped with compasses and a rudder for guidance. A plainer mug using the same emblems was produced. The thimble features the rose and leek and the Institute's emblem to highlight their work in England and Wales.

Along with the plate for St Peter's School, which Harold produced before his retirement, he also produced one for Charterhouse and one for Marlborough College. The latter portrays the arms of the college in the centre surrounded by a wreath of laurel. The border features the symbols of the twelve senior houses. The use of symbols to represent houses within a school is apparently unusual. The house symbols are linked in a decorative gothic style that forms an ornate letter M. The Charterhouse plate features the school's arms in the centre. The border is composed of one of Harold's favourite motifs, the oak leaf and acorn. It alludes to the ancient Charterhouse oak tree, which stands in the centre of the school. The main border is edged with two bands of Charterhouse colours, the inner border displaying the names of the

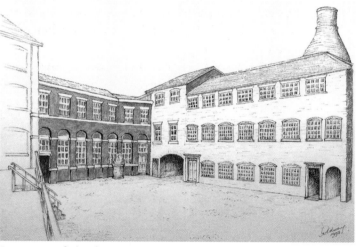

Drawings of the factory drawn from photos and period plans of the factory.

Floral studies, painted during his retirement.

Above: The china terrace in front of the museum (grey building) and Harold's former office above the arch.

HRH Prince Charles and Lady Diana's wedding plate, 1981.

Below: Building that used to house a china slip kiln, now warehousing.

eleven school houses.

As can be appreciated, a lot of research had to be done to come up with the designs for the commemoratives. Harold was not an armchair designer. He would make several visits to the location to find inspiration from architectural detail; would research the history to discover significant events, dates, saints, symbols, etc. that could be used artistically; and would study the art of heraldry from books and in libraries to ensure that all the details were correct. A lot of background research had to go into the commemoratives before the sales team could write the spiel that accompanied the plate.

Even when Harold could no longer chase around researching commemorative designs he remained artistically active. His motto was, 'Age is in the body, youth is in the mind.' Not only did he design greetings cards for his family, he produced numerous watercolour studies of flowers and drew detailed reconstructions of the Spode factory. These achievements were not easy.

Not long after he retired, the health of Betty, his wife, deteriorated. Harold lovingly cared for her until she passed away of cancer in May 1984. He had been given a book of walks by his department on his retirement, which he had been looking forward to doing. Unfortunately he was never able to use this book to its potential as Harold's mobility became severely affected by arthritis, which confined him to the house after 1986. He was quite content, researching and writing his memoirs, painting flowers that people brought into the bungalow for him and answering queries for numerous people on the history of the pottery industry. He continued to add to his extensive collection of antique Spode of which he was trying to obtain an example of each blue and white pattern produced. He stubbornly persevered, even after he was confined to a wheelchair from 1996. Harold wrote in a letter in 1996:

"This June I shall hopefully reach the grand age of 83 years and to date I have made more studies than in recent years. To have retained most of my faculties I am most thankful, particularly sight, pencil and brush control. Although the variety of subjects are not as plentiful as I would wish I still am able to satisfy my needs."

Harold was also very active in helping other people with their research of Spode and Copeland, especially Vega Wilkinson with *Spode–Copeland–Spode: The Works and its People 1770–1970*. He did several pen and ink drawings of the factory which he reconstructed from old photographs and plans. He also researched and charted the developments of the factory on colour-coded plans. He loved to reminisce about the factory and these memories occupied his days.

The greatest blow of all, however, was when he discovered that he had practically lost his eyesight in April 1998. Despite not being able to paint or write he remained very independent and kept his mind active. My uncle, Arthur Clarke, sums up Harold's determination in his obituary, (*The Guardian* 27th September 2002):

"Holdway mastered the infirmities of age with tenacity and determination: his life was filled with hobbies, and as each affliction struck, he adjusted with cheerful and irascible independence."

Harold Holdway peacefully passed away on 31st August 2002.

Appendix 1
An Extended Family

"To perpetuate the memory of men who contributed so much to the glory of Spode Copeland wares." Harold Holdway

Numerous people who have worked at W.T. Copeland & Sons and Spode over the last century have commented on what a friendly, family atmosphere there was on the factory. Even today, there seems to be a sense of belonging at the factory, rather than it being merely just a place of work. Miss Jean Bettany, secretary to Len Whiter, who worked at Spode for 22 years, felt that it was as if you belonged to the factory or as if you had joined a family. Despite the bad pay, there was a paternal atmosphere and pleasant working conditions. "So many nice things happened it was a joy to work there." The sense of history was never far from the factory. Miss Bettany used to be fascinated with a flight of narrow stone steps that were worn with so many passing people. She felt that the old Copeland people kept the spirit going despite the suspicious nature of Carborundum. They were "characters, not plastic people." Like Harold, Douglas Hawley experienced many changes on the factory. When he started in the 1930s he said it was very smoky but still had a good friendly atmosphere and was a nice place to work, especially under the Copeland's. In his memoirs he wrote:

"I had not been at the factory very long before I realised that everyone had a sense of purpose, and despite the somewhat uncomfortable conditions in which they worked, and their limited private enjoyments, they seemed happy. Many people had worked all their lives on the factory, and in some cases their father and grandfather before them. They all appeared to be inspired by a tradition of good workmanship. As I progressed through the factory, I found that the people also seemed to have a feeling of 'belonging', almost as if they were members of a family. I suppose they could be called the soul of the factory, and were some of those dedicated people who carried on the traditions of craftsmanship handed down from previous generations. They were the true backbone of the pottery industry."

Miss Bettany thought it was wonderful the way Harold always knew all the women on the shop floor and how he went out of his way to be friendly towards them. She felt maybe that he was more familiar to those outside his department as he wanted to maintain his distance with those in his department. Harold had an extensive memory of the many characters of the Copeland/Spode factory and was sad that many of his comrades passed away before him. He left many brief notes about the employees of Copeland/Spode and I have therefore included them for the sake of those who worked alongside Harold. Although there must have been many more memorable characters, this is in no way an exhaustive list, nor have I included people that have extensively featured earlier in the memoirs. As Harold said, it would be a shame for the worker's contribution to be forgotten. Harold's memoirs were not just about pots; they were about people.

Many thanks to Robert Copeland who has augmented Harold's list.

Engravers – "the largest squad employed by any factory"

- Joe Barker: fine engraver.
- Stan Bedwell: used to enjoy a glass of red wine with his lunch.
- Frank Boothby: started in 1929, a master engraver who spent the latter part of his career in Harold's design department. He played the violin as a hobby.
- George Cartlidge: foreman engraver before moving to the prestige department as decorating manager.
- Jim Dunn: died 17.03.02, engraver, deaf and dumb.
- Joe Hassall: a master engraver, Tom Hassall's brother.
- Paul Holdway: Harold's son who joined in 1965 and is now a master engraver.
- Jack Longmore Junior: engraver, died aged 85 on 2.12.95.
- Ken Scarrett: a deaf and dumb engraver. He joined on 19th December 1937 as an apprentice and left in August 1950 to become the superintendent of the Deaf and Dumb Institute at Shelton as he felt he had a calling as a missionary among the deaf and dumb. He passed his Deaf and Dumb Welfare exam with honours.
- John Tomlinson: engraver, died 28.12.96.
- John Walton: engraver. He left to found his own engraving and silk screen printing business with Len Potts.
- James Stanway Wood: 26.09.1875–19.02.1965. He joined Copelands in 1911 and was there until 1955. He was responsible for the development and extension of many famous patterns such as Tower and Italian.

Designers and Painters

- Elsie Astell: underglaze enameller, started in 1935.
- Joe Austin: painter, left in 1947.
- Mrs Ball's Shop: Mrs Ada Ball (neé Dean) married W. Ball, a gilder. (Ada's sister, Gertie Dean, a ground layer, was the sweetheart of Harry Hundley, head ground layer.) Mrs Poppy Wakefield (neé Hall) married Harry Wakefield, a painter, Mrs Mary Edge, Mrs Glover, Mrs Elizabeth Bennett, Mrs Rose Warrillow. Mrs Ball was the senior paintress in this small workroom and was consulted by her fellow paintresses if advice was needed. She was also responsible for the pricing of her type of patterns. The shop remained named Mrs Ball's department long after her departure. She left the employ during the war when decorating goods sales were reduced.
- Charles Barker: painter.
- Michael Brennan: painter.
- Johnny Burgess: post-war modeller with Tom Barlow. A friend of Cyril Ball. Worked at Spode 31.01.55 to 13.04.62. In a reference of 1965 Harold said, "He is a man of excellent character, skilled in his profession, diligent and industrious. I was very sorry to lose his services on his taking a new appointment."
- Miss Mary Caldwell, 'Cordie': In 1959 she was Spode's oldest employee and celebrated her 85th birthday at work. It was her 49th year as an underglaze paintress. Her photograph was featured on the dustcover of Godfrey Wynn's book *The Queen's Countrywomen* 1954.
- Florence May Clarke: on-glaze enameller, started 27.4.25.
- Mrs Madelane Coxon: specialised in painting orchids and camellias. Born 14.3.00.
- Jane Dennis: Paintress from age 14, showroom assistant, etc. She was a work's nurse before she retired in 1982. Married and divorced from 'Arnhem' hero who was badly injured. Very attractive, red-haired girl who was chosen as a model, photographed against a background of Gainsborough. Died February 2006 aged 83.
- Lilian Edge: on-glaze enameller, started on 17.8.25.
- Mary Green; underglaze enameller, started in 1912.
- Winifred Green: underglaze enameller, started in 1912.
- Maurice Hancock: painter.
- Billie Hand: painter.
- Iris Jepson: underglaze enameller, started in 1935.
- Eric Olsen: Norwegian sculptor-modeller, joined before Harold in the 1930s and appointed designer

Gilding a Maritime Rose teapot.

on 23.04.40. After the war Eric was very successful in the United States. He became design director of a large pottery factory, Haegar Potteries, New Jersey.

- Arthur Perry, worked for forty years at Spode as a painter, then worked nineteen years at Doulton, retiring aged 75. He started at Spode in 1885. Famous patterns include Rockingham and Buttercup.
- Fred Robinson: painter.
- Rene Shipley: crowned Pottery Queen in 1937. Worked as a paintress before switching to the wages department.
- Beryl Sidlet, paintress in 1953.
- Alice Trimble: on-glaze enameller, started 1914.
- Annie Trimble: on-glaze enameller, started in 1911.
- Arthur Vitta: painter.
- Post-war Billingsley Rose painters and paintresses: Cyril Ball (commenced 9.7.46), Reg Bowden, Doris Thomas, Lily Edge, Doris Beck and Hilda Viggars. The men including Cyril Ball, Arthur Gaskell, E. Bate and H. Wakefield, were later replaced by women; Iris Jepson, Alice Wagg, Doris Thomas, Lily Edge and Hilda Viggars. Later, two girls were placed to paint leaves and the men to paint the roses until it was made into a silk screen by Johnson Matthey.

Kilns

- Sam Bradbury: foreman glost placer, started on 23.7.25.
- Clem Burrows: china biscuit 'cod placer'. Retired in September 1966 after 52 years' service in the pottery industry, 47 of which were at W.T. Copeland & Sons. Started in 1940.
- Bill Clay: china biscuit 'cod placer'.
- Jim Evans: lit an Aladdin lamp from hot coals from the china bottle ovens and Lord Mayor Sir Harold Clowes lit a modern gas poker, then Ian Forse applied it to the firing jets of the new china bisque oven on 11th May 1961. Jim's son, Ron Evans, recently retired after 48 years as a polisher. He went to work at the mini Spode factory at Carborundum Museum of Ceramics at Niagara Falls for $2^1/_2$ years.
- George Gibson: earthenware glost placer, started in 1921.
- Arthur Grimshaw: earthenware biscuit placer, started in 1920.
- Jim Jervis: was a china fireman for 50 years. His wife, Mabel Jervis was a freehand paintress who left school aged 14 to become an apprentice at Copeland's and stayed for 10 years.
- Walter Lambert: earthenware biscuit 'cod placer'.
- Ashton Maskery: earthenware ovens. Retired Sergeant Major, veteran soldier of WW1, awarded a Military Medal and Croix de Guerre for bravery in action. States that the middle oven was rebuilt

during the Boer War and the other three rebuilt after WW1.

- Frank Simpson, Henry Davenport, Sam Sparks: enamel kiln firemen, bottle ovens and rotalec.
- Twin tunnels earthenware bisque kiln lighting ceremony, 01.10.51. Mr and Mrs Gresham, Ian Forse, Spencer Copeland, Robert Copeland, John Copeland, Gordon Hewitt, Frank Thorley, Sid Thompson & Geoffrey Cholerton attended.

Managers and Foremen

- Charles Audley: pre-war North of England & Scotland representative for Copeland. Drove a large Humber saloon car. "Audley" pattern was named after him which was introduced in earthenware in 1938/9 and in china in 1953/4.
- John Barnish: clay manager, died 20.03.02.
- Michael Bachelor: home sales manager after John Docherty.
- Sam Bloor: works manager, started in 1935.
- George Cartlidge: decorating/prestige manager, died aged 81 on 8.4.94.
- Harold Cheshire: started on 28.1.24 and by 1960 he had been at Spode for 36 years. He started as general assistant to the works manager and served in various manufacturing departments. He became a salesman for the Greater London area in May 1959. He was very good at organising exhibitions.
- Peter Coleman: assistant to Michael Bachelor. Married a Cheshire girl, daughter of a leading agent for JCB. Peter later bought and ran Cloverleaf table mat firm.
- Wilfred Duckers: assistant and successor to Jimmy Upsdell. Wilf died at work aged 45 on 4.1.68.
- Arthur Durose, in charge of earthenware transfer printing until he joined the sales staff. He then moved to china printing and then, due to Carborundum cuts, he then became a training officer under Robert Copeland. Arthur died aged 82 on 23.5.91. His wife, Gladys also worked at Spode. His son, Trevor Durose was an engraver, whose daughter Joanne, now works in the shop. At one point all three generations were working at Spode together.
- Hilda Finney: forewoman transferrer.
- Ian Forse: tunnel ovens specialist. Retired after 48 years in the pottery industry on 17.06.80 as a technical and development officer of Enoch Wedgwood, Tunstall. He became work's manager after 27 years at Spode.
- Brenda Greenberg: in charge of Spode shop and transferred to London office for a while. "A feisty women." Died 2003.
- Douglas Hawley: assistant to Audley, then foreign and export sales representative. Died 22.07.03 aged 87.
- Ted (Arthur) Hewitt: joint managing director with Gresham Copeland.
- Mrs Holland: in charge of colour shop.
- Bill or Will Johnson: 1934 china making foreman, "the finest manager", succeeded by David Titley who was foreman just before January 1948, "not in the same street."
- Cecil Leese: foreman polisher, started on 21.7.24.
- Billy (William) Longsdale: general manager in 1934. Replaced S. Smith who was demoted and put in charge of the bisque warehouse.
- Cyril Marsh: chairman in about 1964.
- John Robinson: started as a painter at the same time as Robert Copeland, about Christmas 1947. He went into the pattern safe to keep the pattern books before becoming decorating manager of the prestige department, left to create his own factory; very good at modelling. Was succeeded by Colin Fletcher. Colin died of a heart attack aged 58 on 24.10.96.
- Sidney Smith: "a veritable mine of information". Was earthenware clay manager, later became personnel manager.
- John Talbot: sales manager, died aged 68 July 1997.
- Frank Thorley: sales director, came from Wedgwood circa 1933 until he retired in 1956.
- Alan Tucker-Feltham: accountant who introduced first accounting system. Appointed after Mr William (Bill) Newton became chairman of Copeland's on Ronald Copeland's retirement until 1955.
- Jimmy William Upsdell, "Uncle": contracts manager, responsible for samples. He was a Merchant

Seaman and previously an Acting Paymaster in the Royal Army Pay Corps in WW1, stationed at Lichfield. He was a prominent Freemason and was awarded an MBE. He joined Copeland's on 21.3.21 working in the cashier's office before transferring to the estimating department. He later became curator of the museum. He married a local girl. He died 24.09.63 aged 71. Harold wrote of Jimmy Upsdell's death in a letter: "The circumstances of his death were so tragic – one day at the factory with a cheery goodnight and next morning quietly and peacefully passing away. I was by his side when he died after receiving a call the previous evening from his wife saying he was not too well and it was only by chance, or guidance, that I visited him when I did. For Jimmy it was a wonderful way to go for he always dreaded the day of his retirement."

- Jes Yates: ex-glost foreman.

Administration

- Miss D.H. Bettany: works secretary, started on 25.8.24.
- Miss Jean Bettany, secretary to Len Whiter and others. At Spode from 1969–1987 when she retired on her 60th birthday. All the admin was moved down to Worcester and Spode was just a shell. When they decided to move the admin back in 1988 she was invited back and worked until 1992. As she was only allowed to go on a casual rate, her wage of £2.62.5 per hour was   somewhat of a joke.
- Phyllis Cheshire: wife of Harold Cheshire, ran wages office. Just four women for about 950 employees.
- Elsie Clowes: personal assistant to Ronald and Gresham Copeland for 25 years. Died in her 102nd year on 01.06.96.
- George Morrison: sales clerk responsible for American market.
- Lottie Pickin: worked in the office.
- William Pilgrim: Arthur Hewitt appointed him as a secretary who went on to become work's purchasing officer – "very efficient." Harold called him Midnight as he was black. He had a daughter who he said had to do extra well because of her colour.
- James Rushton: invoice clerk for 46 years, a Dunkirk veteran, married to Doris Rushton who spent five years in the sorting office. In March 2003 they celebrated their diamond wedding.

Various Clay Production Jobs

- Ernie Bates: china plate maker.
- Eric Beard: earthenware plate maker.
- Frank Biddulph: china plate maker.
- Kenny Boswell: china dish presser, died 04.03.95.
- Charlie Brian: china thrower and his younger brother Bill Brian.
- Charlie Brennan: caster.
- Harry Collins: the last presser retired aged 65 in August 1990.
- Handle finishers: Marion Cotgreave, Mrs Amis Slater, Rene Morrerion, Ada Shenton. Ada later married and became Mrs Gourley. She worked until retirement age and then became a factory guide.
- Albert Davies: earthenware caster, started in 1920.
- Jack and Bill Eccles: both brothers were cup makers since a boy. Both sportsmen with a sense of humour. Jack started on 20.9.25. Bill started on 16.6.24 and later became a glost warehouseman.
- Roy Harlnet: modeller, went to Lenox USA, a big success; blonde sweetheart, Rita, who worked in Sam Bloor's shop selling hotdogs. He brought her to the factory to act as secretary to Cartlidge. Sam signed him on as assistant modeller.
- Joe Hirst: china plate maker.
- Hector Lamond: earthenware presser, started in 1921.
- Jack Lea: china turner.
- Ernie Mellenchip: caster.
- Tom McCue: dish presser, taught Robert Copeland to press.
- Len Potts: china plate maker, started in 1932, last hand plate maker at Spode before they used

press and moulds, died 01.04.94.
- Arthur Steel: caster, specialised in birds and figures, "The Bullfinch Man".
- Arthur Talbot: earthenware turner.
- John Viggars: earthenware presser, started on 10.8.20.
- Frank Wakelin: china plate maker.
- John Walley: died before 1953, plate maker, a favourite of Ronald Copeland.
- Albert Wright: earthenware caster.

Warehouse workers

- Marjorie Bates: finished china warehouse, started on 26.1.25.
- Albert Bowden: earthenware printed warehouse.
- Bill Finney: finished china warehouse.
- Eric Brayford: china biscuit warehouse.
- Betty Cartwright: china white glost warehouse, overlooking.
- Harry Cooper: china white glost warehouse.
- Jack Dabbs: finished china warehouse. Husband of Barbara Dabbs who also worked on the factory.
- Anne Eccles (neé Halfpenny): died 21.07.02, wife of Bill Eccles, both worked in warehouse.
- Jack Goodyear: white china glost warehouse, started on 20.8.23.
- Fred Roberts: white china glost warehouse.
- Delia Swift: earthenware biscuit warehouse, started on 12.9.23.

Gilders

- Tom Brough: gilder, along with his sisters, Mary Wycherley and Louie Edwards.
- Charles Deaville: gilder, died 04.01.39. His son, Lesley, was an engraver who rode round the factory naked on a bike on wartime night-time fire duty.
- Bob Marshall: pre-war gilder.
- Patty Roper: gilder.
- Jack Stone: gilder.

Dipping and Sliphouse

- Mr Coxon: china sliphouse.
- Bill Faulkner: earthenware sliphouse.
- George Harrison: china dipper.
- Ethel Perry: china dipping house, started in 1920.

Ground Layers and Burnishers

- John (Jack) Booth: ground layer.
- Mrs Griffiths: ground layer.
- Fred Jones: ground layer.
- Ken Kimberley: ground layer who had a crippled foot and walked with a limp, died aged 66 on 20.10.95.
- Dolly Parker: head burnisher, died aged 74 on 1.6.85.
- Nancy Powell: burnisher forewoman.
- Burnishers: Nellie Beck, Nelly Roberts, Marian Beckett (neé Birks), who became Lord Mayor of Stoke-on-Trent in 1993. She started at Spode aged 15 and spent more than twenty years there becoming departmental manager.

Ken Kimberley groundlaying.

Printers

- Jack Amos: earthenware printer, one of over 30 or 40.
- Ernest Boult: china printer, started on 16.7.24.

- Ralph Farmer: gold and fine printer.
- Percy Grindley: printer or fitter, died 87 years.
- Albert Procter: print foreman, conductor of the Spode Copeland choir.
- Albert Shenton: gold and fine printer. His wife Ada was a transferrer.

Packers

- Russell Angove: packing department along with his wife.
- Bill Finney: packing department, started in 1920.
- Geoff Gifford: head packer (still there in 2003).
- Charlie Mansfield: packing department.

Various Other Jobs

- Olive Astley: ran shop.
- Hilda Beech: showroom, started on 24.1.14.
- Bill Bourne: traveller in home market, died 16.12.86.
- William Broomfield: mould maker, started in 1920.
- The Burton family: saggar makers.
- John Dodd: labourer, started in 1920.
- John Dono: saggar maker, started on 24.11.21.
- Francis succeeded Strathern as works engineer who walked into the sea and committed suicide. Was a ship's engineer previously.
- John (Jack) Glover: mould maker, started in 1935.
- Ron Hassall: second son of Tom Hassall. Worked for Copeland and Thompson in America. Died 10.01.95.
- Mrs Hill: liner.
- George Moore: storeman, started on 23.2.21.
- Geoff Parry-Thomas: colour shop, prepared colours for Ted Wright.
- Joe Parton: polisher and grinder.
- Lt Commander Geoffrey Reid: works engineer. His assistant was Harry Convey, a stoker, who was a Chief Petty Officer who served with Reid during the war. He left to go to Florida. Reid left in a hurry and Convey and Webster took over the engineer's job. Reid's secretary, "a lovely girl" also left in a hurry (instant dismissal by DHB) because of her behaviour with the maintenance squad.
- Bill Storer: front lodge man. Later became the Lord Mayor's Toastmaster. Bred Bull Terriers. Came to Copeland's in the early 1950s from the Army as either a Sergeant or Sergeant Major.
- Alan Webster: a chief engineer. Was found guilty in November 1963 of stealing scrap materials from the factory by selling them but not accounting for the money to his employers.
- Ted Wright: earthenware colour mixer for printers and copper plate room key keeper.

Cricket Team – Pre-war

- Geoff Cholerton, artist; Percy Grindley, fitter; Stan Degg, printer; Harold Holdway; Arthur Gaskell, artist; Albert Smallwood, polisher; Joe Lee, warehouse; George Morrison, foreign sales office; Jimmy Upsdell, costing/sales; Frank Thorley, director; Jack Booth, ground layer; Billy Eccles, warehouseman.

Snooker Teams

- Copeland snooker champion team 1937: Harold Holdway; Percy Grindley, fitter; Stan Bedwell, engraver; Geoff Cholerton, artist; Joe Lee, biscuit warehouse; Jack Wieuker or Wenker, artist; Jack Booth, ground layer; Albert Shenton, printer; Albert Proctor, print foreman; Ronald Copeland, chairman; Tom Hassall, art director; Jack Goodyear, china warehouse; Joe Fenn, artist. They were Snooker League champions in May 1939.

George Jones

- Dorothy Chorlton: apprentice gilder 1930, Harold's first sweetheart.
- Bill Brain: owner of Longton Foley China factory. At the final closure of the George Jones group of factories the Coalport name was acquired by Bill Brain who named his factory Coalport and deleted his own name. "This was a very smart move and his business prospered and he eventually sold his factory to Wedgwood and he retired in luxury to Scotland." The old name misled, W. Brain and Co.
- Kathy Dudley: head gilder, equal to male pattern gilder. Six ladies all lost sweethearts in WW1 – "widowed maids".
- Mr Mills: decorating manager who came from Ridgway's.
- Annie Shepard: 1st Pottery Queen July 1934.

Other Factories

- James Davies: owner of lithograph manufacturers of Longton. Also owned Sinclair and Co. of Shelton, colour and glaze suppliers to ceramic manufacturers.
- Gordon Evans: traveller to local firms (from James Davies?)
- Tony Greenwood: independent. Was selling Spode and others' best ware to American forces. He took the money on the spot but used the money before the goods were delivered and ended up committing suicide.
- Ron Hopkinson, modeller, Jack Ratcliffe, and Arnold Machin, both artists: In 1932 when they all reached the age of 21 years, they all left Minton's as the end of their apprenticeship meant extra pay. During the course of his apprenticeship, Arnold attended modelling instruction at Stoke Art School. Ron went on to Wedgwood's and Jack and Arnold went to Crown Derby as artists. Although Arnold was a qualified painter, he continued to attend modelling classes at Stoke and Derby and was finally awarded a scholarship as a sculptor at RCA, London. He left Derby to teach at Derby Arts School.
- Harry Koskie: (Leon Henry) sales director who supplied colour from Blythe Colour Works. A keen swimmer and trainer for Olympic swimming team. He and Harold "got on like a house on fire."
- Raymond Loewe: American designer of all things, designed 'Script' for Rosenthal China, Lenox, USA.
- John Wadsworth ARCA: who was for many years the eminent art director of Minton's who was succeeded by Stanley Woodman ARCA, who during the early 1920s produced, in Harold's opinion, some of the finest ceramic designs of this period. He, however, was dissatisfied with his remuneration and workload.

APPENDIX II
W.T. COPELAND & SONS
WAGE SUMMARY 1942

Direct Wages[13]

Average per week

Painters, gilders	£120.	4.	6.
Burnishers	17.	10.	0.
Paintresses Glost	157.	2.	6.
Paintresses Biscuit	110.	10.	0.
Enamel Kilns	19.	3.	6.
China painters	117.	11.	7.
Biscuit Placers E'ware	57.	6.	0.
Biscuit Placers China	24.	2.	0.
Glost Placers & Dip			
E'ware & China	134.	15.	1.
Saggarmakers	12.	14.	2.
Settermakers	8.	4.	5.
Marlgrinders	10.	3.	2.
Mill	31.	14.	3.
Pressmen, Puggers &			
Slipmakers	33.	3.	8.
Mouldmakers	31.	10.	2.
Pressers & Casters	61.	11.	7.
Jiggerers & Jolliers	132.	0.	0.
Throwers & Handlers	75.	9.	1.
Printers Biscuit	186.	19.	6.
China potters	115.	3.	0.
Foremen	35.	4.	0.

Indirect Wages

Average per week

Foremen	£63.	17.	7.
Engravers	37.	7.	0.
Warehouse China Bis.	13.	15.	9.
Warehouse Ch. Gl. Wh.	15.	15.	6.
Warehouse Ch. Finished	17.	18.	6.
Warehouse E'W Enam.	53.	18.	6.
Warehouse E'W Printed	17.	11.	9.
Warehouse E'W Biscuit	26.	6.	0.
Warehouse E'W Drawing	30.	14.	4.
Warehouse E'W Sorting	15.	11.	9.
Polishers	57.	17.	4.
Maintenance	142.	7.	8.
Packers, Carriers, Clerk	35.	11.	8.
Lodge	18.	13.	10.
Tractor driver	4.	0.	3.

Bottle ovens and coal at W.T. Copeland & Sons.

[13] Wages are for the whole department.

APPENDIX III
LIST OF PAINTRESSES AT
W.T. COPELAND & SONS 1941

Surname	Christian	Married	D.O.B	Age	Type of work & Dept	Domestic Particulars
				Underglaze Paintresses		
				Apprentices		
Hammonds	Edith	Yes	1.8.91	50	Supervisor, training of girls etc & Colour Shop	Husband in Navy
Stoner	Hilda	Yes	13.1.18	24	Buttercup, Cowslip, Rosalie, oddments & general work	Husband in Forces
Pomelli	Mary		5.11.22	19	Buttercup, Cowslip, Rosalie, also some women's work	
Brough	Gwen		20.5.23	18	Buttercup, Cowslip, Rosalie, also some women's work	
Pratt	Joan		20.5.23	18	Buttercup, Cowslip, Rosalie, also some women's work	
Higginson	Betty		26.9.23	18	Buttercup, Cowslip, Rosalie, also some women's work	
Turner	Hilda		16.8.24	17	Buttercup, Cowslip, Rosalie, also some women's work	
Smith	Vera		21.12.24	17	Buttercup, Cowslip, Rosalie, also some women's work	
Griggs	Vera		5.5.25	17	Buttercup, Cowslip, Rosalie, also some women's work	
Poole	Dorothy		13.2.25	17	Buttercup, Cowslip, Rosalie, etc	
Steele	Joyce		29.10.25	17	Buttercup, Cowslip, Rosalie, etc	
Stanley	Vera		18.7.25	16	Buttercup, Fairy Dell	
Walkendon	Joan		21.8.25	16	Buttercup, Fairy Dell Put on release list, waiting to be called upon	
Ryder	Joan		7.10.25	16	Buttercup, Fairy Dell	
Marks	Alice		29.1.25	16	Buttercup, Fairy Dell	
Clamp	Helen		19.11.25	16	Buttercup, Fairy Dell	
Snape	Irene		22.1.26	16	Buttercup, Fairy Dell	
Bott	Lilian		20.3.26	16	Buttercup, Fairy Dell	
Cliffe	Ivy		27.3.26	16	Buttercup, Cowslip, Rosalie	
Mott	Joan		16.9.25	16	Buttercup, Cowslip, Rosalie	
Hough	Doreen		7.11.25	16	Buttercup, Cowslip, Rosalie	
Garner	Ethel		17.5.26	15	Fairy Dell etc	
Chell	Edith		9.8.26	15	Cloverlly	
Tunstall	Doris		3.9.26	15	Buttercup, Cowslip, Rosalie	
Hyde	Jean		15.8.26	15	Buttercup, Fairy Dell	
Kelter	Iris		1.11.26	15	Buttercup, Fairy Dell	
Skeoch	Ivy		7.11.26	15	Buttercup, Fairy Dell	
Wood	Beatrice		18.12.26	15	Buttercup, Fairy Dell	
Brough	Joan		5.1.27	15	Buttercup, Fairy Dell	
Boulton	Eileen		3.2.27	15	Buttercup, Fairy Dell	
Brocklehurst	Doreen		11.3.27	15	Buttercup, Fairy Dell	
Cottam	Jean		16.8.27	14	Buttercup, Fairy Dell	
Edge	Cecily		6.12.23	18	Lining, Sketching for printers	
		Embossed Shop: Reynolds, flower centres, Toby Jugs, all handle decoration				
Morrey	Avis		10.12.93	50	Settling, counting, giving out work	
Bloor	Mrs	Yes	8.6.70	71		
Lamonby	Mrs	Yes	9.2.87	57		
Caldwell	Mary		30.4.74	68		
Boothby	Mrs	Yes	23.9.94	48		
Green	Mary		24.10.98	43		
Green	Winnifred		9.10.97	44		
Holford	Ethel		1.8.96	45		
Finney	Hilda		1.9.96	45	Quality Supervisor, also enamelling	
		General Underglaze Painting Shop: Gainsborough, Reynolds, Rose Briar, Strathmere, Mayflower etc				
Griffin	Mrs	Yes	28.3.04	38		
Cresswell	Mrs	Yes	12.11.04	37		
Roberts	Mrs	Yes	18.3.03	39		

Surname	Christian	Married	D.O.B	Age	Type of work & Dept	Domestic Particulars
Galley	Mrs	Yes	26.1.04	38		
Till	Nellie		5.12.19	22		
Sheldon	Fanny		9.3.89	53		
Wood	Mrs	Yes	15.11.18	23		
Shenton	Connie		14.3.13	29		
Roper	Mrs	Yes	26.1.12	30		unfit
Ball	Mrs	Yes	8.2.13	29		
Eccles	Mrs	Yes	26.5.86	58		
Russell	Mrs	Yes	15.10.07	34		
Drinkwater	Mrs	Yes	11.6.15	26		
Booth	Eva		14.11.94	48		
Copestake	Mrs	Yes	14.6.93	49		
Swann	Mrs	Yes				
Parks	Florence		5.9.91	48		
Harper	Nellie		27.1.07	35		
Mellor	Nellie		22.10.94	48		
McQuade	Mrs	Yes	17.3.08	34		
Buckles	Mrs	Yes	25.7.89	43		
Rhead	Maud		16.6.88	44		
Heath	Mrs	Yes	7.3.13	29		
Weaver	Mrs	Yes	7.1.05	37		
Clewes	Mrs	Yes	10.7.15	26	Leaving, housing war workers	

On Glaze Enamellers China and Earthenware

Mrs Trimble's Dep't: 90% e'ware patterns: HB, 8411, India Tree etc. 10% china patterns: Peacock, China Pheasant, Chelsea, Peplow etc

Surname	Christian	Married	D.O.B	Age	Type of work & Dept	Domestic Particulars
Gratton	Brenda		10.8.27	14		
Ogden	Bertha		21.8.27	14		
Keates	Hilda		14.9.27	14		
Ecclestone	Pauline		28.10.27	14		
Morrey	Iris Betty		11.11.27	14		
Parry	Joan		3.12.27	14		
Deaks	Joyce			14		
Jones	Doreen Elsie		27.2.28	14		
Wooley	Nellie		15.2.28	14		
Allen	Iris		11.4.28	14		
Wood	Betty		18.5.27	14		
Boardman	Emily		31.5.27	14		
Darlington	Freda		7.6.27	14		
Steele	Laura		29.7.27	14		
Vyse	Beryl		6.8.27	14		
Billington	Florence, B		9.7.26	15		
Davis	Florence, Ada		1.11.26	15		
Clamp	Edith		28.2.27	15		
Edwards	Alma May		7.5.25	16		
Holmes	Dorothy Veron		17.3.26	16		

Mrs Challoner's Dep't: Types of patterns as above, but slightly advanced stage. 90% e'ware, 10% china

Surname	Christian	Married	D.O.B	Age	Type of work & Dept	Domestic Particulars
Hill	Irene Florence		1.7.26	15		
Conway	Iris		4.7.26	15		
Boyle	Audrey		13.7.26	15		
Baddeley	Iris		1.8.26	15		
Wilson	Elsie Lilian		2.8.25	16		
Tipper	Irene		15.10.25	16		
Copeland	Joyce Mary		15.11.25	16		
Williams	Gladys					

China Bob Shop: 100% China: Chelsea Garden, Chelsea Peplow, Chelsea Iris etc

Surname	Christian	Married	D.O.B	Age	Type of work & Dept	Domestic Particulars
Hardy	Ann		23.4.15	26		Fit
Hughes	Mabel		6.9.15	26		Fit
Robinson	Norah		30.4.15	26		Unfit
Barker	Phylis	Yes	5.6.15	26		
Atkinson	Emily	Yes	12.2.20	21		Leaving for Leicester

Surname	Christian	Married	D.O.B	Age	Type of work & Dept	Domestic Particulars
Wood	Francis	Yes	17.1.16	25		
Vickers	Hilda		4.9.06	35		
Puddle	Olive	Yes	4.12.16	25		Unfit
Tilstone	Joyce		6.9.16	25		fit
Kelly	Mary		19.8.21	20		
Wright	Mabel		10.2.20	21		Birmingham: training ROF
Battle	Olive		28.12.19	22		Birmingham: training ROF
Palin	Annie		4.3.00	41		
James	Elsie		16.3.96	45		
Holland	E	Yes	14.7.94			mending and looking after them
Rose Leaf Paintresses: Billingsley Rose 2/8867, Maritime Rose etc. 80% e'ware, 20% china						
Wagg	Alice		24.1.21	20	Most of them can do china enamelling	Left to work at Swynnerton
Stephan	Iris		23.9.21	20		fit
Wagg	Dora		18.9.21	19		fit
Robinson	Dorothy M	Yes	21.11.22	19		fit
Wright	Margaret		23.11.22	19		fit
Rhead	Margaret		24.2.22	19		fit
Partington	Nancy		8.8.22	19		fit
Edwards	Jane		15.12.22	19		fit
Hand Craft Shop: Geisha Blue, china; Dimity, china; varied birds, e'ware; 0.1010 & Claudia patterns (Jewel), Moss Rose etc. 60% China, 40% E'ware						
Holmes	Jessie		18.2.22	19		Unfit
Byrne	Kathleen		4.9.20	21		
Ellis	Beatrice Mary		9.8.20	21		
Elsby	Phylis	Yes	23.10.19	22		
Sale	Joyce		17.7.18	23		
Vyse	Nellie		14.1.09	32		
Beck	Doris		27.2.06	35		
Jepson	Louisa	Yes	3.2.06	35		
Highest Class China: Fruit & Flowers, Orchids etc, Camellia, Billingsley Rose e'ware. 95% china, 5% e'ware						
Adams	Phylis	Yes	4.9.12	29		fit
Goodwin	Charlotte	Yes	20.7.13	28		unfit
Coxon	Madelane	Yes	14.3.00	41	All china	
Goodyear	Maud	Yes	20.3.01	40	China Birds Figures etc	
Taylor	Madge	Yes	17.6.13	28	China Birds Figures etc	Husband in Navy
Colclough	Hannah	Yes	30.5.06	35	Churchill & Roosevelt figures (faces)	Husband (MOS) & son going to school
Sunderland	Ada		6.7.10	31	50% China: flower centres, gold printed sets. 50% E'ware: Buchard, Heath & Rose	Invalid Mother
Thomas	Doris		28.4.10	31	50% China: flower centres, gold printed sets. 50% E'ware: Buchard, Heath & Rose	
Finney	Phylis	Yes	1.10.10	31	50% China: flower centres, gold printed sets. 50% E'ware: Buchard, Heath & Rose	Husband (bricklayer)
Oliver	E	Yes	20.12.11	30	50% China: flower centres, gold printed sets. 50% E'ware: Buchard, Heath & Rose	Husband (joiner)
Edge	Lilian		13.6.11	30	50% China: flower centres, gold printed sets. 50% E'ware: Buchard, Heath & Rose	Fit
Mrs Ball's Shop: Best class china & e'ware, flower centres & groups, Billingsley Rose etc 50% china, 50% e'ware						
Jepsom	Iris		24.8.21	20		Left to work at Swynnerton
Brown	Jessie		9.6.21	20		
Veron	Matilda		4.4.22	19		
Bennett	Elizabeth		7.1.03	38		
Trimble	Alice		18.1.99	42		
Stone	Mary		14.4.92	49		
Edge	Mary A		26.4.88	53		
Glover	Edith		11.3.82	59		
"The Villa": 100% e'ware: Red Indian Tree, Christmas Tree, Byron, Korea, Chinese Rose						
Lowe	Vera		20.12.17	24		Cripple
Trigg	Millicent	Yes	2.11.13	28		Husband (ROF)
Clark	Florence	Yes	27.5.10	31		Husband (driver)
Cartlidge	Florence	Yes		29		Husband in Air Force, expectant Mother
Miller	Evelyn		9.8.10	31		

Surname	Christian	Married	D.O.B	Age	Type of work & Dept	Domestic Particulars
Walton	Doris	Yes	5.5.08	33		
Hughes	Lilian		20.10.07	34		
Baskerville	J	Yes	16.4.98	43		
Richards	G	Yes	26.5.97	44		
Cleeton		Yes	29.7.95	46		
Oldfield		Yes	4.2.89	52		
Arrowsmith		Yes	27.8.85	56		
Smith	W	Yes				Left on doctor's orders, eyesight
Banders, Liners, Gilders: 50% e'ware, 50% china						
Forester	Irene		1.6.23	18	Edger, colour	
Palmer	Stella	Yes	20.4.15	26	Edger & liner colour	Fit, husband in Forces
Webster	Dorothy	Yes	7.5.15	26	Liner & edger, also gold	Unfit, husband electrician at WTC
Alcock	Doris		5.3.18	23	Liner & edger	Unfit,
Cotgreave	Marion	Yes	23.2.12	29	Bander & liner	To stay at WTC, husband(bricklayer), young daughter
Roper	Martha		27.3.06	35	Bander & liner, also gold	
Gourley	Ada	Yes	22.10.07	34	Handles & finishing best work	
Smith	Mary	Yes	25.12.21	26	Gilder	Left
Roberts	Nellie		30.9.84	57	Bander, & ivory wash, cobalt blue	
Edwards		Yes	19.10.07	34	Gilder	
Wycherley		Yes	19.2.90	51	Gilder	
Astley		Yes	2.10.11	30	Gilder	

* Note: ROF = Royal Ordnance Factory, based at Swynnerton.

Appendix iv
Decorating Piece Rates 9.11.46

Earthenware (* = added at a later date in ink)

No.	Pattern	Temporary Rate	Revised rate*
S117	Heath & Rose	3/-	3/3
2/9617	Moss Rose	2/3	3/-
2/8949	Claudia	3/-	
0.1010	Ann Hathaway	4/-	
S.427	Star of Bethlehem	2/3	3/-
2/9051	Patricia	5/-	7/-
S.2375	Strawberry	6/6	
S.2375	Du-Barry	2/-	2/6
2/9165	Hollyhock	9/9	13/-
S.2287	Hollyhock	9/9	13/-
S.2393	Christopher Wren	6/6	
2/8369	Antoinette	7/6	
2/9253	Chinese Rose	5/9	5/-
S.306	Korea (apple)	5/-	6/6
S.307	Burlington	10/6	
S.2248	Lauriston	7/6	6/-
S.1393	Eden	6/6	7/-
S.2401	Audley	7/6	
S.2133	Christmas Tree	7/9	
S.1870	Clovelly	6/3	
S.518	Byron Scenes	3/3	
2/4088	H.B	2/9	
2/8411	Florence	3/-	
S.798	Bermuda	4/6	
2/4191	Mandalay	5/3	
2/6459	Shanghai	7/9	9/-
2/9040	Basket	5/-	
2/8100	Crimson Black-bird	5/-	7/6
2/7832	Crimson Vienna Bird	3/3	3/6
S.138	Game Plate, Aster border	7/9 centre, 6/6 border	
2/5526	Game Plate, blue border	7/9 centre, 6/6 border	
2/6770	Marlborough	5/9	
2/3993	Tower (painted)	9/9	
2/8374	Sorrento	3/-	
2/959	India Tree	6/6	6/9
2/9265	Hunting Scenes	6/6	
2/9344	Hunting Scenes	6/6	
2/8867	Billingsley Rose 'roses'	1/6	1/9 men
	'leaves'	1/5	
2/4074*	Bang Up	7/6	
2/6040*	Bang Up (coloured)	6/6	
2/9043*	Chatsworth	4/6	
S745*	Sydney (yellow & orange)	4/7	

China (* = added at a later date in ink)

No.	Pattern	Temporary Rate	Revised rate*
R.9781	Chelsea Garden	5/3	
R.8542	Peplow	7/6	9/-
R.5321	Shanghai	7/6	9/-
R.4535	Currants	7/6	8/-
Y.5194	Rockingham	6/3	6/6
Y.6586	Pink Spray		
Y.4840	Iris	7/3	7/-
Y.6533	Dorothy Perkins	6/9	7/9
Y.4973	Queen's Bird	2/9	3/3
Y.6754	Famille Rose	9/9	12/-
Y.5920*	Famille Rose	12/-	
R.9641	Gobelin	7/6	11/-
R.8152*	Gobelin	11/-	
Y.2999	Forget-me-not	4/-	5/-
Y.3710	Jeannette (Savoy)		
Y.2971	Farne		
Y.6525	Vine	5/-	7/6
R.9289	Rising Sun	20/-	21/-
Y.5764	Dimity	4/-	6/-
Y.5831	Minerva	11/9	
Y.4584	Eden	6/6	7/6
Y.6278	Audley	7/-	7/9
Y.5922	Strathmere	7/-	7/9
Y.5926	Chinese Rose	7/3	7/9
Y.3456	Blanche-de-Chine	3/3	3/9
Y.6170	Blue Acorn	-	
Y.6568	Red Acorn	-	7/6
Y.5171	Green Acorn	-	7/6
Y.6606	Blue Acorn	-	
2218	Peacock	9/-	
Y.6426	New Lens (basket)	4/6	
Y.4881	Chinese Figures (stone) 10/9	11/9	
	Card Bowls* 12"	6/-	
	Card Bowls* 10"	5/6	
Y.6575	New Iris	4/6	5/-
Y.5954	Lauriston	7/-	8/-
C.1703	Kiota	10/9	11/9
1/8135	China Basket	4/6	5/-
R.2241	Dresden Rose	9/-	9/9
	Card Bowl 10"*	3/6	
	(with extra sprig in centre)*	10/6	
Y6859*	Dresden Rose	9/9	
Y5741	Dresden Rose	9/-	9/9
Y.5758	Dresden Rose	9/-	9/9
Y.6470	Irene	5/3	
C.S.584		10/9	11/9
Y.5373	Concord	6/-	8/-
R.4118	Roses	1/6	1/9 Women 2/- Men

China (* = added at a later date in ink)

No.	Pattern	Temporary Rate	Revised rate*
R.4118	Leaves	1/6	1/9
Y.3186	Berwick	6/3	6/6
Y.3182	Oaklea	2/9	
Y.3697	Tittensor Sprays	6/6	7/3
Y.4626	Browns Plants	7/-	7/9
Y.4626	Regent	3/3	
Y.5137	Pearl	5/3	5/9
	Rosalie	5/3	5/9
Y.2788	Bridal Rose (same as R.4118)		
Y.6447	Old Colony (same as R.4118)		
R.7137*	Blue Scale border & centre	6/6	
Y.6059*	Double Camellias	24/-	
Y.6060*	Single Camellia	18/-	
Y.5552*	Orchids	14/-	18/-
	Soup tureen complete	15/-	
Y.6612*	Fruit & Blossom	14/	18/-
Y.6180*	Single Camellia		
	(stripped assorted colourings)	8/-	
Y.4061*	Card bowls (flower centre)	6/-	
Y.6689*	Fortnum & Mason centre	9/-	
1/9504*		12/-	
Y.4133*		2/3	
Y. 4315*		12/-	
Y.2986*		8/-	
Y.5780*	Oak & Vine	6/-	
R.9486*	Songster (ivory)	4/6	
	Marco bowl 10" (ivory)	2/3	
Y.2684*	Willis on stone china	10/-	
Y.4895*	Briar Wood	9/-	
Y.3130*		14/6	
	Marco bowl 12"	7/6	
	Marco bowl 10"	5/6	
Y.6684*	New Shanghai (almond)	8/6	
Y.4785*		6/6	
	Marco bowl 12"	3/3	
	Marco bowl 10"	2/2	
Y.4758*	Shanghai centres		
	Songster border	10/-	
R.8479*	Kings	12/-	
W43*	Stone China (B.Room)	6/6	
Y.6883*	New Iris type coffee set 8/-		
R.5008*		8/6	
R6434*	Gold Edge Rockingham 7/6		
Y.5868*		4/6	
R.7680*		3/6	
Y.5695*		7/6	
Y.6466*	American Birds (Audubon)	27/-	
R4434*	Watteau	18/-	

China (* = added at a later date in ink)

No.	Pattern	Temporary Rate	Revised rate*
Y6851*	Bow pot	1/6	
R3210*	Mosaie Blushing	10/-	
Y.3495*	Blanche (coloured)	5/6	
W48*	Willis (stone) Slight	10/-	
Y.4744*	Black Sprig	15/-	
1.9720*	Ting	8/-	

ART DEPARTMENT DESIGNS AND DEVELOPMENTS 1962–63

Pattern Name & Description	Date & Authority for Proving Pattern	Proofs Received	Date Approved	Date & Authority	Layouts Approved for Ordering Range of Items	Promised Delivery of Sheets
Gothic Pattern by Mike Kitt		Jan 1962 (J&M)	Jan 1962 (HH)	16.05.62 refit for RCA	05.08.62 (HH, WD, GC)	
Christmas Tree		01.06.62	18.06.62 (HH, G. Thompson)		05.07.62	27.08.62
Persia by D. Jackson		22.01.62 (J&M)	24.01.62 (HH)	16.05.62 refit for RCA	02.10.62	11.01.63
Pique by M. Kitt		22.01.62 (J&M)	24.01.62 (HH) on ice 16.05.62			
Gold Leaves & Berries by D. Jackson		16.03.62 (J&M)	20.03.62 on ice 16.05.62			
Sycamore by D. Jackson		16.03.62 (J&M)	20.03.62 on ice 16.05.62			
Vielle France	1961	16.02.62 (J&M)	21.02.62		Layout completed by engraving dept. WTC 29.06.62	
Nursery Set, 3 items, D.Jackson	12.03.62	27.06.62	02.07.62 V. good	TRC will sell 20,000 but requires a little more forceful colouring	05.09.62 (HH, GC) sets in 12 months	19.11.62
Green Velvet Gold border	15.01.62	06.03.62 (J&M)	24.09.62 (MC)	15.02.63 Fits taken 15.11. .62(HH, WD, GC)		
Bel Paesaggio		17.01.62 The chromo transfer cold	25.01.62			
Rockingham (Conversion from print and enamel)	03.09.62	1st proof 18.08.62 2nd proof scheme E2 27.02.63	Not approved too weak 22.01.63. Not approved much better but cold 07.03.63			
Billingsley Rose	10.04.62	22.06.62	25.06.62 hold until futher notice for E/W & china			
Billingsley Rose, Gift ware		1st proof recieved 8.11.62 needs attention. 2nd proof recieved 19.12.63	20.12.62	28.08.62	Drawing Charge £103 24.04.6	Promised delivery date 12 sheets 28.01.63
Thistledown, conversion from colour and gold print	10in plate selection 26.09.62	22.11.62	26.11.62	13.03.63		

Pattern Name & Description	Date & Authority for Proving Pattern	Proofs Received	Date Approved	Date & Authority	Layouts Approved for Ordering Range of Items	Promised Delivery of Sheets
Darlington blue colouring conversion	10in plate selection 08.11.62	04.03.63 07.03.63	Not approved			
Green Garland	10in plate selection & 9 piece place setting 29.01.63	10.04.63, refits 14.05.63	Colouring approved, fit not right.	08.05.63	Approved final 18.07.63	
Gold Pendant border	10in plate selection & 9 piece place setting 29.01.63	12.03.63	1st proof 14.03.63 2nd proof 08.04.63			
Red Pendant border	10in plate selection & 9 piece place setting 29.01.63	12.03.63				
Trapnell conversion from existing pattern	10in plate	29.01.63				

Key	
HH	Harold Holdway
WD	Wilf Duckers – sales
GC	George Cartlidge
TRC	Thomas Robert Copeland
J+M	Johnson and Matthey
WTC	William Taylor Copeland
MC	?

APPENDIX VI
HAROLD HOLDWAY'S DIARY DATES

20.2.34	HH started at Spode.
7.4.40	Tom Hassall died, after 30 years as art director.
18.9.40	Holborn London showroom and office bombed, unfit for habitation and closed down.
6.11.40	Spencer Copeland and Sonia Chambers married.
1941	HM King George VI and Queen Elizabeth II visit Spode.
19.2.41	Arthur E. Hewitt presented with an illuminated scroll and commemorative bowl in recognition of being elected Lord Mayor of Stoke-on-Trent.
19.3.43	Letter from G.M. Forsyth asking HH to take drawing and design class at Stoke School of Art for young pottery apprentices.
1946	Electricity fired tunnel kiln installed for firing glost earthenware.
28.2.47	Geoffrey Cholerton appointed art director, HH assistant.
11.47	Princess Elizabeth's wedding – two designs were created for HRH to choose from.
1949	Bowl presentation at Buckingham Palace.
11.3.49	Visit to Royal College of Art to see Prof Baker.
25.10.49	Paid £1000 for Henshall's photographers
29.9.52	Jubilee Dinner and presentation in honour of R.R.J. Copeland at Stoke Town Hall for 50 years' service.
1952	Opening of new earthenware production departments including twin gas-fired tunnel kiln for firing biscuit earthenware.
9.3.53	Gresham Copeland: vice chairman, Arthur Hewitt: managing director.
1953	Spencer's car given to Geoffrey Cholerton, old Singer to replace Lancaster.
1954	New decorating shop finished, housing apprentices, ground layers and Indian Tree paintresses.
1954	Murray Curvex printing machine installed and developed.
1955	Development of plastics and epoxy resins for the use of making moulds.
29.3.56	Sam Bloor presented with *News Chronicle* 'Be Your Own Boss' prize.
26.6.56	Sam Bloor appointed works manager.
26.1.57	HH's first driving lesson.
6.3.57	Saw Prof Baker at RCA and saw work of two students: "Partridge good draughtsman, Young has creative ability".
18.5.57	Continental trip with R.S. Copeland and wife Sonia to Paris, Amsterdam, Milan and Florence.
15.7.57	HH passed driving test.
28.11.57	HH presented to Princess Margaret during her private visit to the works.
1958	Closure of grinding mill at Spode to release space for new production.
1958	Brussels International Exposition: Spode awarded a Diploma of Honour.
11.7.58	HH received a letter of thanks from HRH Princess Margaret regarding her tea set from the Hon. Iris Peake MVO.
28.2.59	Cyril Ball given notice to leave – economy drive per R.S. Copeland.
Autumn 1959	Len Whiter joined W.T. Copeland & Sons.
9.9.59	Trip to USA: visited Preswick, New Jersey, Empire State Building, Tiffany's, Atantic City, New York, Philadelphia, returned 3.10.59.
9.10.59	Moved to bungalow in Oakhill.
1960	Gas-fired open flame type tunnel kiln installed for firing biscuit china.
1960	Granted Duke of Edinburgh Award for Elegant Design for Royal College Shape in bone china.

11.5.61	Ian Forse lit Jubilee Oven for china biscuit.
28.6.61	Presentation of 12th Milan Triennale silver award to HH and T.R. Copeland at Ministry of Education, London.
23.10.62	Cyril Ball died aged 50 years.
7.3.62	HH attempted to give up smoking.
10–14.5.62	Fine China and Earthenware Manufacturers Association Trip to Cong, Ireland, Ashford Castle, Galway, etc. with Arthur Dutton, Len Whiter and Spencer Copeland.
24.9.63	Jimmy Upsdell, responsible for samples, died aged 71.
13.12.63	Wedgwood & Spode merger announced in *Financial Times*.
30.6.64	Ada Copeland died at home, aged 88.
8.5.65	R.S. Copeland visit and Mike Kitt's wedding.
28.1.66	R. Spencer Copeland and Jean Smith married.
21.6.66	Attended Westminster Abbey 900th anniversary garden party with wife, Betty.
5.4.66	Carborundum visit, top brass, W.H. Wendel, G. McKensize, Williamson, US president of Carborundum.
1.7.66	Carborundum take over Spode.
1.11.66	W.H. Wendel to visit.
21–26.11.66	Canada trip to Buffalo and Toronto.
1.12.66	G.E. Thompson resigned.
4.12.66	Dinner for Len Whiter on his leaving at the Royal George Hotel, Knutsford.
18.12.66	Works dance.
19.12.66	Carborundum Belle Vue dance.
1967	Len Whiter returned to Spode as commemorative ware sales manager until 1972.
1.2.67	Livery dinner, Goldsmiths' Hall.
21.2.67	Gresham Copeland died.
24.2.67	Gresham's funeral, Prestatlyn.
25.9–11.10.67	Brussels British Week.
26.5.67	Luncheon at Iolanthe room, Savoy Hotel for presentation to Master Gunner.
28.9.67	Sir Robert Mansergh, President and Council of the British Chamber of Commerce for Belgium and Luxembourg hosts British Week ball in Brussels.
29.9.67	Lunch given by President of Board of Trade on the occasion of the British Week in Brussels.
26.11.67	Spode sold to Carborundum Inc.
4–8.1.68	Trip to Hamburg.
4.1.68	Wilf Duckers died at work aged 45.
5–16.2.68	1st visit of George Barker, US president of Spode, & Dick De Natale, design manager of Carborundum.
8.3.68	USA samples sent.
1969	Completion of extensive enlargements of production facilities including fully equipped modern sliphouse, advanced making machinery and new gas-fired tunnel kiln for firing glost ware with up to date accommodation.
5.2.69	John Docherty, home sales manager – given a day's notice to leave.
1970	Bicentenary of founding of firm.
26.4.70	Trip to Paris and Hannover.
1.5.70	Goldsmiths' Exhibition open to public until 12th June.
14.5.70	Goldsmiths' Hall bicentenary banquet attended by Princess Anne.
1.7.70	Princess Margaret visits Spode at 11.00am.
10.7.70	Summer Ball, Trentham Gardens.
5.10.70	Spode Ltd: announcement of change in company name.
23.10.70	Civic dinner celebrating Spode bicentenary at Jubilee Hall, Stoke.
26–28.4.71	St Ives visit to Barbara Hepworth to approve sculptures: also 7–8.4.71; also 14–16.10.71 presentation of Gemini.
4.5.71	HH visit to Nuremberg regarding lithographs for Alan Lowden.

Special Offer
Christmas Tree
10" Plates
Seconds £8.05
Now
£1.50
No Further Discount

7.8.71	Alan Lowden back from USA.
23.6.71	USA trip.
27.7.71	Trip to Ripon Cathedral (Mr Hodgson, Dean and Canon) and Richmond (Green Howards plate) Col J. Forbes Ashworth.
18.11.71	Trip to Ripon (photography).
12.71	R. Spencer Copeland retired.
2.10.72	Alan Lowden left.
2.12.72	Paul Holdway and Kathleen Dawson's wedding day – off to Paris for honeymoon.
20.8.73	Arrived home from Carmarthen (Welsh Fusiliers plate) at 8.15pm, Betty admitted to hospital at 9.00pm.
10.8.74	Tom Barlow died aged 68.
4.11.74	John Bullock starts at Spode.
6.1.76	Given go-ahead for Persian 50 Year plate, price for plate £5.27.
7.2.75	Hereford visit: research with Len Whiter for commemorative plate.
9.3.75	August Warnecke died aged 72.
7.6.75 11am	Spode for sale announced Paul Thompson.
8.6.75	Len Whiter leaves for Persia – seeks approval for sample plate.
19.9.75	Black Watch design approved by Queen Mother.
10.2.76	St John's Ambulance artwork completed – shown to Len Whiter.
27.2.76	Visit to St John's Ambulance headquarters, presentation of design with P. Raynor & M. Stroud of Goodes Ltd.
20.5.76	Presentation of Gordon's Highlanders Aberdeen plate, one for the Queen and one for Bishop.
27.5.76	Handed in 3-month notice to John Bullock to finish 31.8.76.
14.7.76	Spode merge with Worcester, agreement signed 27.6.76. MD: J. Collis, deputy MD: Paul Thompson.
28.7.76	Wimbledon plate – delivered proofs to V & A, liked by curator and chairman.
	End of July 76 Withdrew notice – car and directorship offered.
9.9.76	Directorship confirmed.
6.12.76	Dinner dance to celebrate retirement of W.J. Whatmore from board of directors of Carborundum Co. Ltd.
21.12.76	Wendle bowl finished "looks good!".
11.1.77	Photo session at St Albans with Roy Trigg and Len Whiter.
1.3.77	Visit to York re St Peter's plate for M. Sinclair (Worcester plate request).
14.6.77	Thomas Goode and Co. London Ltd 150th anniversary.
22.6.77	St Albans Day plate ready for dispatch, Archbishop of Canterbury visit.
16.11.77	*Financial Times* reports Kennecoft Copper's offer of $530 million for Carborundum.
22.11.77	Paul Thompson resigns, Roy Fraser of Carborundum assistant chief to Davies.
3.5.78	Ada Copeland died at home.
16.6.78	HH's last day at Spode, 44 years 4 months, farewell party at Talbot Hotel.
2.8.78	Research visit to Charterhouse.
8.11.78	Research visit to Winchester.
15.12.78	Michael Sinclair visit re Winchester plate & decanter & wine glass, sent to Len Whiter.
23.8.79	Roy Fraser left Royal Worcester Spode suddenly.
24.5.81	HH gave up smoking.
1981/2	HH very busy with designs for Michael Sinclair and Len Whiter.
13.8.82	Barbara Dabbs died.
2.10.82	Reg Wallbank died.
18.1.84	Mollie Jenkinson died aged 68.
4.5.84	Wife, Betty died.
18.2.85	Phyllis Cheshire died, wages department.
1.6.85	Dolly Parker, head burnisher, died aged 74.
24.3.86	Spode changes administration to be at Worcester, 40–60 redundancies.

26.3.86	Spode management changes, home sales manager and Hugh Padley, managing director, given minutes' notice to quit.
5.5.86	Harold Cheshire died aged 79 suddenly on motorway – collapse. Tony Parr died aged about 63.
8.5.86	HH's arthritis becomes severe.
8.10.86	Wedgwood sold to Waterford Glass.
8.10.86	Billy Borne, traveller in home market, died.
12.86	Ray George out as chief executive.
10.7.87	Gresham Hassall died aged 80 years in USA.
2.12.88	Reginald Haggar, art master, died.
23.1.89	Frank Boothby died aged 73, engraver.
14.2.89	Spode to revert to own complete running of factory, sales and production at Stoke.
15.2.89	Spode and Worcester separate entities, Paul Wood appointed managing director, Palissy to be sold.
13.3.90	William Whatmore (Spode and Carborundum) died aged 78.
14.5.90	Spode workers on strike for 24-hours pay claim.
23.5.91	Arthur Durose died aged 82.
18.1.91	Harry Koskie died, aged 91, Blythe Colour Works.
6.8.91	Arnold Mountford, curator of Hanley Museum died aged 68.
29.6.93	Len Whiter died aged 62, born 3.8.30.
11.2.94	Jack Glover, Spode mould maker, died aged 74.
8.4.94	George Cartlidge died aged 81, decorating/prestige manager.
1.4.94	Len Potts, china plate maker, died aged 84.
5.10.94	Joseph White, post-war lodgeman at Spode and Mace Bearer for SOT Corporation, died.
4.3.94	Ken Boswell, china dish maker, died.
10.1.95	Ron Hassall, son of Tom Hassall, who went to work for Copeland and Thompson in USA, died.
8.10.95	Ken Askew died aged 79.
20.10.95	Ken Kimberly, ground layer who walked with a limp, died aged 66.
2.12.95	Jack Longmore died aged 85, engraver.
16.2.96	HH's wheelchair arrived.
1.5.96	Miss Elsie Clowes died aged 101, secretary to R.R.J. Copeland and A.G. Copeland.
24.10.96	Colin Fletcher, prestige manager, Spode, died of heart attack aged 58.
28.12.96	John Tomlinson, engraver, died aged 54.
7.97	John Talbot, sales manager, died aged 68.
4.98	HH's eyesight failed.
12.5.99	Ian Forse died aged 80.
13.11.99	HH fell out of chair – leg wounds/diabetes discovered.
8.3.02	R. Spencer Copeland died aged 83.
17.3.02	Jim Dunn, engraver died.
20.3.02	John Barnish, clay manager, died.
21.7.02	Anne Eccles, wife of Bill Eccles, both worked in warehouse, died.
31.8.02	Harold Holdway died aged 89.

INDEX